空间法评论 第6卷
Space Law Review Vol.6
（第2版）

赵海峰　主编

哈尔滨工业大学出版社

图书在版编目(CIP)数据

空间法评论 第6卷/赵海峰主编. —2版. —哈尔滨：哈尔滨工业大学出版社,2016.8(2018.10重印)
ISBN 978-7-5603-6165-9

Ⅰ.①空… Ⅱ.①赵… Ⅲ.①空间法－文集 Ⅳ.①D.999.1-53

中国版本图书馆 CIP 数据核字(2016)第 191739 号

责任编辑	田新华
封面设计	卞秉利
出版发行	哈尔滨工业大学出版社
社　　址	哈尔滨市南岗区复华四道街10号　邮编150006
传　　真	0451-86414749
网　　址	http://hitpress.hit.edu.cn
印　　刷	哈尔滨圣铂印刷有限公司
开　　本	880mm×1230mm　1/32　印张7.25　字数234千字
版　　次	2016年8月第2版　2018年10月第2次印刷
书　　号	ISBN 978-7-5603-6165-9
定　　价	45.00元

(如因印装质量问题影响阅读,我社负责调换)

编委会

顾　问
　　李　巍　　工业和信息化部政策法规司司长
　　赵宏瑞　　哈尔滨工业大学人文社科与法学院院长、教授、博导

主　编
　　赵海峰　　国家法官学院教授,哈尔滨工业大学空间法研究所原所长

副主编
　　李　滨　　北京师范大学法学院教授,哈尔滨工业大学空间法研究所副所长
　　Fabio Tronchetti　哈尔滨工业大学空间法研究所副所长

编　委
　　马新民　　外交部条法司副司长
　　张振军　　中国空间法学会秘书长
　　王冀莲　　中国长城工业集团有限公司总法律顾问
　　Armel Kerrest　法国西布列塔尼大学航空与空间法研究中心主任、教授
　　Marco Pedrazzi　意大利米兰大学国际研究系副主任、教授
　　Stephan Hobe　德国科隆大学法学院教授,科隆大学航空与空间法研究所所长
　　Joanne Irene Gabrynowicz　美国密西西比大学法学院荣誉教授,密西西比大学国家遥感、航空与空间法研究中心前主任
　　Frans von der Dunk　美国内布拉斯加大学法学院空间法教授
　　Setsuko AOKI　日本庆应义塾大学教授
　　Sang–Myon Rhee　韩国首尔大学法学院教授
　　Ram Jakhu　加拿大麦吉尔大学航空与空间法研究所教授、所长
　　Tanja Masson–Zwaan　国际空间法学会主席,荷兰莱顿大学航空与空间法研究所副所长
　　V. S. Mani　印度斋浦尔(Jaipur)国立大学法律和治理学院院长、教授
　　Lesley Jane Smith　德国吕内堡(Luneburg)大学教授

Steven Freeland　澳大利亚西悉尼大学教授
Stephen Barnes　中国政法大学法学院客座教授
李寿平　北京理工大学法学院副院长、教授、博导，北京理工大学空间法研究所所长
张会庭　中国航天系统科学与工程研究院航天信息中心研究员、副所长
龙卫球　北京航空航天大学法学院院长、教授、博导
凌　岩　中国政法大学国际法学院教授、博导，中国政法大学航空法与空间法研究中心副主任
尹玉海　深圳大学法学院教授，深圳大学空间政策与空间法研究中心主任
赵　云　香港大学法律学院教授
高国柱　北京航空航天大学法学院副教授、北京航空航天大学空间法研究所副所长
李居迁　中国政法大学国际法学院教授、中国政法大学航空法与空间法研究中心副主任
侯瑞雪　哈尔滨工业大学法学院副教授、哈尔滨工业大学空间法研究所副所长
荣吉平　哈尔滨工业大学法学院副教授、哈尔滨工业大学空间法研究所副所长
吴晓丹　中央财经大学法学院副教授，哈尔滨工业大学空间法研究所研究员
高立忠　哈尔滨工业大学法学院副院长、副教授
李晶珠　哈尔滨工业大学法学院讲师
左晓宇　中国航天员训练中心助理研究员
蔡高强　湘潭大学法学院教授、博导
王国语　北京理工大学副教授

主编助理：张　宇　哈尔滨工业大学法学院教学秘书

主　　办：哈尔滨工业大学空间法研究所

Editor in Chief
Prof. Haifeng Zhao, Director of Space Law Institue of Harbin Institute of Technology (H.I.T.), School of Law, H.I.T.

前　　言

《空间法评论》第 6 卷首篇发表了马新民副司长的《国际外空立法发展与我国的外空政策和立法》，此文在原作的基础上做了一些必要的更新，其观点尤其值得我们在研究外空法律政策时多加注意。

接着给大家提供的是日本著名空间法学家青木节子教授所研究的《外空交通管理:改善国际合作与安全的探索》(英、中文)。青木节子教授对外空交通管理这个专题做了专门的研究,提出了此问题上的研究方向。

本书作为中英文的发表平台，正在不断提升英文来稿的数量，本卷发表的若干篇论文就是这种稿件的结晶。这一类稿件，有的翻译成中文，有的则以英文呈现在大家的面前，都体现了本书作为中英文发表平台的特征。大家可以在其中发现一些名流的著作，如 Lotta Viikari 和 Fabio Tronchetti 的作品。其中 Lotta Viikari 的作品研究了空间碎片减缓中撞击影响的评估程序，作为空间法学者，她在空间环境方面的研究很有名。Fabio Tronchetti 的作品则探讨了深海海床和南极的矿物资源开发以及地球静止轨道的分配对管理和商业化利用月球和其他天体自然资源所启示的问题。

同时，本书还登出了《欧洲航天政策决议》《俄罗斯导航定位活动法》和《2011 年中国的航天》等外空领域的重要政策文件和法律草案。

《空间法评论》是哈尔滨工业大学空间法研究所主办的连续性文集。它的出版，得到了中国空间法学会、国防科工局、外交部、中国国际法学会、各兄弟院校、国外空间法研究机构和各位名家学者的大力支持，我们表示衷心的感谢！

赵海峰
国家法官学院教授
哈尔滨工业大学空间法研究所原所长、
人文社科与法学院特聘教授

注：本书在第 2 次印刷中对部分内容进行了补充及删减，原作者单位、职称和个人简介等，除主编更新外，其他仍保留第 1 次印刷时的信息。

目 录

□ 论文

国际外空立法发展与我国的外空政策和立法　　　　马新民
………………………………………………………（1）

外空交通管理:改善国际合作与安全的探索(中、英文)
　　　　　　　　　青木节子 著　李晶珠 译　李滨 校
………………………………………………………（14）

深海海床和南极的矿物资源开发以及地球静止轨道的分配:是否是管理和商业化利用月球和其他天体自然资源的有效经验?（中、英文）
　　　　　　　　Fabio Tronchetti 著　聂明岩 译
………………………………………………………（61）

Impact Assessment Processes in the Mitigation of Space Debris
　　　　　　　　　　　　　　　　　Lotta Viikari
………………………………………………………（142）

□ 学术信息

第54届国际空间法研讨会在南非开普敦举行 ………（167）
国际空间法当前形势和未来发展学术研讨会在哈尔滨
　召开………………………………………………（168）

第一届亚太空间合作组织法律与政策论坛在北京举行
……………………………………………………………（169）
联合国外空委及外空安全形势研讨会在北京举行……（170）
第55届国际空间法研讨会在意大利那不勒斯举行 …（171）
第49届国际航空与航天法会议在韩国首尔举行 ……（172）

□ **法律文件**

俄罗斯导航定位活动法……………………贾雪池 译（173）
Draft Code of Conduct for Outer Space Activities(2008)
……………………………………………………………（177）
《2011年中国的航天》白皮书(中、英文)……………（186）

Contents

☐ **Thesis**

The Development of the International law – making on Outer Space and China's Law and Policy on Outer Space
.... by Ma Xinmin(1)

Space Traffic Management: The Quest for Improvement of International Cooperation and Security (Chinese & English)
　　by Setsuko Aoki, translated by Li Jingzhu, revised by Li Bin
.... (14)

The Exploitation of the Resources of the Deep Seabed, Antarctica and the Allocation of the Geostationary Orbit: Valuable Lessons for the Management and Commercial Use of the Natural Resources of the Moon and Other Celestial Bodies? (Chinese & English)
　　　　by Fabio Tronchetti, translated by Nie Mingyan
.... (61)

Impact Assessment Processes in the Mitigation of Space Debris
　　　　　　　　　　　　　　　　by Lotta Viikari
.... (142)

☐ **Academic Information**

The 54th Annual Meeting of International Space Law held in Cape Town, South Africa .... (167)

The Conference on the Current Status and the Future
Development of International Space Law held in Harbin
.... (168)
The 1st Forum on Law and Policy of APSCO held
in Beijing .... (169)
The Conference on UNCOPUOS and the Security
of Outer Space held in Beijing .... (170)
The 55th Annual Meeting of International Space Law held in Na-
ples, Italy .... (171)
The 49th Meeting on International Aviation and
Astronautical Law? held in Seoul, Korea .... (172)

□ Documents

Russian's Legislation on Navigation and Positioning Activities
　　　　　　　　　　　　　　translated by Jia Xuechi
.... (173)
Draft Code of Conduct for Outer Space Activities(2008)
.... (177)
China's Space Activities in 2011 (Chinese & English)
.... (186)

国际外空立法发展与我国的外空政策和立法

马新民[①]

近年来,外空的战略地位日益受到各国重视。外空不仅是国家战略和安全的重要空间、社会可持续发展的资源宝库、高科技的聚集点,也正在日益成为外空大国经济乃至世界经济发展新的增长点,许多国家已把外空作为其崛起的新机遇。当前,围绕着外空战略、安全、经济、资源利益等展开的政治和法律博弈值得高度关注。

一、当前国际外空政策和立法的发展

1. 各国普遍重视制定空间政策和法律

外空政策是国家或国际组织进行空间活动的指导方针,决定着国家和国际组织空间活动的发展方向。随着外空对国家的战略地位和经济价值的大幅提升,越来越多的国家认识到,谁能有效利用外空,谁就能拥有更多的安全和财富。为了抢占空间科学和应用的制高点和制天权,许多国家或国际组织近年来纷纷出台新的

[①] 马新民,外交部条法司副司长。本文完成于 2007 年 5 月,曾发表于 2008 年《中国航天》第 2 期,此次应邀发表时对有关资料稍做了必要更新,在修改过程中得到外交部条法司周丽鹏的协助,在此表示感谢。

外空战略和政策文件。如欧盟国家2003年通过了指导其航天发展的《航天:扩充中的欧盟新疆域——欧洲航天政策行动计划》白皮书,并于2007年提出《欧盟空间政策》。1978年以来的美国历届政府都高度重视外空政策,并根据国家利益的需要不断调整相关政策,已相继颁布了多个国家空间政策并制定了外空商业、遥感等专项政策。2010年出台《国家航天政策》,关注外空环境日益拥挤、外空武器化日益加剧和竞争日益激烈三大发展趋势,提出维护外空环境安全性和稳定性、维持和提升美国外空军事和情报优势以及重整美国外空行业活力三大战略目标,计划于2025年启动月球外天体载人飞行计划,到21世纪30年代中期实现将人类送入火星的目标。俄罗斯公布了《2006—2015年航天发展计划》和太空军事复兴计划,并正在制定2030年前航天活动发展战略,包括研制空间站、载人登月和飞向火星计划。目前,加拿大、英国、日本、印度等国已出台或正在制定新的空间战略。

同时,各国日益重视空间国内立法。据不完全统计,现已有20多个国家或地区制定了空间法,绝大多数都是20世纪90年代以后制定的,具有代表性的有2005年比利时《空间物体发射、飞行操作与导航活动法》、2006年荷兰《空间活动和建立空间物体登记册的规定》、2008年法国《空间活动法》、2011年奥地利《外空活动授权及设立国家登记处法》等。

美国在空间探索和应用方面处于全球领先地位,建立了坚实的民用、商用和军用基础。美国视外空为其科技、经济和军事的命脉,高度重视外空战略规划和外空立法,已建立了较完备的外空政策和法律体系。美国于1958年通过了世界上第一部外空国内立法——《国家航空航天法》,此后又制定了1962年《通信卫星法》、1984年《商业外空发射法》、1984年《陆地遥感政策法》、1998年《商业空间法》、2000年《商业空间运输竞争法》等,目前正在审议《空间投资法》《空间旅游促进法》《遥感应用法》等。

2. 如何落实两大外空法律原则问题

(1)共同利益原则的实施问题

《外空条约》第 1 条第 1 款规定,探索和利用外空,包括月球和其他天体在内,应为了所有国家福利和利益,而不论其经济或科学发展程度如何,这种探索和利用应是全人类的事情(the province of all mankind)。这就是著名的"共同利益原则"。该原则的核心是共同所有、分享利益。其立法本意是,对外空的探索和利用只有在造福全人类利益的情况下才是合法的,任何不顾他国和全人类的利益,为谋求单方面利益进行的外空活动,包括以商业或军事目的而利用,都是滥用权利的行为,有悖这一原则的精神。原则上讲,任何单方面探索和利用外空的活动只有在确保所有国家公平分享有关利益的情况下,才符合全人类共同利益原则。1996 年联合国大会通过的《外空国际合作宣言》更进一步将这一原则引申为包括应特别照顾到发展中国家的需要和利益。

但由于《外空条约》对如何实施这一原则缺乏明确具体的规定,各国往往都以平等、自由探索和利用外空原则为由,做出对自己有利的解释。共同利益原则在国际实践中还远未落到实处,如何明确该原则的内涵并在实践中加以遵行,任重而道远。

(2)外空国际合作原则的具体化问题

促进外空领域合作是国家承担的一项义务。国际合作原则贯穿于 1967 年《外空条约》各项条款之中。该条约除序言外,还有 6 个条款规定了国际合作义务。其中第 1 条规定,各国应便利并鼓励外空国际合作。第 3 条规定,各国对外空探索和利用应为增进国际合作和谅解进行。第 5 条规定,各国对遇难的宇航员和空间物体应予以援助的义务,《营救协定》对此作了具体规定。第 9 条规定,外空探索和利用应以国际合作为原则,并规定发射国应充分注意他国利益,就外空活动或试验可能产生的危险,主动或应他国请求事先与他国磋商。第 10 条规定,各国应为其他国家提供机会观察空间物体的飞行。第 11 条规定,各国应在最大可能和实际可行的范围内,将外空活动的性质、进行情况、地点和结果通知联合国秘书长,并通告公众和国际科学界。同时,联大还通过了 1996 年《外空国际合作宣言》,强调外空利用应该特别考虑发展中国家的需要。因此,如何使国际合作原则规范化和制度化,大有文章可做。

3. 通过或制定四项国际立法

(1) 通过了《空间资产特有事项的议定书》

2012年2月,国际统一私法协会在德国柏林通过了《移动设备国际利益公约关于空间资产特有事项的议定书》,并于2012年3月开放签署。议定书主要规定了适用于空间资产跨国融资的实体法律规则,内容包括空间资产的定义和识别、融资债权人的权利登记及优先权制度、债权人违约时的救济措施等。根据议定书建立的专门电子登记系统,空间资产跨国融资活动中的提供融资方可将其享有的权利登记为国际利益,并享有议定书赋予的保护,如出现债务人违约时,债权人可按登记先后顺序直接诉诸救济措施进行维权。该议定书是近30多年来外空商业领域第一部国际立法,为空间资产融资和商业化发展创造了更加透明、公平的法律环境,有利于促进外空商业活动的发展。

(2) 推动制定外空行为准则

近年来,美欧国家积极推动制定不具有法律约束力的行为准则。其中一个是2007年美国著名军控研究智库史汀生中心推出的《空间大国行为准则》。该准则规定了空间大国的四项权利和七项义务。

四项权利包括:进入空间从事包括军事支援职能在内的和平探索、利用外空活动的权利;行使《联合国宪章》所规定的自卫权;基于准则之目的及宗旨的知情权;就涉及准则的各种关切和执行情况进行磋商的权利。

七项义务包括:应尊重其他空间大国及合法利益相关方的权利;应指导合法利益相关方在其领土内开展活动或在使用空间发射设施时遵循准则的目的和宗旨;应完善并遵守空间行动安全与交通管理的规定;应共享空间行动安全和交通管理信息,并加强有关空间合作;应减缓并最大限度地减少空间碎片;应防止对空间物体实施有害干扰;应与其他空间大国就相关空间活动展开磋商并加强合作。

该文件虽只是美国学术机构的立法建议,但其对有关国际外空立法的影响不容忽视。

另一个是欧盟于 2008 年提出的《外空活动行为准则》。该准则包括前言和以下四个部分的主要内容：一是核心原则与目标，包括自由探索和利用外空原则、保障空间物体安全原则、承认《联合国宪章》赋予的自卫权原则、善意合作与避免对空间活动造成有害干扰原则、和平利用外空并避免外空冲突原则。二是一般性措施，包括空间操作措施、控制和减缓空间碎片措施。三是合作机制，包括空间活动的通报、空间物体登记、空间活动信息、磋商机制、调查机制等。四是组织层面，包括审议准则会议制度等。当前欧盟正在积极推动启动该准则多边谈判进程。2012 年 6 月，欧盟在维也纳主办国际外空行为准则首次多边专家会，并计划于近期召开部长级会议通过该准则。

（3）制定防止外空武器化和军备竞赛条约问题

1967 年《外空条约》第 4 条确立了外空非军事化的两个体制：在整个外空实行部分非军事化原则，只禁止大规模杀伤性武器，而不禁止其他武器；在月球及其他天体实行全面非军事化原则，即"专为和平目的"而利用。多数发展中国家认为，该规定意味着禁止各种军事活动。因此，对整个外空而言，不禁止进行试验、部署和使用大规模杀伤性武器以外的其他武器，包括反卫星武器。我国、俄罗斯等国认为，《外空条约》没有禁止在整个外空部署大规模杀伤性武器以外的常规武器，也未涉及对外空物体使用或威胁使用武力问题，是严重的漏洞和缺陷，因此应积极推动制定防止外空武器化和军备竞赛的法律文件。

该项立法建议最早是苏联在 1981 年第 36 届联合国大会提出的，在该届联合国大会通过的《防止外空的军备竞赛决议》中，请裁军委员会审议如何就旨在防止外空军备竞赛的协定进行谈判的问题。多年来，我国与俄罗斯一直在日内瓦裁军谈判会议上积极推动制定防止外空武器化和军备竞赛法律文书，已提交了多份工作文件。2002 年 6 月，两国向裁谈会提交了"防止在外空部署武器、对外空物体使用或威胁使用武力的法律文书要点"。2007 年 8 月，两国在裁谈会上向部分国家非正式散发了《防止在外空放置武器、对外空物体使用或威胁使用武力条约草案》。2008年两国向裁谈会共同提交了《防止在外空部署武器、对外空物体使用或威胁使用武力的条约草案》。该草案由序言和14个条款组成,主要内容包括以下几项:一是明确了外空、外空物体和外空武器的定义;二是规定了缔约方的三项义务,包括不在绕地球轨道、天体放置或部署任何武器,不对外空物体使用或威胁使用武力,不协助、不鼓励其他国家或国际组织参与这些活动;三是规定缔约方应采取措施防止在其领土或其管辖的地方发生本条约禁止的活动;四是规定本条约不妨碍各国依据国际法对外空进行研究和利用的权利,也不妨碍各国依《联合国宪章》行使自卫权等。此外,还就外空透明和建立信任措施、争端解决机制等做出规定。多数裁谈会成员对草案表示支持和欢迎,但美认为该草案内容将限制其外空活动,一直明确反对。美国2006年《国家航天政策》明确指出,美国具有在空间不受阻碍地通行或运作的权利,并将蓄意干扰其空间系统的行为视为对其权利的侵害,将采取必要措施保护其在空间活动方面的权利、能力和自由。该文件还提出,美国反对任何禁止或限制美国进入或利用外空的新的法律机制或措施,任何军备控制条约不得损害美国在外空进行研究、发展、试验、作战或其他活动的权利。

2006年美国的航天政策带有明显的空间霸权和单边主义性质,在一定程度上意味着美国的外空武器化政策公开化,可能引发新一轮空间军备竞赛,加速外空军事化的进程。事实上,该政策出台后,俄罗斯、欧盟等随即做出反应,纷纷表示将调整航天发展战略和政策,以适应国家安全的需要。美国这一单边主义外空政策,不仅对各国空间战略产生冲击,而且也使裁谈会短期内难以启动这项条约的谈判工作。

(4)制定全面外空法公约问题

近年来,俄罗斯、乌克兰等国极力在外空委法律小组委员会推动制定一项全面外空法公约。俄国曾在2002年外空委法律小组委员会上散发了其草拟的全面外空公约大纲。俄认为现行有关外空条约存在明显缺陷,外空条约中的许多概念应予明确。如"发射国""空间物体"等;外空活动中的新问题需要予以规范,如外空商业化和私营化、空间碎片等。俄国还认为,通过分别修改现有各项外空条约来解决以上问题并不现实,因为现有各项条约相互关联,修改其中之一必将牵涉其他条约,但各项条约的缔约方不尽相同,要进行统一的修改非常困难,唯一可行的是拟定全面公约。

但此项建议遭到了美、日等国的反对。美认为,谈判制定新外空条约将危及现行外空法律制度,当务之急应是推动各国加入现行外空条约。在最近几次外空委法律小组委员会会议上,俄国都提出应先讨论制定全面外空法公约的适当性和可行性建议,我国与乌克兰、哈萨克斯坦等均作为共同提案国予以支持。

我国政府的立场是,现行外空条约虽存在不足,但并不过时,特别是1967年《外空条约》确立的外空活动的基本法律原则,仍是外空法的基石及其发展的法律框架。我国主张,在不损害现有外空条约确立的外空法基本原则的前提下,可以适当方式完善有关外空条约,包括可考虑制定全面外空法公约。但也有学者认为,制定"外空条约附加议定书"更为可行。由于外空委采用"协商一致"的决策程序,目前看,启动制定全面外空法公约短期内难以取得突破。

4. 密切关注有关外空国际文件

(1)2007年联合国外空委《各国和国际组织登记空间物体方法的做法工作组的结论要点》

该文件主要针对当前各国和国际组织在登记空间物体方面存在的故意不登记或登记不完整等问题,提出了许多新的建议。主要内容有:一是提供登记空间物体的资料统一类别,如所适用的空间研究委员会国际代号,作为发射日期参考时间的协调世界时,作为基本轨道参数标准单位的公里、分和度等。二是提供下列附加资料:所适用的地球静止轨道位置、运行状态的任何变化,衰变或重返的大致日期,将空间物体移至弃星轨道的日期和实际状况,空间物体正式资料的网络链接,等等。三是实现空间物体的最完整登记,如若事先没有就登记达成协议,空间物体从本国领土或设施发射的国家应与有资格作为"发射国"的国家或国际组织联系,共同确定由哪个国家或实体登记该空间物体;在同时发射若干空间物体的情况下,每个空间物体应分别登记,并在不妨碍各国的权利和义务的情况下,应依照有关外空条约将空间物体列入根据《外空条约》第6条对该空间物体的经营负有责任的国家的相应登记册中;各国应鼓励属于其管辖的发射服务提供商向空间物体拥有者和/或经营者提供咨询意见,以就空间物体登记事宜与有关国家联系。四是在轨道空间物体的监管发生变化后要进行变更登记,如监管变化的日期、新的拥有者或经营者的身份、轨道位置的任何变化、空间物体功用的任何变化等。

该结论要点有助于促进各国和国际组织登记实践的一致性,也有助于促进《登记公约》的更好履行。该结论要点虽不具有法律约束力,但对各国和国际组织登记空间物体具有重要的指导意义。

(2) 2007年联合国外空委《空间碎片减缓准则》

该准则规定,在航天器和运载火箭轨道级的飞行任务规划、设计、制造和操作(发射、运行和处置)阶段,应考虑以下七项准则:一是限制在正常运作期间分离碎片;二是最大限度地减少操作阶段可能发生的分裂解体;三是限制轨道中意外碰撞的可能性;四是避免故意自毁和其他有害活动;五是最大限度地降低剩存能源导致的任务完成后分裂解体的可能性;六是限制航天器和运载火箭轨道级在任务结束后长期存在于低地轨道区域;七是限制航天器和运载火箭轨道级在任务结束后对地球同步轨道区域的长期干扰。该准则虽无法律约束力,但反映了现行的国际标准,具有重要影响力。

(3) 2009年联合国外空委和国际原子能机构《外空核动力源应用安全框架》

为了确保外空核动力源安全,联合国外空委与国际原子能机构联合起草并于2009年共同发布了《外层空间核动力源应用安全框架》,旨在为外空核动力源应用的相关发射、运行和寿终阶段的安全防护提供指导,以及为空间核动力源设计、制造、测试和运输等活动提供安全管理和技术建议。该安全框架规定了核动力源安全应用领域的技术标准,对于发展和使用空间核动力源应用具有重要指导意义。该安全框架不具有法律约束力。

(4)1984年国际法协会《关于解决空间法争端的公约草案》

该公约草案包括七章和一个附件。主要内容有:争端的范围(第1~2条),不具有法律约束力的争端解决程序(第3~4条),具有法律约束力的争端解决程序(第5~13条),调解程序(第14~23条),仲裁程序(第24~26条),国际空间法法庭(第37~68条),最后条款(第69~76条),另有示范性争端解决条款作为附件。

该草案适用于国家间的空间法争端,而不适用于私人实体从事空间活动产生的争端。目前,该草案还没有引起联合国外空委及其会员的重视。

(5)1994年国际法协会《关于保护环境免受空间碎片损害的国际文书》

该文件规定了空间碎片责任和损害赔偿的法律原则,共包括16个条款。主要内容有以下几项:一是明确有关概念。关于"空间碎片",是指外层空间的人造物体,不包括正在运行或有其他用途的卫星,包括航天运载工具或火箭级残余以及正常调整操作过程中释放的物体、在轨爆炸和卫星解体、碰撞所生碎片、微粒和其他形式的污染、废弃卫星;关于"环境",包括外层空间环境和国家管辖范围之内及之外的地球环境;关于"损害",是指生命丧失、人身伤害或其他健康损伤,或国家、自然人或法人的财产或政府间国际组织的财产的损失或损害,或任何对国家管辖或管制的区域之内及之外的环境造成的不利改变。二是规定了适用范围。本文书应适用于对环境、人身或物体造成或可能造成损害的空间碎片,包括直接或间接、即时或延后的损害。三是规定了缔约方和缔约国际组织一般合作义务以及善意地防止、通知、磋商和谈判的义务。四是规定了空间碎片造成的损害的国际责任和赔偿责任原则,即发射或促使发射空间物体的本文书的缔约方或缔约国际组织,应承担国际责任。如发射或促使发射空间物体的缔约方或缔约国际组织的空间物体产生的空间碎片对另一国家、人员或物体或参加本文书的国际组织造成损害,则其应承担国际赔偿责任。

该文书是目前国际上关于空间碎片责任和损害赔偿问题唯一的国际文件,虽不具有法律约束力,但是对该领域国际法规则的形成和发展有一定的影响。

(6)外空委法律小组推动制定外空国内立法建议

目前,外空委法律小组委员会下属的"与和平探索和利用外层空间有关的国家立法问题工作组"正在研究外空国内立法问题,并于2012年结束其五年工作计划,作为最终的工作成果。该工作组提出了《就与和平探索和利用外空有关国家立法所作建议》,有关国家或地区正积极推动联合国外空委通过该建议。该立法建议敦促各国依据本国法酌情颁布外空活动监管立法,就外空活动的管理、许可、登记、监督、责任和保险等做出规定。

二、我国的外空立法与有关外空条约的实施

我国航天事业开始于1956年,已走过了60多年的光辉历程,我国的空间政策和立法在此间也取得了一些成绩。我国于1983年加入《外空条约》,1988年加入《营救协定》《责任公约》和《登记公约》。我国于2000年、2006年和2011年先后发表了三个《中国的航天》白皮书,提出了中国的航天的基本政策和发展目标。2001年和2002年先后颁布实施了两项行政法规,即《空间物体登记管理办法》《民用航天发射项目许可证管理暂行办法》,以规范有关空间活动,履行有关条约义务。目前我国有关部门正在加紧制定《发射空间物体涉外损害赔偿条例草案》和《空间活动管理条例草案》等。但必须看到,我国的空间政策和立法与我国迅速发展的空间事业相比还比较滞后,还存在一些问题。

1. 国际条约在我国的实施尚缺乏明确的法律依据

我国《宪法》中没有关于国际条约在国内适用的专门规定。根据我国的法律实践,条约在我国的适用大体上有两种不同的方式:

一种是直接适用。我们不少内法律都规定,我国参加的国

际条约与我国法律有不同规定的、优先适用国际条约的规定,我国提出保留的除外。这一规定明确了国际条约在我国适用的两项基本规则:一是条约优先适用;二是条约直接适用。

另一种是转化适用。如我国在加入《维也纳外交关系公约》和《维也纳领事关系公约》之后,分别制定了《外交特权与豁免条例》和《领事特权与豁免条例》;在加入《联合国海洋法公约》之后,分别制定了《领海及毗连区法》和《专属经济区和大陆架法》。以上可被视为转化适用的方式。

但在外空法领域,我国现行的两项外空行政法规,即《空间物体登记管理办法》和《民用航天发射项目许可证管理暂行办法》,都没有专门条款对外空条约的适用做出规定。因此,有关国际条约在我国的适用问题,目前还缺乏明确依据。

2. 国内法中还没有关于外空法律地位的规定

对于包括月球及其他天体在内的外空的法律地位,我国现行法律没有明确规定。在我国法律中,是否有必要以及如何界定外空的法律地位问题,是一个值得深入探讨的问题。

如何界定外空的法律地位,在理论上,国际上有两种代表性的主张。一种认为外空是"共有物",其地位类似于公海,主张各国对外空有权平等和无歧视地探索和利用、自由探索和利用、不得据为己有(non-appropriation)和以和平目的探索和利用。另一种认为外空是"人类共同继承财产"(common heritage of mankind),类似于国际海底区域,主张各国对外空不得据为己有、共同开发、分享利益和专为和平目的的利用。

从现行外空条约的实际内容看,外空的法律制度大体分为两个部分:一是适用于包括月球和其他天体在内的整个外空的法律制度和规则,以1967年《外空条约》为核心。二是专门适用月球和其他天体的法律制度和规则,以1979年《月球协定》为依据。两者的法律地位和制度是有所区别的。从理论上讲,两者的关系是一般法与特别法的关系。对月球和其他天体来说,首先应适用《月球协定》确立的月球及其他天体的专门法律制度。主要有两项特殊制度:一是月球及其他天体及其资源属于人类共同继承财产,各国承诺将来通过建立月球资源的国际开发制度进行利用,即须遵循统一的国际开发制度。二是月球及其他天体应"专为和平目的"而利用。对《月球协定》没有规定的事项,原则上仍应适用作为外空一般法的《外空条约》的规定。

就包括月球和其他天体在内的整个外空而言,将其界定为类似于国际海底区域的"人类共同继承财产"并不适当,认为外空类似于公海也不够准确。尽管外空与国际海底区域和公海都不属于任何国家的主权管辖范围,但外空应属自成一类的国际公共区域,应适用共同利益原则,其法律地位的具体内容主要应包括以下几点:(1)各国平等和无歧视探索和利用;(2)各国自由探索和利用;(3)各国为全人类共同利益探索和利用,特别是要顾及发展中国家的利益;(4)各国不得据为己有;(5)各国为和平目的探索和利用;(6)各国以国际合作方式探索和利用;(7)各国探索和利用外空应遵守包括《联合国宪章》在内的一般国际法。

3. 规范外空活动的国内立法有待进一步完善

主要涉及两方面的立法:一是应健全规范外空活动的公法制度。二是应建立规范外空商业活动的私法制度。就公法而言,现行的两个行政法规适用范围有限,仅限于对外空发射活动的监管,应逐步扩大到所有外空活动,包括外空遥感、外空旅游等。同时,需要进一步完善有关从事外空活动的人员、外空物体的管辖(包括登记)以及外空国家责任方面的制度。

4. 进一步完善和健全我国的空间政策

与美、俄等空间强国相比,我国关于空间政策和战略的研究起步较晚。《2000年中国的航天》《2006年中国的航天》和《2011年中国的航天》白皮书宣示了我国的一些空间政策,但还比较原则和粗疏,需要进一步深入和完善。必须从国家发展战略的高度认识和重视外空事务,充分利用现行外空条约赋予的权利,统筹规划,各部门协调,制定中长期的国家外空战略和方案以及相关配套政策和法律,不断增强我在外空事务上的能力和话语权。当前,除了要不断完善空间科学探索方面的政策外,还应健全空间技术开发和利用方面的政策,特别是空间产业政策。如外空安全政策、民用航天政策、商业航天政策、空间资源、环保政策、空间产品及技术出口政策、空间合作政策等。在产业政策方面,可考虑扶持大型国企和民企参与有关外空活动,扩大我国在外空的活动空间和利益。

5. 缺乏反映我国国家利益的外空法理

在重视参与制定国际外空立法的同时,也应注重现行国际外空立法的解释和适用。空间法适用的关键是如何解释有关国际条约问题。要切忌把外空法规则绝对化,要充分认识适用国际条约在很多情况下并不存在"非白即黑""是非分明"的界限,在很大程度上取决于如何解释这些规则,而如何解释在很大程度上又取决于价值观、国家利益和政策取向,这是适用包括外空法在内的所有国际法规则的核心。同样的国际法规则,基于不同的利益、政策和价值观,可能得出截然相反的结论。在外空法领域,我们尤其要平衡好国际社会共同利益、国家利益和非国家实体三者的关系,逐步建立一套服务于我国外空战略利益需要的外空法理。

外空交通管理:改善国际合作与安全的探索

青木节子 著[①]　李晶珠 译　李滨 校[②]

摘要:进入 21 世纪以来,出现了外空交通管理(STM)的概念。2006 年国际宇航科学院(IAA)的报告将外空交通管理的概念界定为:"用以促进安全进入外空,在外空进行操作和从外空返回地面的过程中不受物理或无线电频率干扰的一整套技术上或制度上的规定。"外空交通管理包括从发射阶段,在轨运行阶段,到再入阶段所采用的交通规则和规则的实施。本文注意到了外空交通管理对进一步促进外空发展和利用的重要性。首先,本文将研讨第一个有关外空交通管理的国际宇航科学院的报告。在评价国际宇航科学院的报告后,为了找到实现外空交通管理制度的条件,本文将探讨现有的法律和软法框架,也包括对一些国际组织的发展趋势的研究。作为结论,到 2020 年,有五个条件可以用来构建第一阶段的外空交通管理制度。由于有关外空交通管理(外空安全)与武器控制(外空安保)的必要措施在很多方面是重叠的,成功的外空交通管理制度的关键在于对外空军事利用实行部分豁免措施。

[①]　青木节子,日本应庆义塾大学教授。
[②]　李晶珠,哈尔滨工业大学法学院讲师。李滨,北京师范大学法学院教授,哈尔滨工业大学空间法研究所副所长。

1. 为什么需要"外空交通管理"

毫无疑问,外空活动的第一个 50 年是非常成功的。虽然繁荣的外空活动意味着引入外空的人造物体数量的不断增加,但由于人们已经习惯于把外空看作无限的和不可估量的广袤无边的领域,倾向于认为没有为了未来外空活动安全而采取立即行动的必要。事实上,乍一看,每立方公里只有 10^{-7} 个外空物体的数字更增加了这种放心感。然而,进一步观察外空形势获得的信息向我们显示了值得警惕的现实,那就是强烈要求整个国际社会要认真地去关注这个问题了。

由美国国防部操作的美国的外空监视网络(SSN)的报告指出,截止到 2009 年 1 月 1 日,在低地球轨道(LEOs)上可以跟踪和统计到 12 743 个大约 10 厘米或更大的外空物体[1]。尽管没有既定的定义,低地球轨道通常是指在地球表面上 2 000 公里以下的轨道,其中达到 400 公里的轨道和 800 ~ 1 000 公里周围的极地轨道是最有价值的[2]。据估计,在这些可跟踪到的外空物体中,只有不到 10% 的(可能是 6% ~ 7%)的物体是有用的[3],其余的可以被称为是空间碎片或轨道碎片[4]。

据估计,有 300 000 个直径在 1 到 10 厘米的外空物体无法被

---

[1] 美国国家航空航天局,"美国空间碎片环境和可操作的更新资料",在联合国和平利用外层空间委员会科学技术小组会议第 46 届会议上的报告,2009 年 2 月 9—20 日,第 5 页。

[2] 在地球静止轨道上,据说直径达到 1 米或更大的物体是可以被外空监视网络跟踪到的。

[3] Spacesecurity. org. , ed. , Space Security Index 2008 , at 2.

[4] 严格来说,不发挥作用的物体是不是空间碎片取决于空间碎片的定义。参见 Lboboš Perek,"外空交通的早期概念",国际空间法学会和欧洲空间法中心主办的"关于外空交通管理的前景"的研讨会上提交的论文,2002 年 4 月 2 日,第 6 ~ 7 页。

追踪到,并且在被观测的同一外空区域有数以几十亿计的更小的外空物体①。这样的事实使我们意识到,在低地球轨道的有用区域内充满了空间碎片。目前,直径在 1 到 10 厘米之间的外空物体是很成问题的,原因在于正在运行的卫星既不能被强化到可以抵抗这些空间碎片,也不能灵活地移动去避开这些空间碎片,因为这些碎片太小以至于无法被外空观测网络追踪到。没有被追踪到的小的空间碎片以每秒 7.5 公里的速度高速飞行,不仅可以造成人类生命和财产的损失,也将严重损害有价值的空间财产。

被追踪到的外空物体在 2004 年 6 月底统计为 9 148 个②,到 2005 年底为 9 428 个③,到 2006 年底 9 948 个④,到 2008 年 1 月 1 日 12 456 个⑤,而到 2009 年 1 月 1 日则为 12 743 个。

正是因为知道在有限的有用轨道上有不断增加的外空物体在运行,空间物体之间时常发生碰撞并不奇怪。其中最早的例子包括苏联的宇宙 1275 号卫星(Kosmos1275)被所有者不明的空间碎片所毁灭,以及法国的军用卫星 Cerise 与火箭 Ariane 在上升阶段的碰撞,都是发生在 1996 年⑥。调动卫星有时可以避免其与空间

---

① 见第 15 页注释①。

② Spacesecurity.org., ed., *Space Security* 2004, (Northview Press, 2005), at 3.

③ Spacesecurity.org., ed., *Space Security* 2006, (2006), at 36.

④ Spacesecurity.org., ed., *Space Security* 2007 (2007), at 23.

⑤ 美国国家航空航天局,"美国空间碎片环境和政策更新",联合国和平利用外层空间委员会第 45 届科学技术小组会议上的报告,2008 年 2 月 11~22 日,第 3 页。2007 年可跟踪到的外空物体的激增是因为中国在 2007 年 1 月 11 日进行了反卫星(ASAT)试验,根据美国外空监测网络的数据,增加的碎片达到了 2 600 个,是有史以来最大的增加。同上,第 11 页。Spacesecurity.org,同前注解 1,第 2 页。

⑥ Spacesecurity.org. ed., 外空安保 2003 (艾森豪威尔研究院,2004 年),第 1~4 页。

碎片碰撞①。据报告,每隔一年或两年,美国国家航空航天局就会根据外空监测网络提供的信息,在轨道上调动航天飞机来避免与即将到来的空间碎片发生碰撞②。因为大多数的民用和商用卫星不具有机动能力并且也没有被设计来抵抗物体的冲击与干扰,所以空间碎片的威胁在任何时候都必须被充分认识到。对目前形势符合逻辑的结论应该是,寻求一个更好的有关外空交通的国际管理体制。

2. "外空交通管理"概念的出现

2.1 有关"外空交通管理"第一次全面研究工作的开展

在这样的背景下,"外空交通管理"的概念逐渐进入学术研究的视野。在这方面,尤其值得注意的是美国航空航天研究院(AIAA)在1999年和2001年组织的两次重要的研讨会③。在2001年的研讨会期间,有建议认为国际宇航科学院(The International Academy of Astronautics,简称IAA)应该对外空交通管理展开深入研究。IAA在2001年末接受了这个建议并建立了一个大概由20个专家组成的跨学科的研究组④。IAA的报告在2006年以《外空交通管理的广泛研究》为题目出版⑤。但是事实上,在这项工作完成前,IAA的工作就吸引了广泛的注意,这些关注来自国际社会的不

---

① 欧空局的 ERS – 1 卫星在 1997 年和 1998 年被分别移动两次,法国的 SPOT – 2 在 1997 年被移动。

② Steven Mirmina,"减少轨道碎片的扩散:有法律约束力的文件的替代",美国国际法杂志,2005 年,99 卷,第 652 页。

③ 美国航空航天研究院,"国际合作:解决全球问题的会议记录(1999)",第 35~59 页;美国航空航天研究院,"国际合作:新千年的挑战的会议记录(2001)",第 7~14 页。

④ 参见,Corinne Contant, Petr Lála, Kai-Uwe Schrogl,"国际宇航科学院研究组关于外空交通管理规则的研究状况",IAA 03 – 5.5a06,"空间碎片与外空交通管理专题报告(2003,IAA)",第 576~577 页。

⑤ 国际宇航科学院,"外空交通管理的广泛研究(IAA,2006 年)"。

同层面,包括和平利用外层空间委员会(COPUOS)、国际空间法学会(IISL)、欧洲空间法中心(ECSL)和机构间碎片协调委员会(IADC)①。

为了实现 IAA 研究报告的目的,"外空交通管理"被界定为"用以促进安全进入外空,在外空进行操作和从外空返回地面的过程中不受物理的或无线电频率干扰的一整套技术上或制度上的规定"②。鉴于对外空交通管理没有确定的定义,本文对于外空交通管理可行性和挑战的思考也是建立在这个定义基础上的。

2.2　IAA 报告的范围、调查结果和结论③

2006 年 IAA 报告旨在建立 2020 年外空交通管理体制的框架。研究方法具有两个特点:一是未来的管理体制包括广泛的空间活动。具体而言,包括从发射阶段,到在轨运行阶段和最终的涉及运载工具再利用和脱离轨道的再入阶段(三个阶段)的所有外空活动。二是外空交通管理制度的管理维度,包括科学技术领域,也包

---

①　早期的一个里程碑的事件是,2002 年 4 月联合国和平利用外层空间委员会法律小组会议的第 41 届会议的开幕式上,国际空间法学会和 ECSL 赞助的"外空交通管理的前景"专题报告会。参见,IISL/ECSL "外空交通管理的前景"专题研讨会会议记录,2002 年 4 月 2 日,A/AC. 105/C. 2/2002/CRP. 7,2002 年 4 月 4 日,A/AC. 105/787,2002 年 4 月 19 日,第 10 段。专题研讨会的发言人大多是 IAA 研究组的成员。参见,Peter Van Fenema,"统一外空法议定书,'发射国'的概念,外空交通管理和外空的界定",《空气空间与外层空间法》,2002 年 28 卷,第 267～268 页。

②　国际宇航科学院,同上页注释 5,第 10 页和第 18 页。在美国航空航天研究院 2001 年的研讨会上,外空交通管理被定义为,"外空交通包括一个空间物体寿命的所有阶段,从发射到清理。它由防止损害的各种活动组成。"

③　除了 2006 年国际宇航科学院的报告,参见,Petr Lála,"外空活动的交通管理规则"《外空政治学》,2004 年第 2 卷,第 121～132 页;Petr Lála,"国际航天学会关于外空交通管理的研究",《庆祝空间时代:空间技术 50 年,外空条约 40 年会议报告》,2007 年 4 月 2—3 日(UNIDIR,2007),第 179～187 页。

括法律制度领域(两维度)。在 IAA 的报告中列举了对这种两维度三阶段活动的分析结果。

2.2.1 法律制度要求:各个不同的点

报告以外空活动的现状分析为起点,既从技术的维度,又从法律的维度分析。对具有可比性的空气空间和海洋的交通管理体制的分析,也对未来的外空交通管理体制的特点和任务提供了启示(第 2 章)。然后,报告列举了通过分析三个阶段中现有的和将出现的外空活动所得出的调查结果。这些调查结果体现了未来外空交通管理体制的技术和法律要求(第 3 章)。根据报告的调查结果,可以对有效的外空交通管理体制的法律制度要求总结如下[①]:

A 发射阶段

(1)引入安全保证制度。

(2)明确"外空物体"的概念。

(3)重新审视关于空气空间和外层空间的界定问题。

(4)明确"发射国"的概念。

(5)除了《反对弹道导弹扩散国际行为守则》(被周知为海牙行为守则,HCOC)之外,需要建立发射前通知制度,因为 HCOC 只包括没有约束力的条款和适用于有限的情形。

(6)损害发生时必要的通知制度[②]。

B 在轨运行阶段

在这个阶段的活动中,没有提到特别的法律要求,而是国际电讯联盟(ITU)规定的外空活动的成就和限制被重申[③]。

C 再入阶段

(1)外空法和空气空间法必须解决关于外空物体经过空气空间的这个开放性问题。

---

① 国际宇航科学院指出了 21 项调查结果,其中有关外空法在以下被引用。国际宇航科学院,同第 43 页注解 5,第 64 页,75 页和 89 页。

② 同前注,第 64 页。

③ 同前注,第 75 页。

(2) 如果能够建立某些国际承认的下降通道和一些其他交通工具不经常使用的受冲击的区域，并且这些通道和区域可以有助于外空交通的运行，对这个问题应该加以讨论①。

2.2.2　2020年的外空交通管理模式

报告最后预计了2020年的一个内容广泛的外空交通管理模式。第4章根据报告，外空交通管理体制将包括四个要素：

第一个要素是信息需求的保证。毫无疑问，有关外空物体正在哪里飞行的信息是任何可以成功控制交通的制度的首要基础。报告指出，为了满足第一个要素的要求，以下四个问题必须解决：(1)对必要的数据的界定。(2)数据的提供。(3)数据库和数据分配机制的建立。(4)外空气象信息服务机构的建立②。目前，有关外空态势感知（Space Situational Awareness，简称SSA）或者有关外空的精确知识仅仅由俄罗斯和美国掌握③。因此，建立一个和美国外空监视网络信息系统一样好甚至更好的技术基地，使其信息能对所有的外空活动主体，包括国家、组织和私人实体都开放和可以获得是一项艰巨任务④。

第二个要素是通知制度。目前，通知是《登记公约》⑤的任务，截止到2009年4月，该公约共有51个成员。但该公约并不令人满意。一方面是因为公约的强制性通知义务的规定（Art. IV 1 (a)-(e)）不充分；另一方面是因为成员国（或地区）没有很好地遵守公约规定的要求。必要的通知事项包括：(1)发射前对有关参

---

① 同第19页注释①，第89页。
② 同第19页注释①，第14页和第91页。
③ 俄罗斯外空监测系统（SSS）被评价为比美国的外空监测系统敏感度稍差一点。参见，Nicholas L. Johnson，"外空交通管理：概念与实践"，《外空政策》，2004年第20卷，第82页。
④ 国际宇航科学院，同第43页注解⑤，第14页和第91页。
⑤ 《关于射入外空的物体的登记公约》（1976年9月15日生效）1023 U.N.T.S. 15。

数的充分通知。(2)对轨道上的机动性和主动脱轨的事前通知。(3)对外空物体寿命结束和再入的通知①。

第三个要素是具体的交通规则。在 IAA 报告中列举了一些外空交通规则的例子:(1)有关载人外空飞行和非载人航天器发射的安全规则。(2)分区规则(轨道的选择)。(3)在轨运行阶段的可通行规则。(4)机动性的优先次序区分。(5)地球静止轨道(GEO)和低地球轨道(LEO)卫星星系的操作规则。(6)减少空间碎片的规则。(7)再入的规则。(8)在大气中、对流层和地面上的环境保护规则②。

第四个要素是国际控制机制。应该模仿联合国框架下的一些组织,像国际民用航空组织(ICAO)和国际海事组织(IMO),通过一个有关外空交通管理组织的有法律约束力的基本性法案③。2020年以后,期望那时外空交通管理的任务能够被现有的平台或组织(比如,联合国和平利用外层空间委员会、联合国外空事务委员会或者国际民用航空组织)所承担,这些组织将逐渐发展成一个为实现此目的的组织。展望未来 20 年,也可能由《外空条约》成员国(或地区)通过建立一个非政府组织的形式来实现这个任务④。

---

① 国际宇航科学院,同前第 17 页注解⑤,第 14 页和第 91 页。

② 同前注,同时参见,Kai-Uwe Schrogl,"外空交通管理",在乔治·华盛顿大学,空间政策研究院的报告,2008 年 1 月 24 日,第 11 到 12 页。

③ 报告预见到,2020 年后,现在联合国的"外空条约"可能被综合性的"外空公约"所取代。国际宇航科学院,同第 43 页注解⑤,第 15 页和 91 页。

④ 同前注,第 15 页。"外空公约"是未来综合性外空活动条约的临时名称,现在并不存在。同时,IAA 报告也表达了这样的愿望,即私人实体的活动也将发展成与公共外空财产相同的管理类别。空间法可以作为这种推断的范例。

2.3　IAA 报告的评价

就像 IAA 报告的起草者承认的那样,外空交通管理体制的实现需要几十年①,研究并没有急于立即制定规则②,IAA 报告的主要贡献在于它清楚地阐明了这件对于全球具有紧迫性的事项。因此,将报告评价为旨在不远的将来达成外空交通管理的国际协定是不公平的,本部分将在这一前提下对 IAA 报告进行评价。

在理解 IAA 报告所设想的成功的外空交通管理体制时,以下三点似乎是应该加以考虑的。

首先,有趣的是,在 IAA 报告中指出了在外空交通管理方面的三个阶段的法律方面的研究结果和四个要素,而在这些问题上存在的不足并不是外空交通管理制度特有的,一般性的国际外空法也存在着相同的重要问题。并且,联合国和平利用外层空间委员会的法律小组会议正在处理这些问题。发射阶段的一个要求(见本文 2.2.1A(3))已经被列为"外空的定义与界定"的提案 40 多年了,至今没有任何实质性结果。尽管成果不大,较为成功的例子有:关于适用"发射国"概念的协议③(见本文 2.2.1A(4))和加强登记管理的建议④(与可行的外空交通管理制度的第一和第二个要素有关,见本文 2.2.2)被联合国大会决议采纳,决议在整体上认可了联合国和平利用外层空间委员会的报告⑤。这些决议的重要性

---

① Kai-Uwe Schrogl,"外空交通管理:管理外空利用的综合性新办法",《欧洲空间政策研究院快报》,2007 年 10 月,第 3 期,第 3 页。

② Lála,18 页注释③,第 128 页。

③ "'发射国'概念的适用",GA Res. 59/115(2004 年 12 月 10 日)。

④ "加强国家和政府间组织登记空间物体的实践的建议",GA Res. 62/101(2007 年 12 月 17 日)。

⑤ 联合国和平利用外层空间委员会每年的报告会被特别政治与非殖民化委员会(第四委员会)所采纳。尽管由联合国和平利用外层空间委员会没有直接处理"外空物体"的定义问题,但这个概念被看作是逐渐增加的外空商业化利用的关键概念。

将在本文的 3.5.1 部分加以阐述。总而言之,可以说,联合国和平利用外层空间委员会更新联合国过时的《外空条约》的努力仅仅温和地体现在没有约束力的联合国大会决议中。

不能忘记的事实是,自从 1979 年以来,没有一个具有法律约束力的普遍性的法律文件被通过,联合国和平利用外层空间委员会造法活动和任何其他方面的国际组织都难以将外空交通管理纳入其中。因此,必须探索不同的规则制定形式。

第二,对于 2020 年外空交通管理模式,即便不是一个令人讨厌的东西,但是,从事空间活动的国家不愿意受任何额外的在外空自由活动的约束的事实却是构建外空交通管理体制的障碍,这一点是不能被低估的。航天国家的这种态度尤其来自以下两个原因:一是自从空间时代开始以来,自由从事外空活动的观念已经根深蒂固。二是外空是支持地面军事行动终极有效的平台。除非外空交通管理规则的优点能明显超过现有制度的缺点,否则使这些国家放弃长期以来享有的利用外空的自由将是不可能的。此外,外空交通管理的支持者们没有必然地提出明确的以令人信服的技术基础为支撑的实际做法,因此也不会改变现有的状况①。可以说,未来外空交通管理体制的构建,必须以能在整个外空交通管理框架中妥善处理外空军事利用问题为基础。

第三,在遇到有国家不遵守规则时,实施外空交通管理规则和执行惩罚看起来很困难,尤其是没有有约束力的法律文件的情况。既然国内立法可以对实施起关键作用②,因而研究出口管制制度,例如核供应商组织[Nuclear Suppliers Group (NSG)]、澳大利亚组织(Australia Group (AG))、导弹技术控制体制(Missile Technology Control Regime (MTCR))、瓦瑟纳尔安排(Wassenaar Arrangement

---

① 参见:Johnson,同 20 页注解③,第 83~84 页。
② Michael Gerhart,"外空交通管理概念对国内外空立法的影响",IAA 编辑,《2004 年空间碎片与外空交通管理专题报告》(AAS,2004),第 282~284 页。

(WA)》,从这些模式当中吸取有益做法是很必要的。它们建立在有相似观点的国家之间的君子协议之上,通过国内立法,有关出口控制制度在很大程度上得到了执行。正如上面提到的,以坚实的技术基础为支撑的,以行为守则或指导原则(软法)为形式的外空交通管理制度将有助于有效的国内执行。

3. 迈向有效的外空交通管理制度

在对 IAA 报告(见本文 2.3 部分)进行评价的基础之上,本部分将对实现有效的外空交通管理的具体措施进行思考。首先将对现有的外空交通管理活动进行考察,进而找出对未来建立成功的外空交通管理有用的条件,然后对未来外空管理制度的条件提出建议。

3.1 避免无线电频率干扰的协同活动机制

可以说,国际电信联盟已经在通过通知和登记程序这样有限的方式对外空交通进行着管理,因为国际电信联盟对公平、合理有效和经济地使用无线电频谱和地球静止轨道位置负有责任[1]。从20 世纪 70 年代到 80 年代,通过将一定区域的地球静止轨道的位置和频率分配给那些无法与航天国家竞争的国家,国际电信联盟解决了在外空交通管理方面遇到的第一个真正挑战[2]。在这一过程中,《国际电信联盟条约》和后来的《国际电信联盟章程》开始把无线电频率看作"有限的自然资源"[3],1998 年修订后的《国际电信联盟章程》将低地球轨道也列为"有限的自然资源"[4]。"纸卫星"

---

① 参见:《国际电信联盟章程》第 44 条(2),1994 年修订(在下文中《ITU 章程》)。

② 对于直接广播卫星,"先来先得"原则得到了放宽。

③ 《ITU 章程》第 44 条(2),以前是 1973 年《ITU 条约》第 33 条(2)。

④ 《ITU 章程》第 44 条(2)被修订为"无线电频率和任何关联的轨道,包括地球静止轨道卫星轨道,是有限的自然资源。"ITU 的基本修订文本在 1998 年的全体会议上通过(明尼阿波利斯会议),在 2000 年 1 月 1 日生效。

问题是国际电信联盟近期处理的有关外空交通管理的问题之一,在其中列举了使用地球静止轨道位置的条件①。

3.2 空间碎片

作为非政府组织,机构间空间碎片协调委员会(IADC)也以一定的方式管理着外空交通问题。既然在外空发展的现阶段,外空交通管理的目标是"在任何时间减少电子或物理的干扰"②,除了频率管理以外,减少空间碎片的措施应该是外空交通管理的中心问题。到目前为止,最成功的外空交通管理是在减缓空间碎片领域,有关空间碎片的程序和实体规则将有助于制定有效的外空交通管理制度。

直到1988年,美国国家空间政策才将空间碎片当作最大的任务③。跨机构层面的合作工作开始于1987年④,最终在1993年才成立IADC。现在该委员会由11个空间机构组成,毫无疑问是最有实际工作能力的为避免碰撞制定规则的组织,其规则是通过国内机制来实施的。2002年通过了第一个建立在共识基础上空间碎片

---

① Resolution 18 (1994) and Resolution 49 (1997) at ITU; See, also, e. g., A/AC. 705/738 (20 April 2000), paras. 36~49 & Annex III; GAOR 55th Sess. Supplement No. 20 (A/55/20) (2000), paras. 129~135. A/RES/55/122 (27 February 2001), para. 4.

② Johnson, 同20页注解③, 第80页。

③ 《跨机构政策》第9条, 规定在《国内空间法政策总统指令》(1988年2月11日)。然而, 早在1963年, E. W. Peterkin博士在美国海军研究实验室出版了两本备忘录, 对每年空间碎片的增长率进行了预言, 这些预言在后来被证明是非常准确的。David S. F. Portree & Joseph P. Loftus, Jr., Orbital Debris: A Chronology, NASA/TP – 1999 (1999), 第5页。

④ 1987年, 美国国家航空航天局和欧空局工作层面的合作开始了, 两年后, 在美国国家航空航天局和苏联之间, 美国国家航空航天局和日本国家空间发展局之间的双边空间机构合作开始。

缓减指导原则①,这个原则在 2004 年进行了补充②,在 2007 年进行了修正③。

在联合国和平利用外层空间委员会科学技术小组会议(STSC)层面,有关空间碎片问题在 1994 年才被提出④,但该小组会议并没有立即制定联合国和平利用外层空间委员会的缓减规则,而是对当时的空间碎片形势进行了调查,目的是为了培养共识为以后的工作打基础。经过几年的工作,最后在 1999 年形成了"空间碎片技术报告"⑤。STSC 委托 IADC 来制定一套自愿的国际空间碎片缓减指导原则。经过对指导原则草案的进一步修改,IADC 在 2004 年将其提交给 STSC,2007 年 2 月在 STSC 被通过,2007 年 6 月在全体委员会(main Committee)上被通过,最后在 2007 年 12 月被联合国大会核准⑥。虽然没有法律约束力,"联合国空间碎片缓减指导原则"由七项原则组成,具有与 IADC 指导原则不同的普遍适用性的特点。

这七个原则分别简洁地规定了在正常外空活动中减少碎片的建议办法⑦,任务结束后分解阶段的缓减办法,同时也规定了限制地球静止轨道和低地球轨道上无用的外空物体的长期干扰的办

---

① IADC,IADC 空间碎片减缓指导原则(2002 年 10 月 15 日)。

② IADC WG4, IADC 空间碎片减缓指导原则的支持文件(AL.20.3),议题一(2004 年 10 月 5 日)。

③ 从地球静止轨道再入轨的定义和建议措施在 2007 年 9 月修订。IADC,IADC-08-01(2008 年 2 月 8 日出版)。

④ 在那之前,1989 年,瑞典建议空间碎片应被纳入法律小组会议的议事日程,但当时并没有达成共识。澳大利亚、比利时、加拿大、德国、荷兰、尼日利亚共同支持了瑞典的建议。

⑤ See, e.g., A/AC.105/720 (1999)。

⑥ A/AC.105/890 (6 March 2007), para. 99 & Annex IV; GAOR, 62nd Sess., Supplement No. 20 (A/62/20) (2007), II.C.3, paras. 116~128 & Annex 4; A/RES/62/217 (distributed on 10 January 2008)。

⑦ 采取的措施包括降低意外碰撞和避免国际性破坏。

法。相应的实施自愿性的联合国指导原则需要靠 IADC 在其指导原则中规定实践性的标准和配套文件。换句话说,两个文件是互补的,IADC 指导原则对实际减缓措施提供了可操作的技术手段,而联合国的指导原则可以确保其得到普遍适用①。

自从 2008 年 STSC 会议以来,国内的实施情况要报告"空间碎片"议事日程项目中,这可以作为灵活的通过同行来施加压力的方式实施的控制②。不仅是 STSC,法律小组委员会(LSC)也在 2008 年将独立的议事题目"与空间碎片减缓措施有关的国内机制信息交换的一般问题"作为下一届会议的议题③,与 STSC 的技术报告一起提供了同行审查基础上的软压力。因此,可以有理由得出的结论是,在空间碎片问题上存在着一种可取的外空交通管理制度④。

3.3 发射前通知制度:海牙行为守则(HCOC)

2002 年 11 月通过的 HCOC 并不是一个法律文件,而是一个用来阻止和抑制能够运载大规模杀伤性武器的弹道导弹系统扩散的政治宣言⑤。2002 年该文件通过时,共有 93 个成员。尽管到 2009 年 6 月为止,成员已经增加到 130 个,但是,中国、印度、伊朗、朝鲜

---

① 在联合国指导原则的结尾,提到了以下内容:"为了对空间碎片缓减措施进行更深入的描述和建议,成员国(或地区)和国际组织可以参考 IADC 空间碎片减缓指导原则的最先文本和其他的支持文件,这些可以在 IADC 的网站上找到(www.iadc.org)。"A/62/20(2007 年),第 50 页。

② 2008 年,巴西、加拿大、中国、古巴、捷克、德国、希腊、印度、印度尼西亚、意大利、日本、俄罗斯、美国、委内瑞拉和欧空局做了报告。

③ A/AC.105/917(18 April 2008)at 24.

④ 在空间碎片减缓方面,ITU 和 IADC 之间的跨组织关系也是值得注意的。ITU 在 1986 年开始研究地球静止轨道上的物理干扰问题(问题 34/4),所谓的再入轨措施是在 1993 年被提出的(ITU-R S.1003 号建议)。这些措施要求在无用的卫星彻底完结前,将它们移到 300 公里以外的墓地轨道上。接下来,为了适应技术的新近发展和现实的要求,这个建议在 2004 年根据 IADC 指导原则进行了修订(ITU-R S.1003-1 建议)。

⑤ 起草 HCOC 是为了补充导弹及其技术控制制度(MTCR)。

和巴基斯坦这些拥有弹道导弹的国家都不是成员国(或地区)。

由于弹道导弹(BM)与外空发射运载工具(SLV)在工作原理上具有相似性,要求成员国(或地区)不得使用 SLV 项目去掩盖 BM 项目(2g),同时,成员国(或地区)也必须采取必要的警戒措施来协助其他国家的 SLV 项目来阻止导弹的扩散(3d)。为了增加信心和促进弹道导弹和弹道导弹技术的不扩散,进一步要求成员国(或地区)要增强对 BM 和 SLV 项目的采取适当透明度措施的必要性的认识(2h)。

为了上述目的,对于可以扩张的 SLV 项目,根据商业上和经济上的保密原则,要求成员国(或地区)实施:(1)制作一个包括 SLV 政策和陆地发射基地或试验基地的概要的年度报告。(2)提供前一年中有关 SLV 的数目和一般类别的年度信息,就像 HCOC(4iii)中规定的发射前通知机制那样。(3)在自愿的基础上(包括根据许可进入的程度),考虑在它们的发射(试验)基地邀请国际观察员(4 a)ii)。

为 BM 和 SLV 项目而设计的发射前通知机制如下:第一,成员国(或地区)要交换它们之间的关于 BM 和 SLV 发射活动和试飞活动的发射前通知书。第二,通知书应该包括以下信息:BM 和 SLV 的种类,预定的发射时限,发射区域和预定的方位(4 a)iii)。

进一步要求成员国(或地区)批准,加入或者遵守 1967 年《外空条约》①、《责任公约》②和《登记公约》(1975)(3 a),重点在于采纳外空法的基本原则。

HCOC 的年度会议在维也纳举行,在会议上成员国(或地区)商讨实施问题,包括发射前通知和关于 BM 和 SLV 政策的年度报告,并努力使 HCOC 具有普遍性。普遍性适用的挑战是,在航天国

---

① 《关于各国探索和利用包括月球和其他天体的外层空间活动所应遵守原则的条约》(1967 年 10 月 10 日生效),610 U. N. T. S. 205。

② 外空物体所造成损害之国际责任公约(1972 年 9 月 1 日生效),961 U. N. T. S. 187。

家中,中国和印度不是成员国(或地区),而美国推迟了提供发射前通知书,俄罗斯,欧洲国家和日本提交了被要求的通知书①。

除了 HCOC,还有几个双边的事前通知协议,包括美国和俄罗斯之间的和印度和巴基斯坦之间的协议。

3.4 外空安保(space security):裁军会议

值得一提的是,"外空安保"一词有时被解释为"对外空的可靠的和可持续的进入和利用,并且免受来自外空的威胁"②这与 IAA 报告中对外空交通安全的解释相似③。

尽管在裁军会议上没有达成单独的"防止外空军备竞赛"的协定,但在提交给防止外空军备竞赛临时会议(1985—1994)和全体会议的提案中有多种关于外空交通管理的提议。这些提议,既有硬法的形式(条约),也有软法的形式(行为守则,交通规则等),包括禁止"外空武器"到禁止"反卫星武器(ASAT)"、禁止在外空使用武力和敦促透明度与建立信任措施(TCBM)等④。在 20 世纪 90 年代早期,作为相对现实的目标,裁军会议上的重点从裁军的努力转移到建立透明与信任措施上来⑤。以下内容是被看作是外空交通管理的透明度与建立信任措施。

(1)由多边控制组织搜集外空信息

* PAXSAT A,空对空的控制系统,由加拿大在 1987 年首次提

---

① Scott C. Larrimore,"国际外空发射通知与数据交换",《外空政策》,2007 年第 23 卷,第 176 页。

② 例如,在 2007 年联合国外空委科学技术小组会议第 44 界会议上加拿大的报告中所用的定义,也是 spacesecurity.org 所采用的定义。

③ 见本文 2.1 部分。

④ 在 21 世纪,建立信任措施(CBM)的概念逐渐被透明度与建立信任措施(TCBM)所取代。

⑤ 1990 年 12 月 4 日联合国大会 45/55 号决议第一次要求实施建立信任措施的技术内容。

出,并在 2006 年再次重申①。

* 国际传导中心(UNITRACE),由法国提出②。

* 不需要特殊建立一个控制机构,苏联建议成立世界空间组织(WSO)来全面处理外空活动,这个组织也可以作为外空交通管理的平台③。

(2)发射前核查制度

* 国际外空核查团(ISI)④。苏联建议的核心是建立多边的发射前核查制度来实地证明没有外空武器搭载在外空物体上。

(3)加强 1975 年《登记公约》的规定

在过去的几年中,很多国家提出这种建议或支持这种想法。《登记公约》不是控制武器的法律文件,而是为了有效实施 1972 年的《责任公约》而缔结的有关外空物体登记的公约,只是这个公约可以提供透明度这一点被裁军会议注意到了⑤。

(4)卫星之间不干涉原则

* 卫星豁免原则(Satellite immunity)(法国)⑥保留区制度

---

① CD/786 (1987); CD/1785 (2006).

② CD/1092 CD/OS/WP.46 (1991) at 5. Before UNITRACE proposal, see, e.g., CD/937 and CD/OS.WP.35 (1989) and CD/PV.570 (1989);最初由法国在 1978 年在联合国大会裁军会议第一届特别会议上提议的国际卫星控制机构(ISMA),在各种场合包括 CD.A–S 10/AC.1/7 (1978); A/C.1/33/PV.26 (1978); CD/641 (1985), para.4 中被再次提到。ISMA 的任务是控制地球而不是外空,但是成为法国一系列建议的起点,例如卫星图像处理机构(SIPA)和 UNITRACE。

③ CD/639 (1985).

④ CD/PV.385 (1987); CD/817 and CD/OS/WP.19 (1988). 西德也保持着严格的发射前通知制度。CD/905 CD/OS/WP.28 (1989),第 21~22 页。

⑤ 早期的建议可见于 para.27 of CD/641(1985), para.27 of CD/786 (1987) and para.24 of CD/833 (1988).

⑥ CD/905/CD/OS/WP.28 (1989), at 21~22.

(keep-Out Zones (KOZ))(西德)①一直被反复提议和讨论。KOZ 概念的核心是在外空物体之间设定最低限度的距离和对外空物体设定速度限制②。

(5)暂停在外空试验、部署和使用任何类型的武器

与上面提到的建议类似,这一建议也已经被裁军会议反复提及,而且经常是以软法的形式出现的,目的是想让其代替真正的武器控制或裁军协议。不用说,透明度与建立信任措施的目标与外空交通管理的目标不同,但采取的步骤却基本相同。这种现象有两层含义:这意味着外空交通管理的目标可能等同于武器控制措施,将有助于外空的稳定,然而同时,这也将使外空交通管理采取集体行动更加困难,因为这样的措施可能危及对外空的自由军事利用。

3.5 外空安全(Space Safety):联合国和平利用外层空间委员会框架下的外空交通管理

不仅在本文 3.2 部分提到的科学技术小组委员会上,而且在法律小组委员会和全体委员会上,我们都可以发现致力于管理外空交通来促进和平利用外空的趋势。

3.5.1 法律小组委员会

正如本文 2.3 部分提到的一样,每年都有一部分以"和平利用外层空间的国际合作"为题目的联合国大会的决议通过,这些决议对于为建立外空交通管理制度而营造有利的法律环境非常重要。例如,到目前为止,分别在 2004 年和 2007 年通过的"发射国"概念的适用③和有关加强国家和国际政府组织在登记空间物体方面的实践的建议④。

---

① CD/1092 and CD/OS/AP.46 (1991) at 4.
② CD/786 (1987), para.27; CD/905/CD/OS/WP.28 (1989) at 22.
③ A/RES/59/115 (10 December 2004).
④ A/RES/62/101 (17 December 2007).

2004年决议的目的是,尽可能在各种各样的外空活动中确定有责任的国家和应该负责任的国家或者是对某个外空物体有管辖权和控制权的国家。"发射国"概念的这种划分对构建成功的外空交通制度是一个重要前提,因为发射国将负责通知它自己的发射活动,提供和接收外空形势预警系统的信息并且实施具体的交通规则。2007年关于外空物体登记的决议作为外空交通管理的起点,有助于建立更好的外空态势感知系统。

3.5.2 全体委员会的主席报告

受联合国成功通过《空间碎片减缓指导原则》的鼓舞,联合国和平利用外层空间委员会全体委员会主席在他的报告中强调,非常有必要继续致力于某种将外空交通管理包括进去的"交通规则"。他继续指出,联合国外空委的法律小组委员会应承担起这项任务[1],并且国际航天学会的报告为建立这样的"交通规则"已经开了个好头[2]。

目前尚没有这样的议事日程,但是,在几年内就有可能会有这样的议题,尤其是如果外空发生了一个重大的事故对外空物体造成直接的实质性损害时[3]。

3.6 外空交通规则行为守则:联合国大会

在2007年联合国大会的第一次会议上,葡萄牙代表欧盟提交了综合性的、为了防止外空军备竞赛的有关外空透明度与建立信

---

[1] A/AC. 105/L. 268 (10 May 2007) paras. 26~29.

[2] 同前注,28段。

[3] 参见,William Ailor,"外空交通管理:实施与含义",《星际航行学报》,2006年58卷,第279~286页。事实上,在2009年2月,美国商业通讯卫星铱33和俄罗斯失效的军事卫星宇宙2251之间在788公里轨道上发生了第一次主要卫星相撞事件。参见,Becky Iannota & Tariq Malik,"美国卫星在外空因碰撞而毁坏",http://www.space.com/news/090211-satellite-collision.html (2009年3月24日最后一次访问)。

任措施(TCBM)的外空物体和外空活动行为守则的建议①。建议包含了外空交通管理的概念:"这一行为守则规定的主要活动包括,除其他外,避免碰撞和故意爆炸,发展更为安全的交通管理措施,通过加强信息交换,以及透明度和通知措施而获得的保证制度,采纳更严格的减缓空间碎片措施。"②在未来的行为守则中规定了有关实施的最佳方法:(1)避免可以导致空间物体损害和产生空间碎片的危险的机动措施;(2)为避免碰撞在卫星周围设定专门的警戒区;(3)关于发射活动的详细信息的交换;(4)加强登记制度。

可以说,在外空安全保障领域,外空交通安全管理措施也正好符合防止在外空进行军备竞赛的目的。考虑到这些重叠的建议措施不是为了同一目标,成功的外空交通制度将必须建立在这样的认识基础上,即只要对外空的利用是符合现行的国际空间法和与外空活动有关的武器控制法律的,外空的安保利用就不会受到损害③。

4. 结论

从长远的观点来看,越来越多的外空活动主体和更多样化的外空活动使在外空交通规则方面达成某种协议成为必要。因此,在前面研究的基础上,笔者将针对在未来十年中构建有效的外空交通规则提出五个条件:

(1)广为认可的是,外空交通管理是必要的但在此时并不是紧迫的。可是,如果发生了一次重大事故,尤其如果是事故使某个宇航员失去了生命,可能就会改变整个观念。因此,对全面的外空交通管理制度有所准备是第一个条件。这种准备必须包括科学、技术、制度和法律各个领域。必须进行持续地跨学科研究。

(2)关于第(1)点,有关目前形势的技术评价和确定方面需要

---

① A/62/114/ Add.1 (18 September 2007) at 5~8.
② 同前注,第7页。
③ 同前注,第7页,2.9.(c)部分。

改进的地方是应予优先考虑的问题。联合国关于空间碎片减缓的指导原则的成功归功于 IADC 提供的有力的技术背景资料。

（3）为了保证信息要求，应致力于制定以技术为基础的指导原则（软法）。如果外空的某些信息是以技术为支持的，并且如果这些指导原则可以使外空和军事机构相信它们没有被政治化，那么，即使是不情愿的，国家也可以容忍某些对主权的侵蚀。

（4）为了实施有效的外空交通规则，通过符合现有国际空间法的、经过协调的国内通知制度去填补空白是可能的。在这点上，成功的关键在于鼓励更多的国家制定国内空间法，以及建立相应的体现 2004 年和 2007 关于澄清发射国和加强空间物体登记制度的联合国大会决议中包含的建议的登记制度[①]。

（5）为了制定交通规则，必须注意到外空安保和外空安全目前重叠的领域是在增加的，两者有相似的定义和相似的必要的活动。因此，回避外空安保中最敏感的部分是外空交通安全管理第一阶段成功的关键。外空军事活动可能要从外空交通规则中豁免，甚至是在多于几十年的时间里。为了找到合理的解决办法，应对空气空间法和海洋法的先例加以研究。

具有讽刺意味的是，有关外空交通管理或外空安全的工作在为了防止外空军备竞赛而达成有关透明度和建立信任措施的共识上是起关键作用的，而防止外空军备竞赛的目标在裁军会议上 30 年也没实现。

---

① 2006 年，在法律小组会议上讨论加强登记制度时，巴西、印度尼西亚和哈萨克斯坦刚刚通过了国内登记制度，意大利和荷兰的国内法中也反映了法律小组会议讨论的新发展。尽管现在下结论还太早，但是在一定程度上是可以实现调和的。

Space Traffic Management: The Quest for Improvement of International Cooperation and Security

Setsuko AOKI, D. C. L. [①]

Abstract: Since around the turn of the century, the concept of space traffic management (STM) made its appearance. STM is defined as "the set of technical and regulatory provisions for promoting safe access into outer space, operations in outer space and return from outer space to Earth free from physical or radio-frequency interference" in the International Academy of Astronautics (IAA) Report (2006). STM covers the tasks of adopting traffic rules and implementing them from the launch phase, to the in-orbit operation phase, and to the re-entry phase. In this paper, taking notice of the significance of the STM to further promote space development and use, first, the IAA Report, the first comprehensive study of the STM, will be examined. Following the assessment of the IAA Report, in order to find the conditions to realize a STM regime, some of the present legal and soft law frameworks as well as the trends of some international organizations will be studied. As conclusions, 5 conditions would be presented to construct a first

---

[①] Setsuko AOKI, Professor of Policy Management, Keio University, Japan.

stage of STM regime by 2020. Since the required actions of STM (space safety) and arms control (space security) are largely overlapping, the key of the successful STM depends on the construction of the partial exemption measures of military use of space.

1. Why "Space Traffic Management"?

The first 50 years of space activities are, without any doubt, a tremendous success. Although flourishing space activities mean the increasing number of man-made objects introduced into outer space, because we are accustomed to regarding space as the infinite and immeasurable vast vacant area, we tend to think that no imminent steps have to be taken for the future safety of space operations. In fact, the figure that there are only 10^{-7} objects per cubic km would add the sense of reassurance at first glance. A closer look at the space situational information would, however, show an alarming reality that strongly urges the global community to be well prepared to address the issue now.

The US Space Surveillance Network (SSN), operated by Department of Defense (DOD), reports that 12 743 objects, approximately 10 cm or larger, are tracked and catalogued in the Low Earth Orbits (LEOs) as of 1 January 2009[①]. While no established definition exists, LEOs usually indicate orbits below some 2 000 km above Earth's surface, among which orbits up to 400 km and the polar orbits from around 800 km to 1 000 km are most valuable[②]. It is assessed that among tracked

---

① NASA, "USA Space Debris Environment and Operational Updates", presentation to the 46th Session of the Scientific and Technical Subcommittee (STSC) on the Peaceful Uses of Outer Space (COPUOS), 9~20 February, 2009, at 5.

② In GEO, it is said that objects as big as 1 m and bigger in diameter can be tracked by SSN.

objects, only less than 10 percent (perhaps 6 ~ 7 percent) are functional①, and the rests are so called space debris or orbital debris②. It is also estimated that there are over 300 000 objects measuring between 1 and 10 cm in diameter which cannot be trackable and billions smaller in the same area of space③. Such facts lead to realize that the useful parts of LEOs are filled with space debris. Objects between 1 cm and 10 cm are most problematic today because satellites in operation can neither be hardened enough to protect against space debris, nor can satellites maneuver to avoid them since they are too small to be tracked by SSN. Non-trackable small debris could cause the loss of human life and serious damage to valuable space assets, flying as rapid as 7.5 km per second.

The number of the objects actually catalogued stood at 9 148 at the end of June 2004④, 9 428 at the end of 2005⑤, 9 948 by the end of 2006⑥, 12 456 as of 1 January 2008⑦ and 12 743 as of 1 January 2009.

---

① Spacesecurity. org, ed., Space Security Index 2008, at 2.

② Strictly speaking, if all non-functional objects are space debris or not would depend on the definition of space debris. See, e. g., Lobos Perek, "Early Concepts for Space Traffic", paper submitted to the IISL/ECSL Symposium on Prospects for Space Traffic Management, 2 April 2002, at 6 ~ 7.

③ See, e. g., Spacesecurity. org. ed., supra, note 1 above.

④ Spacesecurity. org., ed., Space Security 2004, (Northview Press, 2005), at 3.

⑤ Spacesecurity. org., ed., Space Security 2006, (2006), at 36.

⑥ Spacesecurity. org., ed., Space Security 2007 (2007), at 23.

⑦ NASA, "USA Space Debris Environment and Policy Updates", presentation to the 45th Session of the STSC on the COPUOS, 11 ~ 22 February 2008, at 3. Drastic increase on the trackable objects during 2007 is caused by a Chinese ASAT test on 11 January 2007, which increased debris population close to 2,600 pieces according to the US SSN, biggest increase in history. *Ibid.* at 11; Spacesecurity. org, supra, note 1, at 2.

Because the increasing number of space objects operate in rather limited useful orbits, it is surprising to know that the collision of space objects have occurred. One of the earliest examples would include the destruction of Russian Kosmos 1 275 by space debris the owner of which is unknown and the collision of French military satellite Cerise with the Ariane rocket upper stage, both happened in 1996[1]. Also, maneuvering of satellites is sometimes conducted to avoid space debris[2]. It was also reported that once every year or two, NASA maneuvered the space shuttle away from the trajectory of oncoming debris based on the information given by SSN[3]. Taking into account that the most civilian and commercial satellites do not have maneuvering capability and not manufactured to protect against the physical impact and interference, the threat of space debris must be all the more strongly acknowledged. Logical consequence of the present situation would be the necessity of the quest for a better international management of space traffic.

2. Appearance of the concept of "Space Traffic Management"

2.1 Road to the First Comprehensive Work on STM

Under such circumstances, the concept of Space Traffic Management (STM) was gradually evolved among academic circles, especially through the two important workshops organized by American Institute of

---

[1] Spacesecurity.org. ed., Space Security 2003 (The Eisenhower Institute, 2004), at 1~4.

[2] ERS-1 of the European Space Agency (ESA) was moved twice in 1997 and 1998 respectively and French SPOT-2, in 1997. Ibid.

[3] Steven Mirmina, "Reducing the Proliferation of Orbital Debris: Alternatives to a Legally Binding Instrument", American Journal of International Law, vol. 99 (2005), at 652.

Aeronautics and Astronautics (AIAA) in 1999 and 2001①. During the 2001 workshop, it was suggested that the International Academy of Astronautics (IAA) should conduct an in depth study on STM. IAA accepted it in late 2001 and set up an interdisciplinary study group of approximately 20 experts②. IAA report was published in 2006 under the title of "Cosmic Study on Space Traffic Management"③, but even before the completion of the work, wider and increased attention was paid to the IAA work from various fora of international space community including Committee on the Peaceful Uses of Outer Space (COPUOS), International Institute of Space Law (IISL), European Centre for Space Law (ECLA), and Inter Agency Space Debris Coordination Committee (IADC)④.

For the purposes of the IAA report, STM is defined as "the set of tech-

---

① AIAA, Proceedings of the International Cooperation: Solving Global Problems (1999) at 35 ~ 59; AIAA, Proceedings of the International Cooperation: Addressing Challenges for the New Millennium (2001), at 7 ~ 14.

② See, e.g., Corinne Contant, Petr Lála, Kai-Uwe Schrogl, "Status of the IAA Study Group on Traffic Management Rules for Space Operations", IAA 03 - 5.5a06, Space Debris and Space Traffic Management Symposium (2003, IAA), at 576 ~ 577.

③ IAA, *Cosmic Study on Space Traffic Management* (IAA, 2006).

④ One early milestone is "Prospects for Space Traffic Management" symposium held in April 2002 under the auspices of IISL/ECSL at the opening day of the 41st session of the Legal Subcommittee (LSC) of the COPUOS. See, Proceedings of the IISL/ECSL Symposium on Prospects for Space Traffic Management, 2 April 2002, A/AC. 105/C. 2/2002/CRP. 7, 4 April 2002; A/AC. 105/787, 19 April 2002, para. 10. Most of speakers of that symposium were IAA study group members. See, also, Peter Van Fenema, "Unidroit Space Protocol, the Concept of 'Launching State', Space Traffic Management and Delimitation of Outer Space", Air & Space Law, vol. 28, (2002), at 267 ~ 268.

nical and regulatory provisions for promoting safe access into outer space, operations in outer space and return from outer space to Earth free from physical or radio-frequency interference[①]. Under the circumstances that there is no established definition of STM, the same definition is also used in this paper for the consideration of the possibilities and challenges for STM.

2.2 Scope, Findings and Conclusions of IAA Report[②]

The IAA report in 2006 aims at an outline of a space traffic regime in 2020. The approach of the study has two characteristics. One is the broad scope of space activities covered by the prospective regime. STM in this study covers all space activities from the launch phase, to the in orbit operation phase, and finally to the entry phase concerning reusable vehicles and orbit (three phases). The other is the dimension of management of STM, which comprises scientific and technical area as well as regulatory and legal fields (two dimensions). Results of the analysis of the three phases of activities by the two dimensions are enumerated in the IAA Report.

2.2.1 Regulatory and Legal Requirements: Individual Points

The report begins with the analysis of the present status of space activi-

---

[①] IAA, see note [③] on page 39, at 10 & 18. At the AIAA workshop in 2001, STM was defined as "[s]pace traffic encompasses all the phases of a space object's life, from launch to disposal. It consists of activities intended to prevent damage".

[②] In addition to the IAA Report in 2006, see, e.g., Petr Lála, "Traffic Management Rules for Space Operations" Astropolitics, vol. 2 (2004), at 121 ~ 132; Petr Lála, "Study on Space Traffic Management by the International Academy of Astronautics", Celebrating the Space Age: 50 Years of Space Technology, 40 Years of the Outer Space Treaty, Conference Report, 2 ~ 3 April 2007 (UNIDIR, 2007), at 179 ~ 187.

ties in both in the technical and legal dimensions. Study on the comparable traffic regimes including air and sea is also provided to highlight the characteristics and challenges for the future STM (chapter 2). Then, the findings analyze current and emerging activities in each of the three phases. Such findings show the technical and legal requirements for a future space traffic regime (chapter 3). Among the findings in the report, regulatory and legal requirements for an effective STM are summarized below[①]:

A. The launch phase

(1) Safety certifications should be introduced.

(2) Clarification of the term "space object" is needed.

(3) The question of delimitation of air space and outer space should be revisited.

(4) The concept of "launching State" has to be clarified.

(5) A pre launch notification system is necessary in addition to the International Code of Conduct against Ballistic Missile Proliferation (widely known as Hague Code of Conduct: HCOC), because HCOC includes only non-binding provisions and only in limited cases.

(6) Obligatory information in cases of damage is relevant[②].

B. The in orbit operation phase

In this phase of activities, no specific legal requirements are mentioned. Instead, the accomplishments and the limitations of the activities by the International Telecommunication Union (ITU) are speci-

---

① IAA Report points out 21 findings, among which those related to space law are cited below. IAA, see note ③ on page 39, at 64, 75 & 89.

② Ibid., at 64.

fied①.

C. The re entry phase

(1) Space law and air law have to resolve the open issue of passage of space objects through airspace.

(2) The question should be discussed if a certain internationally recognized descent corridors and possibly even impact areas which are not frequently used by other traffic should be established, and if such corridors and areas could contribute to the space traffic②.

2.2.2 **STM Model for** 2020

The report finally estimates how a comprehensive STM model in 2020 will look like (chapter 4). According to the Report, a STM regime will comprise four elements: (1) the securing the information needs; (2) a notification system; (3) substantive space traffic rules; and finally (4) mechanisms and organizations for implementation.

On the first element, needless to say, the correct information where a space object is flying should constitute a sound basis for any successful traffic control. In the report, it is stated that the following issues have to be addressed for satisfying the first element: (a) definition of necessary data; (b) provision of data; (c) establishment of a database and distribution mechanisms for data; and (d) establishment of an information service on space weather③. Presently, space situational awareness (SSA), or the precision knowledge about the space traffic is only in the possession of the US and Russia④. Thus, it seems quite a challenge

---

① See note ① on page 41, at 75.
② Ibid., at 89.
③ Ibid., at 14 & 91.
④ Russian Space Surveillance System (SSS) is evaluated slightly less sensitive than the US SSN. See, e. g., Nicholas L. Johnson, "Space Traffic Management: Concept and Practices", Space Policy, vol. 20 (2004), at 82.

establishing a technical basis as good as or better than the US SSN information systems open and accessible to all actors, states, organizations and private entities[①].

The second element is a notification system. Currently, it is the task of the Registration Convention[②] to which 51 states are parties as of April 2009, but the Convention has so far yielded the outcome less than satisfactory, partly because the contents of the obligatory notification provisions (Art. IV 1 (a) ~ (e)) are insufficient and partly because the states parties do not necessarily abide by the requirements specified in the Convention. Required areas include: (a) the adequate pre-launch notification of parameters; (b) the pre-notification of orbital manoeuvres and active de-orbiting; and (c) the notification of the end of lifetime of objects, and re-entry[③].

The third element is the concrete traffic rules. Examples of space traffic rules, which are specified in the IAA Report include: (a) safety rules for launches for both unmanned vehicles and manned space flights; (b) rule on zoning (selection of orbits); (c) right-of-way rules for in-orbit phases; (d) prioritization with regard to maneuvers; (e) operational rules for GEO and LEO satellite constellations; (f) debris mitigation regulations; (g) safety rules for re-entry; and (h) environmental protection provisions in the atmosphere, troposphere, and on the earth[④].

---

① IAA, see note ③ on page 39, at 14 & 91.

② Convention on Registration of Objects Launched into Outer Space (entered into force on 15 September 1976) 1023 U. N. T. S. 15.

③ IAA, see note ③ on page 39, at 14 & 91.

④ Ibid., See, also, Kai-Uwe Schrogl, "Space Traffic Management", presentation at Space Policy Institute, The George Washington University, 24 January 2008, at 11 ~ 12.

The fourth element is international control mechanisms. It is maintained that a legally binding constitutive act of a STM organization shall be adopted modeled from the UN family organizations such as International Civil Aviation Organization (ICAO) and International Maritime Organization (IMO)①. After 2020, it is expected that "[t]he operative oversight, i. e. the task of space traffic management, could be taken up by an already existing forum or organization (such as UNCOPUOS/UNOOSA, or ICAO), which would evolve into a body shaped for that purpose. Looking 20 years ahead, it could also be handled by a non-governmental entity tasked by the State parties to an Outer Space Convention"②.

2.3 Assessment of the IAA Report

As drafters of the IAA Report admit that the STM regime would be realized "for decades now"③, and "the study does not, however, advocate a rush to regulation"④, the primary contribution of the IAA Report is to clearly identify the pressing issues for the global society and indicate a model procedure to address them. Thus, it would not be fair if the Re-

---

① The Report foresees the possibility that the present UN space treaties could be superseded by a comprehensive "Outer Space Convention" after 2020. IAA, see note ③ on page 39, at 15 & 91.

② *Ibid*, at 15. "Outer Space Convention" is a provisional name for a future comprehensive treaty on space activities, which does not exist now. Also the expectation is expressed in the IAA Report that the private sector activities will develop into the same category of control as the public space assets. The air law can be a precedent for such speculation.

③ Kai-Uwe Schrogl, "Space Traffic Management: the New Comprehensive Approach for Regulating the Use of Outer Space", ESPI Flash Report, No. 3, (October 2007), at 3.

④ Lala, see note ② on page 40, at 128.

port were evaluated by the possibility of reaching an international agreement of space traffic rules in the near future. Noting that, the IAA Report will be assessed in this section.

The following 3 points seem to be taken into consideration for realizing a successful STM regime envisioned in the IAA Report.

First, interestingly, legal findings pointed out in the 3 phases and 4 elements in the IAA Report as areas of insufficient regulation for the appropriate STM are not unique for STM, but shared as crucial issues in the international space law in general. And as such, those issues have been currently being dealt with at the Legal Subcommittee (LSC) of the COUPOS. One of the requirements in the launch phase (see, A (3) of 2.2.1 of this paper) has been an agenda item named "definition and delimitation of outer space" for more than 4 decades without any tangible results. Although modest, more successful examples are the agreement on the application of the concept of the "Launching State"[1] (see, A(4) of 2.2.1 of this paper) and the recommendation on the enhancement of the registration practices[2], (in relation to the first and second elements of a possible STM regime, see, 2.2.2 of this paper) are adopted as the part of the UN General Assembly (GA) Resolution that endorses the COPUOS report as a whole[3]. The signifi-

---

[1] "Application of the Concept of the 'Launching State'", GA Res. 59/115 (10 December 2004).

[2] "Recommendations on Enhancing the Practices of States and International Intergovernmental Organizations in Registering Space Objects", GA Res. 62/101 (17 December 2007).

[3] The COPUOS Report of the each year is endorsed at the Special Political and Decolonization Committee (Fourth Committee). The issue of the definition of "space objects", while have not been directly dealt with at the COPUOS, is being paid attention to as one of the key concepts which should be clarified in the age of increasing commercial use of outer space.

cance of those resolutions will be revisited in 3.5.1 of this paper. In a word, it can be said that efforts at the COPUOS to update the partly outdated UN treaties on Outer Space have been only mildly rewarded in the form of the non-binding GA resolutions.

Mindful of the fact that not a single legally-binding instrument of universal nature has been adopted since 1979, treaty making at the COPUOS and any other international fora on any subject would be most difficult including that of a STM. Different modality of rule-making must be explored.

Second, as for a model space traffic regime in 2020, if not an aversion, at least the reluctance of spacefaring nations to any additional restraints in the freedom of activities cannot be underestimated as a challenge in constructing a STM regime. Such attitude of spacefaring nations seems to stem from, especially, the following two reasons: first the notion of freedom of space activities strongly embedded since the advent of the space age; second, the extreme usefulness of outer space as a platform to support terrestrial military operations. Unless the merits of traffic rules clearly exceed the demerits of the current regime, the giving up of the long cherished freedom of space would not be possible[①]. It can be said that the reasonable basis for a future STM has to be constructed in a manner that could deal with military use properly in a whole scheme of STM.

Third, it seems difficult to implement space traffic rules and enforce sanctions in case of the non-compliance with the rules, especially when no binding instruments exist. Since national legislation would play a

---

① See, e.g., Johnson, see note ④ on page 42, at 83~84.

critical role for the implementation①, it seems to be desirable that the export control regimes such as Nuclear Suppliers Group (NSG), Australia Group (AG), Missile Technology Control Regime (MTCR), and Wassenaar Arrangement (WA) be studied to make them possible models to follow. Based on gentlemen's agreements among like minded countries, decisions at the export control regimes have been implemented, through national legislation, to a considerably reasonable degree. As mentioned above, STM rules provided for in codes of conduct or guidelines (soft law instruments) with the firm technical basis would be able to serve for an effective national implementation.

3. Toward an Effective STM Regime

Based on the assessment of the IAA Report (see, 2.3), concrete measures toward an effective STM are considered in this section. At first, current STM operations are revisited to identify the conditions to make a future STM successful, and next, the conditions for a STM regime for tomorrow would be proposed.

3.1 Mechanisms for the Compatible Operations Avoiding the Interference of Radio Frequencies

It can be said that ITU has been managing space traffic in a limited way through the notification and registration procedure, because ITU is responsible for the equitable, rational, efficient and economic use of radio frequency spectrum and GEO positions②. The first real challenge

---

① Michael Gerhart, "Consequences of a Space Traffic Management Concept for National Space Legislation", IAA, ed., Space Debris and Space Traffic Management Symposium 2004 (AAS, 2004), at 282~284.

② See, e.g., Art. 44 (2) of the Constitution of the International Telecommunication Union, in 1994 as amended[hereinafter the ITU Constitution].

ITU had faced in its version of the STM had been addressed from 1970's to late 1980's by way of the allocation and allotment of a certain GEO slots and frequencies to the countries not being able to compete on par with spacefaring nations①. In the process, ITU Convention and later, ITU Constitution came to regard the radio frequencies and the GEO as "limited natural resources"②, and the 1998 amendment of the ITU Constitution includes LEOs in the category of "limited natural resources" as well③. "Paper Satellite" issue should be categorized as one of the recent STM addressed at the ITU in that it enumerates the conditions to use a GEO position④.

3.2 Space Debris

IADC, a non-governmental organization, is also managing space traffic in a specific way. Since the aim of STM is "to minimize the potential for electronic or physical interference at any time⑤" in this stage of space development, space debris mitigation measures should be the central for a STM along with the frequencies management. Because the

---

① "First come, first served" principle was relaxed with respect to the direct broadcasting satellites.

② Art. 44 (2) of the ITU Constitution, which was formerly Art. 33 (2) of the ITU Convention of 1973.

③ Art. 44 (2) of the ITU Constitution was amended as "radio frequencies and any associated orbits, including the geostationary satellite orbit, are limited natural resources." Amendment of the ITU basic texts adopted at the Plenipotentiary Conference in 1998 (Minneapolis Conference) was entered into force on 1 January 2000.

④ Resolution 18 (1994) and Resolution 49 (1997) at ITU; See, also, e. g., A/AC.705/738 (20 April 2000), paras. 36~49 & Annex III; GAOR 55th Sess. Supplement No. 20 (A/55/20) (2000), paras. 129~135. A/RES/55/122 (27 February 2001), para. 4.

⑤ Johnson, see note ④ on page 42, at 80.

most successful STM to date is found in the field of space debris mitigation, the process and substantive rules for debris mitigation is expected to help designing an effective STM.

It was not until 1988 when the US National Space Policy referred to orbital debris as one of the most compelling challenges[1]. Inter-agency working level cooperation started in 1987[2], which eventually led to the establishment of IADC in 1993. IADC, now consisting of 11 space agencies, is undoubtedly the most practical entity to make rules for the collision avoidance which would be implemented through national mechanisms. First consensus based Space Debris Mitigation Guidelines were adopted in 2002[3], which was supplemented in 2004[4], and amended in 2007[5].

At the Science and Technical Subcommittee (STSC) of the UN COPU-

---

[1] No. 9 of the Inter-Sector Policies, specified in Presidential Directive on National Space Policy (11 February 1988). However, as early as 1963, Dr. E. W. Peterkin, at the US Naval Research Laboratory, published two memoranda, predicting the annual growth rate for space debris that proved to be considerably accurate in later times. David S. F. Portree & Joseph P. Loftus, Jr., *Orbital Debris: A Chronology*, NASA/TP – 1999 (1999), at 5.

[2] In 1987, NASA-ESA working level cooperation started, and two years later, bilateral space agency cooperation between NASA-USSR and NASA-National Space Development Agency of Japan (NASDA) started.

[3] IADC, IADC Space Debris Mitigation Guidelines (15 October 2002).

[4] IADC WG4, Support Document to the IADC Space Debris Mitigation Guidelines (AL. 20. 3), Issue 1 (5 October 2004).

[5] Definition and recommended measures of re-orbit from GEO were amended in September 2007. IADC, IADC – 08 – 01 (published on 8 February 2008).

OS, space debris issue made its appearance in 1994①, but instead of immediately making COPUOS mitigation guidelines, the Subcommittee surveyed the current situation of space debris in order to nurture a common understanding that could serve as the basis for further deliberations. The result of multiyear task was recorded in Space Debris Technical Report in 1999②. In 2001, STSC mandated IADC to develop a set of voluntary international debris mitigation guidelines. After the further modification required to the draft guidelines IADC submitted to the STSC in 2004, they were adopted at the STSC in February 2007, the main Committee in June 2007 and finally endorsed by the UN General Assembly in December 2007③. Not legally binding, UN Space Debris Mitigation Guidelines, consisting of 7 guidelines, are characterized by the universal applicability different from the IADC guidelines.

Each of the seven UN guidelines succinctly provides for the recommended practices to minimize debris from the normal operations④ and to post mission breakups, and also to limit the long-term interference of non-functional objects in the LEOs and GEO. Accordingly, implementing voluntary UN guidelines requires the practical standards specified in the IADC guidelines and their supporting documents. In other words, both instruments are functioning complementary; IADC guide-

---

① Prior to that, in 1989, Sweden proposed that space debris should be included among the agenda items at the STSC, but consensus was not reached at that time. Australia, Belgium, Canada, Germany, the Netherlands and Nigeria co-sponsored Swedish proposal.

② See, e.g., A/AC.105/720 (1999).

③ A/AC.105/890 (6 March 2007), para. 99 & Annex IV; GAOR, 62nd Sess., Supplement No. 20 (A/62/20) (2007), II.C.3, paras. 116~128 & Annex 4; A/RES/62/217 (distributed on 10 January 2008).

④ Measures taken includes to minimize the accidental collisions and to avoid intentional destruction.

lines provide the practical techniques for the actual mitigation measures and the UN counterparts grant the universal character①.

At the STSC, since 2008 session, national implementation is reported under the agenda item of "space debris", which may function as a flexible peer-pressure type control②. Not only the STSC, but also the LSC also adopted the issue in 2008 as a single item for discussion for the next session titled "general exchange of information on national mechanisms relating to space debris mitigation measures"③. Together with the STSC technical presentation, it may place a peer-review-based soft pressure. It may be, thus, arguably concluded that one type of desirable STM already exists on space debris④.

---

① At the end of the UN guidelines, references are made as follows: "for more in depth description and recommendations pertaining to space debris mitigation measures, Member States and international organizations may refer to the latest version of the IADC space debris mitigation guidelines and other supporting documents, which can be found on the IADC website (www.iadc.org).", A/62/20 (2007) at 50.

② In 2008, Brazil, Canada, China, Cuba, Czech, Germany, Greece, India, Indonesia, Italy, Japan, Russia, the US, Venezuela and ESA made a presentation.

③ A/AC.105/917 (18 April 2008) at 24.

④ Also notable is the inter-organizational relationship between ITU and IADC in space debris mitigation. ITU began studying the physical interference in the GEO in 1986 (Question 34/4) and the so-called re-orbit measures were recommended in 1993 (ITU - R Recommendation S. 1003). Such measures requested the transfer of a non-functional satellite to grave yard orbit about 300 km away before the complete exhaustion. Then, that recommendation was amended in 2004 in accordance with the IADC guidelines to adapt the latest technical requirements and reality (ITU - R Recommendation, S. 1003 - 1).

3.3　Pre Launch Notification System: HCOC

HCOC, adopted in November 2002, is not itself a space law instrument, but a political declaration to prevent and curb the proliferation of ballistic missile systems capable of delivering weapons of mass destruction[①]. The number of the subscribing states was 93 when the instrument was adopted in 2002. While the number increased up to 130, China, India, Iran, North Korea and Pakistan, all of which have ballistic missiles, are not members as of June 2009.

Because of the similarity in functional principle between ballistic missiles (BM) and space launch vehicles (SLV), subscribing states are obligated not to use SLV program to conceal BM program (2 g), and also have to exercise the necessary vigilance in assisting to SLV programs of other countries so as to prevent contributing the missile proliferation (3 d)). Subscribing states are further resolved to respect the recognition of the necessity of appropriate transparency measures on BM and SLV programs in order to increase confidence and to promote non-proliferation of BM and BM technology (2 h).

For that purpose, with respect to expandable SLV programs, in accordance with commercial and economic confidentiality principles, subscribing states are resolved to implement to: (1) make an annual declaration providing an outline of their SLV policies and land (test-) launch sites; (2) provide annual information on the number and generic class of SLV launched during the preceding year, as declared in conformity with the pre-launch notification mechanism referred to in 4 iii) of the HCOC; and (3) consider, on a voluntary basis (including on the degree of access permitted), inviting international observers to their land (test-) launch sites (4 a) ii).

---

① HCOC was drafted to supplement the task of MTCR.

Pre launch notification mechanisms envisioned with respect to BM and SLV programs are as follows. First, states are to exchange pre launch notifications on their BM and SLV launches and test flights. Second, the notification should include such information as the generic class of the BM or SLV, the planned launch notification window, the launch area and the planned direction (4 a) iii).

Subscribing states are further resolved to implement to ratify, accede or otherwise abide by the Outer Space Treaty (1967)[1], Liability Convention[2] and the Registration Convention (1975) (3 a). The importance is underlined to adopt fundamental tenets of space law.

Annual meetings of HCOC are held in Vienna, where subscribing states discuss implementation issues including the pre – launch notifications and annual declarations on BM and SLV policies and try to universalize the HCOC. The challenge for the universal application is that among spacefaring nations, China and India are not subscribing states, and the US has postponed supplying pre-launch notifications. Russia, European states and Japan submit agreed-upon notifications[3].

Other than HCOC, several bilateral pre-notification agreements are existent including the agreement of the US-Russia and India-Pakistan.

3.4 Space Security: Conference on Disarmament

It merits mentioning that "space security" is sometimes defined as "the secure and sustainable access to and use of space, and freedom from

---

[1] Treaty on Principles Governing the Activities of States in the Eploration and Use of Outer Space, including the Moon and Other Celestial Bodies (entered in to force on October 10, 1967) 610 U. N. T. S. 205.

[2] Convention on International Liability for Damage Caused by Space Objects (entered into force on September 1,1972) 961 U. N. T. S. 187.

[3] Scott C. Larrimore, "International Space Launch Notification and Data Exchange", *Space Policy*, vol. 23 (2007), at 176.

space based threats"[1], which reads similar to that of the definition of STM found in the IAA Report[2].

While no single agreement on the Prevention of Arms Race in Outer Space (PAROS) has been produced at the Conference on Disarmament (CD), the notion of a certain STM can be found in a variety of proposals submitted both to the PAROS ad hoc Committee (1985 ~ 1994) and to the plenary. Such proposals, both in the form of hard law (treaties) and soft law (codes of conduct, rules of the road, etc.) range from the banning of "space weapons", to anti satellite (ASAT) weapons, to the use of force in outer space, and to urge Transparency and Confidence Building Measures (TCBM)[3]. In early 1990's, the emphasis placed at the CD shifted from disarmament efforts to TCBM as a less unrealistic goal[4]. TCBM proposals regarded as a STM would be specified below.

(1) Multilateral monitoring organizations to gather information in outer space

* PAXSAT A, space-to-space monitoring system, proposed by Canada, first in 1987 and resurrected in 2006[5].

---

[1] The definition is used, e. g., in a Canadian statement at the 44th session of the STSC of the COPOUOS on 21 February 2007. It is also the definition of spacesecurity. org, etc.

[2] See, 2.1 of this paper.

[3] The term Confidence Building Measures (CBM) was gradually replaced by TCBM in the 21st century.

[4] GARes 45/55 (4 December 1990) for the first time requested that technical aspects of CBM be conducted.

[5] CD/786 (1987); CD/1785 (2006).

* International Trajectography Centre (UNITRACE) proposed by France[1].

* Not specifically a monitoring agency, USSR proposed a World Space Organization (WSO) to comprehensively deal with space activities that could be also a platform of STM[2].

(2) Pre launch inspection

* International Space Inspectorate (ISI)[3] the core of this USSR proposal is the multilateral on site pre launch inspection regime to verify that no weapon is on board a space object.

(3) Strengthening the 1975 Registration Convention

A number of countries made proposals or supported this idea over the years. The Registration Convention is not an arms control instruments, but a treaty to establish an international registry of space objects for the purposes of effectively implementing the 1972 Liability Convention. However, that the Convention can provide transparency was taken note of at the CD[4].

---

① CD/1092 CD/OS/WP. 46 (1991) at 5. Before UNITRACE proposal, see, e. g. , CD/937 and CD/OS. WP. 35 (1989) and CD/PV. 570 (1989); International Satellite Monitoring Agency (ISMA), originally proposed by France in 1978 at the first Special Session of Disarmament at GA, was repeatedly proposed at various fora including the CD. A-S 10/AC. 1/7 (1978); A/C. 1/33/PV. 26 (1978); CD/641 (1985), para. 4. ISMA is tasked with monitoring the earth not in outer space, but became a starting point of a series of French proposal such as Satellite Imaging Processing Agency (SIPA) and UNITRACE.

② CD/639 (1985).

③ CD/PV. 385 (1987); CD/817 and CD/OS/WP. 19 (1988). West Germany also maintained the necessity of the strict pre-launch notification system. CD/905 CD/OS/WP. 28 (1989) at 21～22.

④ Early days proposals are found at para. 27 of CD/641(1985), para. 27 of CD/786 (1987) and para. 24 of CD/833 (1988).

(4) The principle of non-interference among satellites

* Satellite immunity (France)[1] and keep Out Zones (KOZ) (West Germany)[2] have been repeatedly proposed and discussed. The core concept of KOZ is the establishment of minimum distances between space objects and speed limits to be imposed on space objects [3].

(5) Moratorium of the testing, deploying and the use of any weapons in outer space

Proposals similar to those mentioned above have been repeatedly made at the CD, often in the form of a soft-law-type instrument to make it a substitute for the authentic arms control and disarmament agreements. Needless to say, the goal of TCBM and STM differ, but similar steps seem to be taken. That phenomenon may have two implications: it means that the pursuit of STM may amount to arms control measures and contribute to stabilize outer space. It may, however, make the collective action for the STM more difficult since such measures may compromise the freer military use of space.

3.5 Space Safety: STM found in the UN COPUOS

Not only at the STSC mentioned in 3.2. of this paper, but also at the LSC and the Full Committee, trends can be found to pursue space traffic to promote the peaceful uses of space.

3.5.1 Legal Subcommittee

As briefly mentioned in 2.3 of this paper, a part of the omnibus GA Resolutions adopted every year under the title of "international cooperation in the peaceful uses of outer space", are important to prepare for a desirable legal environment for constructing a STM regime. Up to

---

① CD/905/CD/OS/WP.28 (1989), at 21~22.
② CD/1092 and CD/OS/AP.46 (1991) at 4.
③ CD/786 (1987), para.27; CD/905/CD/OS/WP.28 (1989) at 22.

date, e. g. , the application of the "launching State" concept[1] and "[r]ecommendations on enhancing the practices of States and international intergovernmental organizations in registering space objects"[2] were endorsed in 2004 and 2007 respectively.

The 2004 Resolution is designed to identify the responsible and liable state or the states which hold jurisdiction and control over a certain space object as much as possible in various kinds of space activities. Such clarification of "launching State" concept is an important prerequisite for a successful space traffic regime, because the launching State will be tasked with notifying its own launching, providing and receiving SSA information and implementing the traffic rules. The 2007 Resolution on registering space objects serves to the better SSA as a starting point of STM.

3.5.2 Chairman's Report of the Full Committee

Inspired by the successful adoption of the space debris mitigation guidelines at the UN, Chairman of the COPUOS Full Committee specified in his report that it was imperative to proceed into some kind of "rules of the road" in which a STM is included. He continued that the STSC of the COPUOS should take up the issue[3], and that the IAA Report provided an excellent starting point for the consideration of such a "rule of the road"[4].

STM is not yet an agenda item, but, it will have a possibility to be one within several years, especially if a big accident occurs in outer space

---

① A/RES/59/115 (10 December 2004).
② A/RES/62/101 (17 December 2007).
③ A/AC.105/L.268 (10 May 2007) paras. 26~29.
④ Ibid. , para. 28.

that causes direct substantial damages to space objects[1] would occur.

3.6　Code of Conduct on Space Traffic Rules: UN General Assembly

In 2007, at the first Committee of GA, Portugal, on behalf of the EU, submitted a proposal on a comprehensive code of conduct on space objects and space activities for international space transparency and TCBM for the PAROS[2]. That proposal contains the concept of STM: "[t]he key activities to be covered under such a code of conduct could include, inter alia, the avoidance of collisions and deliberate explosions, the development of safer traffic management practices, the provision of assurances through improved information exchanges, transparency and notification measures, and the adoption of more stringent space debris measures[3]." In the part of the implementation of the prospective code of conduct, planned best practices include: (i) avoidance of dangerous maneuvers for causing damage to space objects and for creating space debris; (ii) creating special areas of caution around satellites for the avoidance of collision; (iii) detailed information exchange on launching activities; and (iv) enhanced registration system.

It may be said that in a field of space security, the very actions falling into STM are recommended for the purposes of the PAROS. In consideration of the overlapping recommended practices not for the identical

---

① See, e. g., William Ailor, "Space Traffic Management: Implementations and Implications", Acta Astronautica, vol. 58 (2006), at 279 ~ 286. In fact, in February 2009, the first major satellite collision took place between the US commercial telecommunication satellite Iridium 33 and Russian defunct military satellite Cosmos 2251 at a 788 km orbit. See, e. g, Becky Iannota & Tariq Malik, "US Satellite Destroyed in Space Collision", http://www. space. com/news/090211-satellite-collision. html (last accessed 24 March 2009).

② A/62/114/ Add. 1 (18 September 2007) at 5 ~ 8.

③ Ibid., at 7.

goal, a successful space traffic regime would have to be founded on the recognition that security use of outer space should be intact as long as such use is in accordance with the existing international space law and laws of arms control relevant to space activities[①].

4. Conclusion

Ever larger number of actors along with a wider variety of activities in outer space would make it imperative to reach a certain agreement on space traffic rules, taking a long-term view. Thus, based on the studies in the previous sections, the present author would like to point out 5 conditions on which effective rules for space traffic could be constructed in the next decade:

(1) It is widely acknowledged that STM are necessary but that their difficulty is not a pressing need at the moment. However, one big accident, especially if that takes the life of an astronaut, may well change the whole perception. Thus, the preparedness for a comprehensive STM system is the first condition. The preparedness has to encompass scientific, technical, regulatory and legal fields. Continuous interdisciplinary research must be conducted.

(2) In relation to (1), the technical assessment of the current situation and the identification of the area to improve should be a top priority. Success of the UN space debris mitigation guidelines was brought by the firmly established technical background that the IADC provided.

(3) In order to secure the information needs, technically based guidelines (soft law) are to be pursued. If certain information in outer space is technically supported and if such guidelines may convince the space and military agencies that they are not politicized, then, the partial en-

---

① see note ② on page 58, at 7, esp. 2.9.(c).

croachment of sovereignty could be tolerated, even if reluctantly.

(4) Through the harmonized national notification systems in accordance with the emerging international space law, filling the gap in order to implement effective space traffic rules is possible. The key to success in this regard is to encourage more nations to enact national space laws and set up registration systems taking note of the recommendations contained in the 2004 and 2007 GA Resolutions on clarifying the launching States and on enhancing the registration of space objects[①].

(5) About the drafting of traffic rules, it has to be noted that the increased area on space security and space safety are currently overlapping, as found in the similar definitions and required conducts between the two. Thus, circumventing the most sensitive part of the space security is a key to success in the first stage of STM. Military space activities may have to be exempted from the space traffic rules even in more than a few decades. Air law and law of the sea precedents should be studied for a reasonable solution.

Ironically, the pursuit of STM, or space safety, may play a pivotal role in reaching the consensus of TCBM for PAROS which has not been accomplished at the CD for about 3 decades.

---

① During the discussion of the LSC on the enhancement of registration, in 2006, Brazil, Indonesia and Kazakhstan newly introduced national registration system, and the national acts of Italy and the Netherlands reflect the development of the discussion at the LSC. Although it is too premature to judge, harmonization may be successful to a certain degree.

深海海床和南极的矿物资源开发以及地球静止轨道的分配:是否是管理和商业化利用月球和其他天体自然资源的有效经验?
(中、英文)

Fabio Tronchetti[①]著 聂明岩 译[②]

摘要:对于月球和其他天体的自然资源的开发是空间法和空间活动领域最令人向往的未来发展方向。在月球表面建设活动站、对月球资源的开发和利用都是吸引国际社会的重要事项。尽管这项活动如此吸引人,对于外空资源用于商业目的的可能性与现行国际空间法能否保证这样的开发,安全以及有秩序地进行联系起来,还没有明确的规则对这种可能出现的情况进行规范。现行的应该用于外空资源开发行为的法律制度的缺失,也会打击投资者的信心。因此,应当制定一个新的规制月球和其他天体自然资源开发的法律框架。

在这个层面上规范深海海床开发活动、南极矿产经营活动以及分配地球静止轨道的法律制度是建立这样一个法律框架的有益参考。本文将对上述三种法律制度做比较分析,以期阐述他们对

[①] Fabio Tronchetti,哈尔滨工业大学空间法研究所副所长。
[②] 聂明岩,德国科隆大学法学院博士研究生,哈尔滨工业大学法学院国际法专业 2010 届硕士毕业生。

于外空开发活动的潜在影响。

一、简介

21世纪一开始,对外层空间进行开发和利用被看作是一个新的和令人激动的时代。一些值得注意的发展和项目,包括私人亚轨道飞行[①]和对于火星的探测计划[②]都将在不远的将来实现。

在所有的发展中,有一个最为引起一般公众和法律界注意的事项,即对于月球和其他天体自然资源的开发。对于月球和其他天体上的自然资源的商业开采和利用的可能性已经不再是一个梦想或者是科幻小说的情节,而是逐渐地成为一个可预见的和具体的选择。国家和私人经营者都开始表现出对外层空间资源开发的兴趣。国家对于这一方面的兴趣在近年来表现得尤为明显,主要的空间大国,如美国[③],

---

① 私人公司 Virgin Galactic 已经宣布于2012年之前为付费客户提供亚轨道飞行服务。参见:www.virgingalactic.com.

② 美国总统奥巴马计划提请美国议会投资建造一个重型发射器,其主要目的是将宇航员带上月球和火星。具体信息参见:http://blogs.sciencemag.org/scienceinsider/2009/12/exclusiveobama.html.

③ 2009年6月18日,美国发射了月球轨道侦察器(LRO)任务,这一任务的主要目的是通过重点观察月球极地地区的方式分析月球的物理结构(参见:http://lunar.gsfc.nasa.gov/)。LRO任务代表了未来外层空间开发的第一步的实现。这一任务是由美国前总统乔治·W·布什在2004年提出的。预计于2020年在宇航员重新登陆月球,并在月球表面建立一个永久性的基地,将月球作为一个未来空间开发的基础。更多的关于未来空间开发的信息参见:http://www.nasa.gov/externalflash/Vision/index.html.

中国[①]，印度[②]和日本[③]都开展了探月工程，其目的在于探索月球的矿物组成及确定最有可能建立永久月球基地的位置。在这一层面，美国和中国确立了最具雄心壮志的目标：前者宣布在2020年之前使人类重返月球，后者计划在2017年之前开展其第一个人类月球探测任务。

全球对于月球和其他天体的高度注意主要是由于受到其自然资源的较高经济价值的驱使。月球上有丰富的矿产资源，它们不规则地分布在月球表面和表层之下。一些月球探测工程已经确定了月球中含有大量的硅、铁、铝、氧、氢、铬、锰和其他矿物质。这些物质既可以运回地球，也可以作为月球上永久站点上工作人员生

[①] 中国可能是在月球探索和月球资源分析领域最为活跃的国家。中国的探月工程希望达到如下目标：1）通过卫星分析月球构成；2）在2012年之前发射一个月球表面探测器；3）在2017年之前建立一个人类站点。2007年10月24日，工程的第一个飞船嫦娥Ⅰ号发射。其目的是分析月球资源的组成和质量。关于此问题参见：http：//www.spacedaily.com/reports/China_Moon_Mission_ChangE_1_In_Good_Condition_999.html. 依据中国国防科工局的说法，中国第二个月球探测器嫦娥Ⅱ号当时预计于2010年底发射，其目的是测试嫦娥Ⅲ号的核心技术并提供其降落地区的清晰图片。参见：http：//luna-ci.com/2009/11/30/china-announces-change-2-launch-date-and-change-3-lander-details.

[②] 2008年10月22日，印度发射了第一个月球探测器，Chandrayaan Ⅰ号。其目的是制定月球表面的全图，包括离地球较近和较远的面，同时对于月球的资源和矿产进行研究和了解，并测试未来人类登陆月球的情形。由于突然出现故障，这一任务于2009年8月29日提前结束，比预计的结束时间早14个月。参见：http：//www.isro.org/Chandrayaan/htmls/home.htm.

[③] 2007年9月14日，日本发射了Selene飞船，其目的是分析月球的历史及其物理组成。参见：http：//www.jaxa.jp/projects/sat/selene/index_e.html.

存的物资或者作为火箭推进剂①。然而,最具价值的月球资源是氦-3。氦-3是一种同位素,这种在地球上很少的物质,在月球上的储量却很大。这种物质与其他矿物质结合(如氘)可以作为核聚变反应堆的原料。最重要的是,氦-3可以产生核能,并且这个核聚变的过程是一个不会产生有毒废弃物的清洁的过程。由于具有这些特点,对于氦-3的开采可能会对地球上的能量产生和创造的方式产生巨大影响。事实上,氦-3可以代替化石燃料和其他物质作为地球能量产生的原始能源②。除了月球之外的其他天体上也包含大量的自然资源。这种说法应当是真实的,因为在地球轨道附近,有大约1 400颗近地行星分布在地球周围。这些行星都富含大量的铁和水。

然而,一方面,对于外空资源的开发不应仅使直接参与者获益,而应该使地球上的大多数人获益,尤其是考虑到氦-3的积极作用之后。另一方面,(这种开发)加强了对于现行的空间法律制度能力的考虑,希望借此保证其有秩序、有益和安全发展。现在,还没有建立一个具体的国际性的关于如何商业性地利用外层空间

---

① 参见:http://www.technologyreview.com/Energy/19296/;http://www.popularmechanism.com/science/air/。NASA 的最近一个任务,月球环形山观测和传感卫星(LCROSS)任务也确认了月球的南极点存在水冰。这个任务包括一个火箭,以及对于月球陨石坑(Cabeus)撞击的设备。于2009年10月9日进行。这个任务所产生的碎片可以在地球上用天文望远镜看到,由此证明水冰的存在。尽管碎片的体积比预计的小,也足以提供科学家希望的证据。此外随着火箭进入环形山的调查工作也取得了巨大的成功。它发现了大量的水冰和水蒸气。关于 LCROSS 任务以及其结果的信息请参见:http://news.bbc.co.uk/2/hi/8359744.stm;http://www.nasa.gov/mission_pages/LCROSS/main/prelim_water_results.html;http://www.space.com/scienceastronomy/090923-moon-water-discovery.html。

② 例如,有研究指出,25吨的氦-3可以满足美国一年的能源需求。关于此问题参见:Sci/Tech. Moon map aids discovery,http://news.bbc.co.uk/1/hi/sci/tech/226053.stm。

资源的规则。在这个层面上,两个最相关的法律文件是1967年的《外空条约》[①]和1979年的《月球协定》[②],但实际上,两个条约并没有设置一系列清晰和细节性的法律框架来处理这一问题。现在的法律框架不仅可能会导致对于外空资源的商业开发陷入风险和不确定性之中,而且可能会阻碍这一活动的发展。首先,由于缺少具体的规则指明在哪种情形下应开展开发活动,参与者的权利和义务都是什么,很难预测这些活动所能带来的后果,同样,其可能产生的利益也难以预测。由于存在不确定性,国家及私人公司不愿意进行投资。还需要注意的是,对于天体资源的开发和利用是存在很大的风险的,而且是造价很高的活动。所以,在没有一个稳定的法律制度的情形下,不会有人为这样的活动投资。有财政和技术投入的保护,才能使从这个活动中获得收益变得可能。其二,适当法律框架的缺失很有可能导致外空开发活动产生紧张和冲突。举例而言,如果两个或多个参与开发者同时看中月球的某个点,那么,这种情形将如何处理?以什么法律为基础才能决定某一主体有权利开发这一地点,而其他主体没有呢?采用先到先得的方法吗?很明显,类似的解决方法应当避免,因为空间经营者会竞相或抢夺他们最喜欢的地点,这样就会在他们之间产生紧张关系并且会危及外层空间原本和平的本质。其三,一些国家和私人经营者会利用规制外空资源开发的法律不确定的这种状况,贪心或仅仅为了利益进行开发活动,而不考虑外空环境和基本空间法原则的规定。这种情形是比较危险的,因为它威胁了原本脆弱的外层空间环境的平衡,也会影响现存外层空间法律制度功能的适当发展。

综上,当解释到设定一个法律制度去规制外空的资源开发时,出现的问题是:这样的制度应当如何建立?应当包含什么样的原

[①] 《关于各国探索和利用包括月球和其他天体在内的外层空间活动的原则的条约》,1967年1月27日,610 U.N.T.S. 205, 18 U.S.T.,2410, T.I.A.S. No. 6347, 6 I.L.M. 386(简称《外空条约》)。

[②] 《规制国家在月球和其他天体上活动的协定》,1979年12月5日,1363 U.N.T.S. 3, 18 I.L.M. 1434(简称《月球协定》)。

则？在这两个问题上，应当指出的很重要的一点是在发展一个新的法律制度时，初始阶段是确定现存的规制在相关国际领域和资源开发的法律上是否可以作为模板使用。在本文讨论的情形下，答案是肯定的。1994年，《海洋法公约》修订后的第十一部分规定的深海海床及超出国家管辖的海底的矿物资源的开发进行管理的法律制度[①]、1988年《惠灵顿公约》[②]中规定的南极矿物开采活动的规则以及地球静止轨道资源的分配和利用的规则，都为发展管理开采外层空间资源的法律框架提供了有价值的参考。

在介绍了现今的规制月球和其他天体的法律框架并不健全的状况之后，本文将对上文提及的三种法律制度做比较分析，以期阐释它们对于规制相应的开发行为秩序的影响。并且，本文还将分析这些制度存在的主要问题及局限，以期避免在规制外空资源的商业利用过程中出现类似问题。

本文的最后一部分将介绍开发外空资源的法律框架应当包括哪些主要的基本原则。

二、空间法和月球及其他天体自然资源的开发：对于法律制度的需求

正如在本文摘要中提及的，现存的空间法律框架并没有为规制月球和其他天体自然资源的开发提供一个适当的法律框架。下文中，有必要分析两个国际条约（即《外空条约》与《月球协定》）的条款，以期更好地理解为什么需要建立规制这类开发的新法律制度。

---

① 《关于实施〈海洋法公约〉第十一部分的协定》，(1994) 33 ILM 1309 (1994)，Sops 49-50/1996。

② 《规制南极矿物开发活动的公约》(通常被称作《惠灵顿公约》)，1988年6月2日，27 ILM (1988) 868。

《外空条约》是规制外层空间活动的主要规则①。它的条款为所有发生在外层空间的活动提供了指南。它的重要性体现在有99个国家或地区,而且主要空间大国都是其成员国(或地区)。

　《外空条约》中规定的几个原则,在外空资源开发的过程中是极为重要的。尤其是其规定的对于外层空间的开发和利用应当是为了所有国家的利益而进行(第一条,第1款),对于外层空间的自由开发和利用(第一条,第2款),外空资源不得据为己有(第二条),国家对于私人空间活动的责任(第六条)以及国家对于其所登记的空间物体的管辖(第八条)。

　《外空条约》的条款所存在的问题是其规定过于宽泛,并且没有为其所使用的术语做出解释。例如,如何理解"利益"的含义? 如何在实践中使对外层空间的利用是为所有国家的利益? 尤其是在开发外空资源的过程中。并且,条约明确规定禁止对外层空间据为己有,那么,存在疑问的是,这样的规定是否也包括位于月球和其他天体的资源呢? 在这个问题上,一些研究者认为,第二条中所规定的限制同时适用于外层空间及其上的资源②。然而,还有人认为,与规制公海自由利用的规则类似,对于外空资源的占有仅仅

---

① 对于外空条约的条款的分析参见:P. G. Dembling & D. M. Arons, "The evolution of the Outer Space Treaty", J. Air & L. Comm. 33 (1967), p. 419; H. Qizhi, "The Outer Space in Perspective", Proceedings of Fortieth Colloquium on the Law of Outer Space (1997), p. 52; C. Q. Christol, The Modern International Law of Outer Space (1982) New York, p. 21 ss; B. Cheng, Studies in International Space Law, p. 215 ss; M. N. Andem, International Legal Problems in the Peaceful Exploration and Use of Outer Space (1992), Rovaniemi, p. 30 ss.; I. H. Ph. Diederikis-Verschoor, An Introduction to Space Law, The Netherlands, (2008), p. 24 ss.

② 参见例如:S. Gorove, "Interpreting Article II of the Outer Space Treaty", in Proceedings of the Eleventh Colloquium on the Law of Outer Space, (1968), p. 40; A. A. Cocca, Report of the 54th International Law Association, (1970), p. 434; N. Markov, ibid, p. 411.

是自由开发和利用外层空间的一个表现形式①。

由于《外层空间》中所规定的原则的不确定和模糊性,对于月球和其他天体自然资源的开发不能仅仅依靠这些原则。为了开发过程的成功和有效规制,需要制定清晰的规则,规制开发过程中可能出现的问题。例如,关于开发活动的持续时间以及开采矿物的财产权属,并且明确哪些事情允许,哪些不允许。因此,应当创造一系列对于《外空条约》内容进行补充和扩展的原则。

《外空条约》并没有为月球和其他大体的资源开发提供充分的法律制度,还表现在人类首次登月成功②不久之后,各国决定进行谈判达成新的具体处理月球和其他天体上活动的新条约。这次协商从 1971 年一直持续到 1979 年,其结果是《规制国家在月球和其他天体上活动的协定》,即我们所熟知的《月球协定》③的出现。《月球协定》从 1979 年 12 月 18 日起开始开放签署,至 1984 年 7 月 11 日第五份批准文书提交之后生效。《月球协定》的主要目标是为人类在月球和其他天体之上的活动,尤其是对其中的自然资源的

---

① D. Goedhuis, "Some recent trends in the interpretation and the implementation of the rules of International Space Law", 19 Columbia J. of Transnational L. 213, 219 (1981); C. Q. Christol, "Article II of the Outer Space Treaty Revisited", 9 Annals of Air & Space L. 217 (1984).

② 1969 年 7 月 20 日,两位美国宇航员尼尔·阿姆斯特朗和埃德温·奥尔德林实现了人类历史上首次登月。

③ 对于《月球协定》的分析参见:G. Zhukov & Y. Kolosov, International Space Law, (1984), Novosti Press Agency, Moscow, p. 173; B. Cheng, supra, footnote 11, p. 246; H. W. Bashor Jr., The Moon Treaty Paradox (2004), Libris Corporation; C. Q. Christol, The Modern International Law of Outer Space, (1982), New York; L. Vikkari, From Manganese Nodules to Lunar Regolith: a Comparative Legal Study of the Utilisation of Natural Resources in the Deep Seabed and Outer Space, (2002), Rovaniemi; H. A. Wassenbergh, Principles of Outer Space in Hindsight, (1991), p. 39; N. Jasentuliyana & R. S. K. Lee, Manual of Space Law, New York, (1979), Vol. I, p. 253.

开采活动设定法律规则。

很遗憾的是与《外空条约》不同,《月球协定》并没有取得成功。至今,只有 13 个国家或地区,且不包括空间大国批准了《月球协定》①。导致其失败的深层原因可以在其第十一条所规定的内容中找到。这一条宣布了月球及其自然资源都是"全人类共同财产",将"全人类共同财产"这一概念引入了这类资源的开发之中②。简单说来,"全人类财产"的概念是建立在这样一个假设的基础之上的,所有人都是人类的成员,无论他们居住在这个世界上的哪个位置,他们都有相同的机会改善他们的经济和居住条件③。以这个假设为基础,应当认为,所有的国家都是团结一致为了全人类的利益

---

① 批准《月球协定》的 13 个国家分别为:澳大利亚、奥地利、智利、墨西哥、摩洛哥、荷兰、巴基斯坦、菲律宾、乌拉圭、哈萨克斯坦、比利时、秘鲁和黎巴嫩。

② 关于《月球协定》第 11 条的意义的分析,参见:B. Rosenfield, "Article XI of the Draft Moon Agreement", in Proceedings of the 22th Colloquium on the Law of Outer Space, (1980), p. 209; R. J. Lee, "Creating an International Regime for Property Rights Under the Moon Agreement", in Proceedings of the Forty-Second Colloquium on the Law of Outer Space, (1999), p. 409; K. V. Cook, "The Discover of Lunar Water: An Opportunity to Develop a Workable Moon Treaty", (1994), 11 Geo. Int'l Envtl. L. Rev., p. 647; S. Hobe, "Common Heritage of Mankind-An Outdated Concept in International Space Law"?, in Proceedings of the Forty-First Colloquium on the Law of Outer Space, (1998), p. 271;

③ 对于"全人类共同财产"的概念的更多解释参见:C. C. Joyner, "Legal Implications of the Concept of the Common Heritage of Mankind", in 35 Int'l & Comp. L. Q. 190, (1986); S. Gorove, "The Concept of the Common Heritage of Mankind: A Political, Moral or Legal Innovation?", 9 San Diego L. Rev. 390, (1972); G. M. Danilenko, "The Concept of the Common Heritage of Mankind in International Law", 13 Annals Air & Space L. 247; C. Q. Christol, "The Common Heritage of Mankind Provisions in the 1979 Agreement Governing the Activities of States on the Moon and Other Celestial Bodies", in 14 International Law 429, (1980); V. Kopal, "Outer Space as a Global Common", in Proceedings of the Fortieth Colloquium on the Law of Outer Space, p. 108, (1997).

而共同奋斗的,由于其(指月球及其他天体)所包含资源的经济和科技价值,应当分享对于这些领域的管理,换言之,它们应为全人类共同财产。并且,这一概念要求,所有在人类共同财产区域开发的活动,尤其是旨在开发本地区资源的活动,应当仅依照已存的国际制度的规定进行,其首要目标是有秩序地管理此一区域,并公平分享对区域开发产生的利益,尤其要考虑发展中国家的需要,而不问其参与的程度如何。"人类共同财产"还包括更进一步的含义。例如,保护本区域的环境,在区域开发活动中应当以和平方式,以及具有科学开发的自由等。

"人类共同财产"的概念存在的问题是,发展中国家和发达国家对其解释和应用持有相反的态度。前者增加了一个"公共财产"(common property)的概念,将其"人类共同财产"的概念解释为超出国家管辖的范围。以"公共财产"的方式要求对于这个区域的共同管理,所有国家共同分享从此区域开采的资源及从其处获得的利益,而无论国家在开发活动中的参与程度如何,并且要强制地要求发达国家将技术转移给发展中国家。

后者(发达国家)尤其是美国,并不同意发展中国家对人类共同财产概念的解释,认为这样的解释对于参与开发活动者有害,并且没有以市场为导向。在美国看来,对于这一概念的解释并不应当改变现在对于国际资源自由进入的现状。并且,这一概念的解释不应当改变传统的公海自由原则,即国家可以自由地开发和利用。同时,发达国家意识到"人类共同财产原则"是对区域进行开发可以对财政做出的贡献以及对其资源开发所能带来的利益。从这一层面讲,发展中国家的特别需要应当加以考虑。但是,只有实际开发资源的国家有权利决定如何分享资源以及什么是公平。

因为对于如何解释"全人类共同财产"原则不能达成一致意见,结果也不能确定如何将其适用于月球及其他天体资源的开发之中,这导致无论是发展中国家还是发达国家都拒绝签署《月球协定》。

也许有人会问,《月球协定》在将来有无成功的可能性,尤其是在过去的五年中,有四个国家成了它的成员国(或地区)①。不考虑最近这几个签署方,许多其他国家是不可能决定加入《月球协定》的。举例而言,美国就曾经宣布对加入《月球协定》不感兴趣。由于《月球协定》的接受者是很受限制的,这就导致它与未来的空间自然资源开发没有关系或者关系很小。因此,由于不能引用《月球协定》的条款,现存的与外空资源开发相关的规则就都包含于《外空条约》之中了。但是,正如之前所解释的。这些原则的内容并不详细,不能保证开发的安全与秩序。因此,需要制定一个新的规制商业开发和利用地球和其他天体的自然资源的法律框架。规制公海矿物开发活动,南极以及对于地球静止轨道利用的规则可以作为制定这个法律框架的例子。

三、《海洋法公约》和不属国家管辖的海床资源的开发:1994年实施协议的影响

(一)1982—1994:通往1994年"实施《海洋法公约》第十一部分协议"之路

对于不受国家主权限制的海床及洋底资源的开采是1982年联合国《海洋法公约》②的第十一部分规定的,并经1994年"实施联合国《海洋法公约》的第十一部分的协议"进行修改。1994年的实施协议为建立规制外空资源开发的法律提供了最有价值的借鉴。因为它为"全人类共同财产"的概念提供了一个全新的解释,并且设置了规制位于国际区域的资源的商业利用的规则。这些都为发达国家和发展中国家所普遍接受。为了更好地解释1994年实施协议的重要性,下面有必要分析一下其通过的过程。

从20世纪70年代开始,需要一个新的全球性条约对在海洋上

---

① 这四个国家分别为:2001年哈萨克斯坦,2004年比利时,2005年秘鲁,2007年黎巴嫩。
② 联合国《海洋法公约》(1982),21 ILM 1245 (1982), SopS 49~50/1996。

的活动进行规制的想法已经在各国之间达成了普遍的共识。这个新条约的谈判于1973年在联合国的框架下开始进行,联合国《海洋法公约》于1982年12月10日开放签署[①]。在谈判的过程中,一个最具争议的问题是关于规制国家管辖权之外的深海海床资源的探索和开发的法律框架的制定,因为发展中国家和发达国家对于如何组织这一法律框架持有相反的态度。得益于数量众多以及联合国大会的投票机制,即给每个国家一个投票的机会,发展中国家也可以参与到《海洋法公约》的最后文本中来。并且,值得注意的是,规制深海海床矿业经营的第十一部分反映了发展中国家的立场及要求。

《海洋法公约》第十一部分宣布海床及其资源是"全人类共同财产"。它为管理和开发共同财产区域及其资源设立了复杂的管理及开发机制。国际海底管理局被授权去管理、控制深海海床及资源的开发。依照"全人类共同财产"重新分配的方式,开发矿产活动的税收在所有公约缔约方之间平摊。管理局本身通过其企业矿物公司参与深海海床的开发。在全人类共同财产区域进行经营的公司应当提供两块价值相同的位置,海底局将在其中挑选一块给那些获得批准的国家的企业进行开发,另一块保留,由海底管理局自己使用,可以通过其矿物公司,或与发展中国家合作进行开发(所以被称作"平行开发机制")。管理局可以强制发达国家在公平的商业环境之下将市场上无法获得的采矿技术转移给发展中国家,以期使它们有能力参与到开发活动之中。并且,管理局的决定(主要机构是理事会和大会)主要是在一国一票的基础上做出的,这就导致了其所做的大多数决定都受到发展中国家的主导和影响。

当1982年《海洋法公约》开放签署时,很明显,发达国家并没有准备接受第十一部分条款的规定。在发达国家看来,这些条约

---

① 关于联合国《海洋法公约》的谈判过程的分析参见:Churchill R. R., A. W. Lowe, The Law of the Sea, 3ed., (1999) Manchester Univ. Press, p. 223; J. T. Swing, "Who Will Own the Oceans"?, 54 Foreign Aff. 527, (1975~1976); B. H. Oxman, "The Third United Nations Conference on the Law of the Sea: the Tenth Session", in 76 A. J. I. L. 1, (1982).

对其政治、经济利益是有害的,对于海底资源的开发是一个阻碍。发达国家对于规制深海海床开发的规则的批判主要可以列为以下几点:(1)决策机制并没有给予工业化国家及其活动或投资以相适应的权利;(2)强制转让技术(规定不合理);(3)规定的经济原则与市场经济原理不符,不利于深海资源的开发。由于上述原因,发达国家拒绝签署或批准《海洋法公约》。

  然而,发达国家一方面拒绝接受《海洋法公约》第十一部分的规定;另一方面也意识到建立一个有效的规制深海矿物开发的法律机制的迫切性。因此,一些西方国家决定在《海洋法公约》生效之前建立一个临时的机制授权并管理开采活动,以期保护其已经向深海开发投入巨资的公司。通过这些被叫作"往复式的国家机制"(Reciprocating States Regime)(1980年)的制度,每个国家都通过了类似的国内立法用以规制深海矿产开发。美国以其《深海海床矿物资源法案》(Deep Sea Bed Hand Mineral Resources Act)首开先河①。接着是同一年制定的《联邦德国规制深海海床矿物的法案》(Federal Republic of Germany's Act on the Interim Regulation of Deep Sea Bed Mining)。之后,英国、法国、日本和意大利通过了类似的法律②。1982年,联邦德国、英国、法国和美国签订了一个关于深海海床锰结核(Poly metallic Nodules)的临时协议。在这一协议的框架下,成员国(或地区)的公民及公司禁止参与深海资源的探索及开发,除非得到其所在国或其他某成员国(或地区)的许可。获得许可的执照持有者应当支付一定的税收,这些钱在联合国《海洋法公约》生效之后发给国际海底管理局。协议条款的规定与《海洋法公约》第十一部分的内容有很大的不同。协议中规定的税款是公约中所规定的一半;协议没有要求选择两块价值相同的地点其中一个

---

  ① 《深海海床矿物资源法案》30 USC 1401 et seq,(1980)。
  ② 这些立法已经被分别转载如下:德意志联邦共和国20(International Legal Materials)ILM 393(1981),21 ILM 832(1982);法国,21 ILM 808(1982);英国,20 ILM 1219(1981);日本,22 ILM 102(1983);意大利,24 ILM 983(1985)。

留给管理局,也不要求发达国家向发展中国家转移技术[①]。

但是,这个往复式国家制度仅是《海洋法公约》生效之前的一个过渡的制度。在20世纪80年代后期,越来越多的发达国家开始达成一致,将在这个制度中建立起来的对《海洋法公约》第十一部分的修订合并到公约本身之中。事实上,发达国家同意制定一个更有效率的管理国家主权范围之外的深海矿物开发的法律制度。这一观点也得到多数发展中国家的认可。对于这一观点的广泛接受,尤其是发展中国家的认可,可以作为解释如下几个因素(20世纪80年代已经不是影响《海洋法公约》谈判的因素的理由):其一,发展中国家不再会作为一个群体有能力影响到联合国的决议。其二,越来越多的《海洋法公约》的国家开始担心公约的财政含义,因为公约要60个国家批准才生效。现在的主要贡献国有美国、德国和英国,已经愈加不能负担管理局的财政需求并使公约规定的控制海底管理的系统起作用了。并且,大多数发达国家拒绝原来的《海洋法公约》第十一部分的规定,并认为公约的其他部分应当更好地组织并发挥更大的作用。

因此,在1990年,发达国家和发展中国家开始了修订联合国《海洋法公约》第十一部分的进程,并在联合国秘书长主持之下开始了正式的协商。这一进程的结果是,联合国大会于1994年7月28日通过了"关于实施1982年12月10日联合国《海洋法公约》第十一部分的协议"(简称《实施协议》)。这一协议于7月29日开放签署,并很快被50个国家批准,其中包括18个发展中国家和18个发达国家。美国同意暂时适用。这一协议。由于《实施协议》的成功,致使《海洋法公约》可以在1994年11月生效。由于美国的临时参加,《实施协议》于1996年生效。

---

① 在接下来几年,往复式国家制度中的成员又签署了一些其他的文件用以处理冲突性的主张以及特别许可等。例如,1994年《关于有关海底区域的主张冲突的谅解备忘录草案》,转载于 Law of the Sea Bulletin (LOSB) 37 (1984),1994年的《关于深海问题的临时性谅解》,转载于 4 LOSB 101 (1985);23 ILM 1365 (1984) 以及1996年的《纽约谅解》,转载于 8 LOSB 38~39 (1986)。

(二)1994 年的《实施协议》

《实施协议》在很大程度上修改了《海洋法公约》第十一部分[①]。它的条款解决了发达国家针对原公约第十一部分罗列的批判意见,并且引入了自由市场机制管理这一区域及其资源。通过这样做,《实施协议》引入了"全人类共同财产"概念的全新版本,这一概念软化了之前刻板的政治和经济需求。

下面是《实施协议》对第十一部分所做的主要修改:

1. 决议的做出[②]

之前的理事会的决议做出的体系应当加以改变,以便于给美国及其他具有主要经济利益者对于决议的做出有更强的影响,使其影响力与其利益及重要程度相适应。协议应该由一致的方式做出。当全体一致的方式不可能达成的时候,涉及实质问题的讨论时,采用出席代表三分之二多数投票的方式。理事会由36个成员组成,分配如下:4个成员来自矿产品最大的消费者和进口商;4个成员来自最大的矿产品出口国;4个成员来自区域活动的准备和开发投资最多的国家;6个成员来自发展中国家;其他的18个成员依公平原则"按地理分配"。这就意味着美国和其他发达国家合作可以阻碍重要决定的做出,例如财政事务。

2. 技术转移[③]

关于强制转移技术的要求被取消了。依据新的规定,发展中国家应当在市场上以公平合理的价格获得深海矿物开发技术,或者通过与工业化国家合作获得。成员国(或地区)应当促进本区域活动的国际科学和技术合作并与国际海底管理局合作,减少企业

[①] 关于1994年"实施协议"的分析参见:C. B. Thompson, "International Law of the Sea/Seed: Public Domain versus Private Commodity", in 44 Nat. Resources J. 843, (2004); A. De Marffy-Mantuano, "Current Development: The Procedural Framework of the Agreement Implementing the 1982 United Nations Convention on the Law of the Sea", in 89 A. J. I. L. 814, (1995).

[②] 附件,第三部分,1994年《实施协定》。

[③] 附件,第五部分,1994年《实施协定》。

和发展中国家获得技术的难度。

3. 产品政策①

深海矿物开发应当依据合理的商业原则进行,不得歧视,倾向于某些特定的国家或产品。

4. 开发生产者②

新的程序规定了确切的被批准者所获得的批准的时间段。每一个批准者获得批准的时间都是 15 年,并可以延长 5 年。这样的程序规定给工程的投资者带来了经济上的确定性。

5. 平行开发制度

为管理局提供一块平行的开发地点的制度取消了。协议事实上是将这个要求改变为每个成员国(或地区)都为企业投资一块矿产区。

(三) 1994 年的《实施协议》:对于外空资源开发的有益借鉴经验

通过对 1994 年《实施协议》及其通过的过程的分析,可以提出如下几个值得借鉴的经验,是我们在制订规制外空自然资源开发的规则的过程中所应当注意的。第一个借鉴经验:管理国际区域开发活动最适合的解决方式是建立一个国际制度。也许有人会认为,没有必要建立任何制度,让国家仅依照自己的国内法律自由、独立地开展活动就可以了。但是,《实施协议》的演进表明这种方式是不可取的。在 20 世纪 80 年代后期通过了规制深海矿物开发的国内法律之后,发达国家开始意识到应当将国内层面建立的法律解决方式转化到《海洋法公约》所建立的框架之下,以便于建立一个单独的、全球性的和具有连续性的法律制度用以规制超出国家管辖之外的海底矿物开发活动。这被认为是保障这些活动安全、协调和有益发展的最佳选择。

《实施协定》同时表明了如何建立一个规制国际资源开发的法律制度以及它应当包含哪些因素。其成功的关键是在发展中国家和发达国家之间找到一个利益的平衡。之前的公约第十一部分失

---

① 附件,第六部分,1994 年《实施协定》。
② 附件,第一部分,1994 年《实施协定》。

败的原因在于没有创立这样一个平衡,具有较强的发展中国家导向性。当要建立一个国际法律框架的时候,很有必要了解是否注意了发展中国家的特别需求,并通过保护、经济奖励等方式促使发达国家接受并到建立起来的框架中来。应当谨记的是,只有发达国家才有财政和技术实力开发国际资源,无论是在公海还是在外层空间层面。没有这些国家的参与,这样的开发永远不可能发生。因此,一个国际法律框架能够使开发活动成为营利的商业活动是至关重要的。

《实施协议》给我们带来的另一个借鉴经验是:保证对于一个国际区域资源开发贡献最多的国家在决议做出机制中具有足够的影响力。对于之前公约第十一部分提出的一个最大的批判是国际海底管理局的决议是在一国一票的基础上做出的,这就是给发展中国家控制甚至是阻碍决议的权利。《实施协议》解决了这个问题,主要是通过给那些在海底资源开发中具有主要经济利益的国家在国际海底管理局决议做出的体系中提供适当的表决权实现的。规制关于月球和其他天体自然资源开发的法律制度,也应采用类似的解决方式。

除此之外,《实施协议》还为探索和开发国家管辖之外的矿物资源许可证的授予和持续性机制提供了有效的解决方式。协议明确规定了获得开发海床授权的执照执有者的开发计划的时间表以及每个被授权计划的持续时间。这一体系具有十分积极的影响,因为它为那些有意投资海底矿物开发的投资者提供了确定性。在开发外空资源的许可证授权及持续性问题上,应当采用类似的做法。事实上,一个法律机制如果清晰地阐明了在一个许可获得同意授权之前,需要等待多长时间以及授权开发活动可以持续多久,可以给参与者创建一个稳定的和明确的法律环境,才有可能促使投资者将他们的资源投入到外空资源的开发之中去。

总而言之,《实施协议》中规定的如下几个因素应当借鉴到外空自然资源开发活动之中:

(1)建立一个规制这种开发的法律框架。

(2)创造发达国家和发展中国家利益和需要的平衡。

(3)通过经济刺激使外空资源的开发成为一个获益的商业。

(4)决议的做出机制中,国家的重要性要与其在开发活动中的影响相适应。

(5)许可的审查和授予的时间框架。

四、南极矿产开发活动:1988《惠灵顿公约》

对于南极活动,由南极条约体系进行规制,这是一个由一系列国际协议①组成的条约体系。南极条约体系被公认为是规制国际区域的最成功的法律框架之一,因为它保证了南极50多年的和平科学探测,并保护南极地区的环境。

南极条约体系以1959年的《南极条约》②为基础,而《南极条约》的规定包括南极应仅用于和平的目的、国家对南极进行的科学考察自由、为所有在南极地区开展的活动提供指导和协助等。在《南极条约》的所有条款中,其中第四条规定的内容尤其重要,因为

---

① 南极条约体系包括:《南极条约》(1959年11月),12 UST 794,TIAS No. 4780,402 UNTS 71(1961年6月23日生效);《保护南极海豹公约》1972年6月1日,27 UST 441,TIAS NO. 8826,ILM 11(1978年3月11日生效);《保护南极海洋生物资源公约》1980年5月20日,TIAS 10240,ILM 19 (1980),841~859(1982年4月7日生效);《管理南极矿物资源活动的公约》1988年6月2日,27 ILM(1988)868(尚未生效);《保护南极环境条约的议定书》1991,30 ILM(1991)1455(1998年1月14日生效)。

② 对于《南极条约》的分析参见:J. Hanessian,"The 1959 Antarctic Treaty",9 Int & Comp. L. Quart. 436,(1960); A. Watts, Internatonal Law and the Antarctic Treaty System,(1992 Cambridge); C. Joyner-S. K. Chopra (Eds.), The Antarctic Legal Regime,(1988 Martinus Nijhoff Publishers); R. Sattler, "Symposium: Issues in Space Law: Transporting a Legal System for Property Rights from the Earth to the Stars", 6 Chi. j. Int'l L. 23,(2005); J. Couratier, Le Systeme Antarctique,(1991) Bruxelles, Etablissement Emile Bruylant.《南极条约》现在有45个缔约方。其中有28个协商方,它们是通过原始批准或者是从事实质的研究的方式获得的协商方地位。这些国家有权利参加由协商方组成的南极条约协商方会议的决议做出。其他国家只是有权利出席会议。

这一条处理了对南极地区的领土要求的问题。南极的法律地位十分复杂。在1959年《南极条约》生效以前,有几个国家在南极的一些地区成功地开展了开发任务。这些开发任务所导致的结果是:a)国家开始对它们开发过的南极大陆主张主权权利[1];b)那些在发现南极大陆过程中起重要作用的国家尽管没有对南极主张主权权利,但是,那些国家并不承认其他国家的主权主张。不过,这些国家保留在将来主张南极主权的权利[2];c)那些不对南极主张任何主权权利,也不保留将来主张权利的国家拒绝接受其他国家的主张[3]。这些国家呼吁对于南极区域的国际管理。

这些潜在的观点使《南极条约》的谈判过程中如何确定南极的法律地位成了最具争议的问题。条约的第四条所采用的解决方式是将领土及主权的主张暂时搁置;简言之,其冷却了于1959年对南极的主权主张及反对意见[4]。第四条之所以至关重要是因为它要求各国暂时将他们的不同意见放在一边,而为了和平的目的合作,对南极进行探索和研究。

---

[1] 第一个权利主张是英国于1908年7月21日提出的,其所主张的南极主权范围涵盖了西经80度和20度之间的扇形区。1923年新西兰所主张的主权权利涵盖的范围从西经150度到东经160度。1924年3月27日法国所主张的主权权利涵盖从东经136度到东经142度的扇形区。1933年2月7日澳大利亚,主张了两个区域,分别从东经45度到136度以及从东经142度到160度。1939年1月14日挪威主张的主权权利从西经20度到东经45度。1939年7月16日阿根廷主张的权利从西经25度至75度。1940年11月6日智利主张权利从西经53度至西经90度。有趣的是,阿根廷和智利所主张权力的区域部分或全部与英国主张的范围重合。

[2] 这些国家包括美国,其权利主张基于1818年对威尔克斯和1840年对帕尔默的探索;还有苏联,其主张理由是1819和1821年其司令别林斯基首次对于南极洲的环绕航行。

[3] 这些国家包括德国和意大利。

[4] 《南极条约》第四条规定,本条约的任务规定不得解释为:"缔约任何一方放弃在南极原来所主张的领土主权权利或领土的要求。"或者"缔约任何一方全部或部分放弃由于它在南极的活动或由于它的国民在南极的活动或其他原因而构成的对南极领土主权的要求的任何根据。"

《南极条约》定义并规制了南极的法律地位,但是它并没有规制南极的矿产的发掘与开发的问题。出现这种情形在很大程度上是因为在谈判签订条约时,还没有充足的地质学数据证明南极地区的矿物资源的存在和价值。但是,自19世纪70年代开始,科学报告表明南极矿物资源经济价值的潜力,《南极条约》的缔约方感到如果不解决这些资源的法律地位的问题的话,可能会重新导致对南极矿物资源和平利用的威胁,因为诸多国家可能会开始争夺对南极地区和其极富价值的资源的主权。因此,这些国家决定探讨如何处理南极矿物开发的问题。

关于规制南极矿物开发的谈判正式开始于1982年[1]。这些协定将协商方(consultative parties)的概念引入《南极条约》之中。具体而言就是,所有的国家都可以依附于条约,而只有那些承担"实质研究活动"的国家可以获得协商方的地位。因为主要的发展中国家都缺少资金执行这种类型的活动,所以协商方主要由发达国家或地区组成。谈判于1988年6月2日结束,并且与惠灵顿通过《规制南极矿物开发的公约》(因此又称作《惠灵顿公约》)。依据第62条的规定,只有参与谈判的所有协商方签署了条约之后,公约才能生效。但是,由于法国与澳大利亚撤销了对公约的支持,导致了整个签署过程的瓦解。这两个国家为其所做出选择的辩护理由是对于南极矿物资源的开发会损害南极的环境。而其他协商方试图向法国和澳大利亚说明《惠灵顿公约》的良好性质的努力也都失败了,因此,最后没有国家签署这个公约。

在《惠灵顿公约》失败三年之后,又通过了一个新的文件,叫作

---

[1] 对于规制《南极矿产资源公约》的谈判的分析可以参见:C. C. Joyner, "The Antarctic Minerals Negotiating Process", 81 AJIL 888, (1987); A. Watts, "Lesson to be learned from the Mineral Resources Negotiations", in R. Wolfrum(ed.), Antarctic Challenge III, p. 319~331, (Berlin 1988); F. Francioni, "Legal Aspects of Mineral Exploitation in Antarctica", 19 Cornell Int'l L. J. 163, (1986); G. D. Triggs, "Negotiations of a Mineral Regime", in G. D. Triggs (ed.), The Antarctic Treaty Regime. Law, Environment and Resources, p. 182~195, (Cambridge 1987).

《南极条约环境保护议定书》,就是我们通常所说的《马德里议定书》[①]。1991年的《马德里议定书》通过宣布:"除了科学研究,一切与矿物开发的活动都应当禁止",终止了以商业目的对南极矿产进行开发和利用的可能性。

尽管没有南极条约体系的成员国(或地区)签署《惠灵顿公约》,但是,由于其对于月球和其他天体的自然资源的开发的法律制度的发展具有潜在的影响,所以,仍有对其条款进行分析的必要。

(一)《规制南极矿产资源开发的公约》(《惠灵顿公约》)

《惠灵顿公约》的主要目的是为规制南极矿物资源的探索和开发设立一个法律框架[②]。公约明确规定不得使南极的和平本质和环境的平衡陷入危险。并且,开发活动不应当被一个或两个国家垄断,而应当在和平的基础上对所有国家开放,并且要在考虑了国际社会利益的基础之上进行。

条约首要考虑的问题是保护南极的环境[③]。为了核实它们对环境的潜在影响,所有矿物开发活动都应当进行一个预防性的评

---

① 对于这个议定书的分析可以参考:L. Pineschi, "The Madrid Protocol on the Protection of the Antarctic Environment and its Effectiveness", in F. Francioni and T. Scovazzi (eds.), International Law for Antarctica p. 377 (2nd ed. 1996); C. Redgwell, "Environmental Protection in Antarctica: the 1991 Madrid Protocol", 43 ICLQ 599, (1994); D. Vidas, "The Protocol on Environmental Protection to the Antarctic Treaty: A Ten-Year Review", Yearbook of International Co-operation on Environment and Development 51, (2002/2003).

② 对于公约条款的解释请参见:例如:C. Joyner, "The Evolving Antarctic Minerals Regime", 19 Ocean Dev. & Int'l L. 73 (1988); J. G. Starke, "International Legal Notes", 62 Austl. L. J. 956, (1988); Note, "Death of a Treaty: the Decline and Fall of the Antarctic Minerals Convention", 22 Vand. J. Transnat'l L. 631, (1989); B. H. Heim, "Exploring the last frontier for mineral resources: a comparison of international law regarding the deep seabed, outer space and Antarctica", 23 Vand. J. Transnat'l L. 819, (1990).

③ 参见《规制南极矿物资源开发的公约》的第2、3、4条。

估。如果被证明对南极生态存在威胁,那么,这些活动将不被授权或是被停止。

在机构设置层面,公约创立了一个南极矿物开发委员会,一个监管委员会以及缔约方科学、技术和环境委员会特别会议。

南极矿物开发委员会由公约刚刚开放签署①时取得协商方地位的国家或地区组成,负责通过决议保护南极环境、指定被保护区域、确认可能的探索和开发区域以及审查协调委员会的行为等。决议通常是在三分之二多数的情形下通过,而有关探索和开发的申请的批准的通过则要求全体一致②。

监管委员会(Regulatory Committee)通常是为了每个指定开发的区域而建立的。它的主要功能是:审查探索和开发申请的许可;通过管理方案以及监视探索和开发③。

缔约方科学、技术和环境委员会特别会议由公约缔约方的科学家组成④。它的功能不仅仅是给出科学和技术咨询意见,也是一种对全体成员决议做出过程的参与。这是在开发委员会中没有的。

缔约方特别会议对所有成员开放⑤。它发起了一个论坛,在这里,非协商方可以主张自己的价值。

矿物开发活动被建议分为三个阶段进行,勘探(prospecting)、探索(exploration)和开发(development)。勘探被定义为这样一种活动:"寻找那些具有潜力进行探索和开发的区域"⑥。第37条(1和2)规定勘探并不赋予经营者对资源的任何权利,勘探行为也无须经过公约设定的机构授权。发起国有义务在勘探计划进行的至少九个月前通知开发委员会。通知的内容应当包括:勘探地区的特征;对所要使用方法的描述以及对可能造成的环境影响的评估。

---

① 参见《规制南极矿物资源开发的公约》的第21条。
② 参见《规制南极矿物资源开发的公约》的第241条,第2款。
③ 参见《规制南极矿物资源开发的公约》的第29条。
④ 参见《规制南极矿物资源开发的公约》的第23条。
⑤ 参见《规制南极矿物资源开发的公约》的第28条。
⑥ 参见《规制南极矿物资源开发的公约》的第21条第8款。

规制探索和开发的法规则更加复杂些。开始探索和开发活动前法律机构需进行事先的评估和评价。在做出了可以开始活动的决议之后,相关机构进一步可能会做出允许矿物探索及可能的情况下的开发许可。

这个过程包括三个阶段:准备(识别相关区域);审查通过探索许可(申请、准备管理方案、批准并发出探索许可)以及授予开发许可(申请、修改管理方案、批准、发出开发许可)。

在准备阶段要求开发委员会的成员国(或地区)"指出一块可能探索,开发特殊矿产或资源的区域"①。与之相伴的还要求将必要的信息②传递给所有的缔约方。开发委员会在考虑了"特别会议和咨询委员会按要求做出的总结的特殊意义"之后,会通过全体一致的方式决定这个区域是否符合公约中所规定的条件。这就意味着开发委员会的每一个成员国(或地区)都可以组织任何行为。在区域确定之后,开发委员会会建立个别咨询委员会。委员会会将这个区域分成几块,并确立可以提交申请的期限。在监管委员会完成准备工作之后,每一个成员国(或地区)都可以为了自己的经营者的利益提出许可的申请。这个申请必须包括计划进行活动的信息并附有一个发起国或地区对于其经营者有能力满足公约要求,有财政和技术实力开展计划活动的证明③。在申请提交之后,咨询委员会有两个选择:(1)以其无法满足法律要求的理由拒绝许可;(2)进入管理方案的准备④。

管理方案是规制探索和开发活动的手段。第 47 条规定了管理方案中必须包括的不可排除的内容清单⑤。管理方案的通过意味着监管委员会将在很快通过授权许可,经营者即可以在此授权下对于指定区

---

① 参见《规制南极矿物资源开发的公约》的第 39 条第 1 段。
② 参见《规制南极矿物资源开发的公约》的第 39 条第 2 段。
③ 参见《规制南极矿物资源开发的公约》的第 44 条。
④ 参见《规制南极矿物资源开发的公约》的第 51 条第 3 款。
⑤ 例如,性能要求,财政义务,管理计划或适用法律的实施等。

域的资源在管理方案的要求之下具有排他的探索权利①。

处理开发许可申请的程序除了不再需要建立的管理计划之外,大体上是依照探索许可决议的程序进行的。取而代之的是,监管委员会可以决定方案是否需要修改。

经过许可管理方案的个别许可可能会因为给南极环境造成不可接受的污染的原因而被改变或暂时停止,而如果这种影响无法避免,许可则可能会被取消。并且,如果经营者没有依据公约的要求活动,咨询委员会也可能会改变、中止或者取消许可。与此同时,还可能会给经营者处以经济制裁。

(二)规制南极矿物资源开发的公约:对于外空资源开发法律制度的影响

规制南极矿物资源开发的公约为外空资源开发的法律制度的建立提供了一个模板。事实上,这个公约中不仅包含一些可以加入这一法律制度中的因素,同时也表明了要制定一个规制国际区域活动的法律框架应当避免哪些错误。

从这个角度讲,第一步需要明确的是公约为什么会失败。失败的真实原因除了是法国和澳大利亚基于环境的考虑拒绝签署公约外,还存在其他原因。这些原因具有政治和经济性质,可以在公约的具体条款具有争议的特征中找到根据。

首先,公约中缺少对矿产经营者的经济刺激。事实上,规制矿产开发活动的公约所建立的体系包含一定程度的不确定性,这可能会导致矿产开发的经营者不营利。从这个角度出发开发委员会关于认定可能探索和开发区域的决定要求在全体一致的条件下做

---

① 管理计划在三分之二多数同意的情形下就可以通过,这三分之二多数中包括对此处提出开发要求的国家简单多数通过和没有提出要求的国家简单多数的通过。因此,也就是说,一个管理计划需要监管委员会(Regulatory committee)中的十个成员的七个投赞成票,并且七个人中有至少两个是来自提出开发要求的国家或地区的成员,三个来自没有提出要求的国家或地区的成员。这样的要求超出了一个申请国家的能力范围,从而也就导致了很难通过一个管理计划。

出,这可能在开发活动的一开始就中断它。尤其是,由于开发委员会一个成员的反对,就可能导致相似要求被拒绝,而不考虑申请者已经完全遵守环境要求很好地完成勘探阶段并已经投入大量的资金和技术,这与通过经济激励开发的观点相去甚远。因为存在上述可能性,所以,没有经营者愿意投资到南极的矿产开发中去。相反,如果一个经营者在某一特定区域的勘探阶段是值得信任的,那么他在探索和开发这一区域中也享有优先权。

其二,规制南极资源开发活动的法律体系存在的另一个问题是它的时间要求。三阶段的审查过程导致通过一个经营的许可十分慢,这不利于鼓励潜在的投资者。

其三,更多的问题则是由公约所创建的机构框架造成的。这些机构不仅复杂而且效率低下。例如,投票程序很复杂,而且机构的权力存在重叠。

其四,公约宣告的主要目的之一是为了矿产开发活动创造公平的机会,而事实上并没有创造这种机会,也没有保护发展中国家的特殊利益需要。

因此,考虑公约失败的原因,很有必要总结。一个规制国际区域的矿产资源的开发的法律应当包括如下要素:

(1)对于经营者的经济鼓励以及规制开发活动的法律制度的确定性。

(2)审查经营者参与矿物开发资格的时间应当合理。

(3)简单的机构框架,每一个机构都应当有清晰的和明确的功能。

(4)有效率和公平的投票程序。

(5)保证矿产开发活动国际参与的机制。

无论如何,即便存在缺陷,公约也为未来要制定的开发外空资源的法律制度提供了有用的借鉴因素。

其一,条约中规定对于南极环境保护的条款可以借鉴。这些条款设定了环境参数,要求在勘探和探索南极时必须遵守。这样的规定也可以引入外空的矿产开发活动之中。事实上,对于月球和其他天体的环境保护也是应当在开发活动进行之前需要考虑的。这不仅仅是出于道德原因的考虑,也是因为对于外空的损害,可能会阻止它们潜在的经济价值的永久性利用或是减少。

其二,公约设立了矿物经营者争端解决机制。在外层空间的资源开发法律制度中,也应当建立相似的机制。事实上,只有包含对于参与者争端解决的程序机制,一个国际制度才最有可能成功。

五、地球静止轨道的分配和利用

(一)作为有限自然资源的地球静止轨道

地球静止轨道指的是,赤道上空 35 757 千米处的环形轨道。在那里,卫星绕地球一周所需的时间是 23 小时 56 分 4 秒[①]。由于这个时间与地球自转一周的时间是同步的,发射到地球静止轨道上的卫星就好像是固定在地球表面上空一样,在赤道上空一个特定的点上固定。因此,这个轨道被称作"地球静止轨道"。

考虑到这样一个事实,在这个轨道上的卫星的视阈是地球的三分之一,三颗相同情形的卫星所提供的信号就可以覆盖极点之外的几乎整个地球。由于这些特征,地球静止轨道是开展通信、广播和气象等活动的战略资源。

很有必要澄清的是,卫星通过无线电信号运行,而无线电频谱是电磁频谱的一个特定的波段,在这个波段,卫星可以与地球通讯。因此,为了在地球静止轨道运营,卫星需要轨道位置和频谱的分配进行通讯服务。

尽管是提供通讯和其他服务最有效率的轨道,但地球静止轨道仍被一些因素影响阻碍了它的继续利用。其一,一旦一个卫星发射至轨道之上,由于诸多因素的影响,例如地球赤道为椭圆形(的影响)、月球和太阳的引力以及阳光的辐射等,这就需要一个有效的维持系统的站点,帮助卫星停留在预定轨道之中,并与地球的

---

① 有关地球静止轨道的特征描述请参见:K. U. Schrogl, "Question relating to the character and utilization of the geostationary orbit", in "International space law in the making: current issues in the United Nations Committee on the Peaceful Uses of Outer Space (K. U. Schrogl-M. Benköeds.)", Frontières, 1993; S. Cahill, "Give me my space: implications for permitting national appropriation of the geostationary orbit", 19 Wis. Int'l L. J., (2001), p. 231; F. Lyall, Law and Space Telecommunications, Dartmouth, (1989), p. 388.

自转保持同步。这个系统是十分重要的,因为卫星位置的每一点的改变都会影响它的功能并增加与其他卫星相撞的危险。其二,由于具有上述的物理学特征,地球静止轨道只能容纳有限数量的卫星。据估算,在现代化技术条件下,卫星可以在 0.1°经度的范围之内保持它的最佳位置。因此,在地球静止轨道上,以每个为 0.2°计量的话,可以有 1 800 个位置用于卫星放置,而不会导致它们撞击。现在发射至这个轨道上的卫星,还远不及这个数字。因此,与现在的一般预测相反,卫星之间发生物理撞击的风险,也就是通常所谓的"物理性拥塞(physical congestion)的风险"还相对较低。可能存在的问题是不同系统之间的无线电频率相互干扰。如果两个不同的卫星在相同的地理地区发射以相同的频率进行,那么,它们可能会相互干扰,导致信号的丢失或损坏。由于地球静止轨道上可使用于空间服务的频谱十分有限,而卫星的数量还在不断增加,无线电频谱的拥堵已经不仅仅是一种风险了,而是变成了现实。

由于存在这些阻碍,地球静止轨道被看作是有限的自然资源[1]。事实上,这些阻碍限制了置于轨道上的卫星的数量,使得这种放置有风险并且昂贵。

(二)地球静止轨道的分配

对于在国际社会上管理和分配用于卫星通信的地球静止轨道的位置和频率负责的组织是国际电信联盟(ITU)[2]。在国际电信联

---

[1] 地球静止轨道被普遍承认是有限的自然资源,这是由 1973 年《国际电信联盟公约》第 33 条的规定造成的,本条将这一轨道冠以"地球静止轨道"之名。

[2] 国际电信联盟是联合国的专门机构。依据 1992 年《国际电信联盟公约》第一条的规定,联盟的主要目的是:a)维持和扩大国际合作,以改进和合理使用各种电信;b)在通讯领域为发展中国家提供技术支持;c)促进技术设施的发展及其最有效的运用,以提高电信业务的效率扩大技术设施的用途并尽量使之为公众普遍利用;d)以促进国际和平的目的促进电信业务的使用。

盟的框架下,管理频谱以及地球静止轨道卫星的位置的工作隶属于无线电通信部(Radio communication sector)。依照 1992 年公约第 7 条的规定,无线电通信部的目标是"保证所有的无线电通信服务提供者合理、平等、有效和经济的利用无线电频谱,包括静止卫星或轨道卫星的利用"。为了实现这些目标,无线电通信部(Radio communication sector)确保"无线电管理条例"(Radio Regulations)(即国际电信联盟政府的条约文本)中包含分配频谱的规则,并且运营者按要求观测技术参数(的内容)。

上述的地球静止轨道物理局限性导致了公平和平等进入轨道与对其有效利用之间的紧张关系。这种紧张关系源于发达国家和发展中国家对轨道位置和频率分配的不同看法,前者支持自由市场竞争的方式,而后者并不认同。

分配地球静止轨道位置及其频率的主要方法被称作"归纳法(a posteriori)",这个方法是以"先到先得"的方式为基础的[①]。这个方法包含如下几个阶段:当卫星经营者希望开发一个通信卫星系统时,它要联系成员国(或地区),成员国(或地区)将告知无线电通信局(Radio communication Bureau),通信局负责指定特定的频率

[①] 对于"归纳法"的分析可以参见:R. S. Jakhu, "The legal status of the geostationary orbit", in 7 Annals Air & Space L., (1982), p. 333; J. C. Thompson, "Space for rent: the International Telecommunication Union, space law, and orbit/spectrum leasing", 62 J. Air L. & Comm., (1996~97), p. 279; J. Wilson, "The International Telecommunication Union and the geostationary satellite orbit: an overview", in 23 Annals Air & Space L., (1994), p. 241; L. D. Roberts, "A lost of connection: geostationary satellite networks and the International Telecommunication Union", 15 Berk. Tech. L. J., (2000), p. 1095; F. Lyall, "Paralysis by phantom: problems of the ITU filling procedures", in Proceedings of the Thirty Ninth Colloquium on the Law of Outer Space (1996), p. 189; O. Fernandez - A. Brital, "The legal status of the geostationary orbit and ITU recent activities", in Proceedings of the Thirty second Colloquium on the Law of Outer Space, (1989), p. 223.

及轨道位置给经营者。这要求重新审查"国际频率登记和分配表"（Allocation and of the Master International Frequency）以确定之前没有人对这个频率提出申请，并且保证预计放置的位置不会干扰已存在的系统的运行。如果在审查过程中没有发现问题，国际电信联盟将会将运营者的报告加入到频率登记之中，相应的频率和轨道位置也随之分配给了这个运营者，运营者对于频率和轨道位置的使用是暂时的，即在卫星系统运营的整个过程中使用。需要提出的是，运营者只是对于使用轨道的某一特定的位置获得了一个临时使用的权利，并没有对这个轨道获得任何财产权。

这个"归纳法"程序是以先注册为导向的。第一个申请频率的经营者在报告和登记过程都成功的情形下是第一个获得使用权的。并且，一旦经营者的系统被允许使用分配到的轨道／频谱资源，即免受后来使用者的干涉。这个体系很明显是受到发达国家欢迎的，因为发达国家有技术和财政资源在地球静止轨道上放置并运行卫星。

在1960年初，"归纳法"程序刚刚建立的时候，由于对轨道频谱资源的利用并不很多，所以用这个程序管理地球静止轨道上的卫星还是合理的。但是，20世纪70年代和80年代时，卫星的数量随着对于卫星服务要求的增加而增加，发展中国家就开始越来越关心轨道／频谱资源的稀缺性以及它的分配方式。因此它们开始批判"归纳法"的程序，并要求以平等进入地球静止轨道的原则为基础，建立一个新的分配程序。在这个方面，发展中国家取得的第一个成果是在《国际电信联盟公约》的文本（第33条）中规定的自由进入地球静止轨道的原则中加入确保"考虑发展中国家以及位于地球静止轨道下的特殊国家的特别需要"。《国际电信联盟公约》第33条的语言十分重要，因为它通过强调平等不仅仅是用效率和经济衡量给予不发达国家对于获得轨道／频谱资源的利用和管理的需要予以完全的承认。之后，在20世纪80年代末，关于分配轨道／频谱资源问题达成了新的协议，这个协议被称作"双重分配"或叫作"演绎法(a priori)"①。这个系统只适用于固定卫星服务(Fixed satellite services)(FSS)②。在这个服务之中,只适用于"扩展带(expansion band)",每个国际电信联盟的成员国(或地区)都有权在预先确定的弧度和波段上使用一个轨道位置。因此,通过"演绎法"的分配计划,每一个国家都至少有一个轨道位置和频率用于通信目的。因为所有的国家,包括后发者,都遵守这个分配计划,并且这个计划不要求国家在任何的特定时间内证明有使用分配资源的能力,所以,新的"演绎法"程序得到了大多数发展中国家的认可。

(三)国际电信联盟分配轨道/频谱资源的体系:一个制定外空资源开采的法律制度的有益参考

需要考虑的是,无论是地球静止轨道的资源还是存在于月球及其他天体表面和地下的物质资源都是"有限的自然资源"。为了

---

① 关于"演绎法"的描述以及其适用过程,请参见 C. Q. Christol, "The legal status of the geostationary orbit in the light of the 1895~1988 activities of the ITU", in Proceeding of the Thirty-Second Colloquium on the Law of Outer Space, (1989), p. 215; S. Ospina, "The ITU and WARC-ORB: will the revised radio regulations result in a sui-generis legal regime for the GSO?", in Proceeding of the Thirty-Second Colloquium on the Law of Outer Space, (1989), p. 247; T. Lozanova, "Legal status of the geostationary orbit in the light of the recent activities of ITU", in Proceeding of the Thirty-Second Colloquium on the Law of Outer Space, (1989), p. 233; S. Wiessner, "Access to a res publica internationalis: the case of the geostationary orbit", in Proceedings of the Twenty-Ninth Colloquium on the Law of Outer Space, (1986), p. 147.

② 1988年的"WARC 最后文件"将固定卫星服务(FSS)的概念定义为:在无线电通信中,当使用一个或多个卫星时,在固定位置的地球站点之间提供服务的;固定位置可能是固定区域的固定地点;在某些情形下,这种服务包括卫星与卫星的连接,可能在卫星间进行操作;固定为性服务可能包含与其他空间通信服务的共用频段(feeder links)。

阻止浪费,最大限度地利用其价值,所有这些资源都需要合理利用和分配。因此,分析地球静止轨道是如何管理的,可以为外空资源的矿物开发提供实用的经验。

其一,规制轨道和频谱资源的法律框架包括平等进入和效率的概念。尽管将这个体系应用至轨道位置和频率的分配问题上曾在发达国家和发展中国家之间引起问题和争议,这两个概念仍应当应用于未来的月球和其他天体的法律制度中。将这两个概念引入法律制度之中可以在发达国家和不发达国家之间寻找需要和利益的平衡,并符合《外空条约》第一条的规定,即要求不歧视地为了所有国家的利益探索和利用外层空间。

其二,分配轨道位置的体系是建立在对于位置和频率的利用都是受时间限制的基础之上的。事实上,没有实体有权利永久利用地球静止轨道资源。这与未来的开发月球和其他天体的制度有根本性的联系。(月球和其他天体的)法律制度的一个十分重要的方面是,应当仅授权实体对其预先确定的位置的有限的时间内进行开发(即便这种授权可以持续)。不应当对这些地点取得任何的永久的特权。类似的这样的条款也符合《外空条约》第二条的要求,外层空间,包括月球和其他天体,不得据为己有。

但是,分配轨道位置的法律体系中的几个要素是不能引入规制外空矿物资源开发的法律制度之中的。包括分配轨道位置和频率的两个程序规则,其中一个是建立在"先到先得"的基础之上的。这样的方法不应当成为外空资源开发活动法律规制的基础。建立在这种方法之上的法律制度,事实上仅对工业化国家有利,因为只有这些国家有经济和技术条件去参与这种类型的活动。相反,发展中国家将会被完全地排挤出外空资源的开发活动,无法从中获利。并且还应当考虑地球静止轨道和月球资源的不同性质,前者是无法耗尽的,后者则是可耗尽的。将"先到先得"的方式引入到外空矿物资源的开发之中,很有可能会导致资源的快速耗尽,并对月球和其他天体造成污染。

需要补充说明的是,分配轨道位置的另外一个程序"演绎法"

也不适用未来的月球开发的法律制度。如之前所说,这个程序给予所有国家至少一部分轨道/频谱资源,而不要求其证明自己的需要以及使用所分配资源的技术能力。这个"演绎法"体系虽然在道德角度看是公平合理的,但是它可能是导致对有效资源的没有效率的利用和浪费,因为大部分发展中国家根本不会去利用分配给它们的资源。所以,这个方法不能用于将来规制外空资源开发的法律制度中。考虑到这种开发活动的高风险和巨大经济利益,应当阻止"演绎法"方式建立起来的体系所可能带来的效率低下和浪费。如果应用于国际电信联盟体系中的"演绎法"程序用于月球的矿物开发之中,在这种情形下,特定的月球上的地区(可能包含有价值的能源)就可能被平等地分配给所有国家,而不考虑它们的技术先进程度,结果是月球这个地区的绝大部分没有被利用,可能会导致没有生产的情形。

因此,未来的规制月球和其他天体资源开发活动的法律制度应当寻找一个替代的方法,这个方法要比现在国际电信联盟法律制度应用的方法更具生产效率,并且要保证所有国家有效和平等的利用。

六、规制月球和其他天体自然资源开发的法律制度

通过对开发和利用深海海床资源的法律制度,南极资源开采的法律制度以及地球静止轨道分配的法律制度进行比较分析,很容易揭示出这些法律制度对于未来的外空资源开发的影响。考虑到对已出现的相关问题的分析,这一开发应当依照如下方式进行:

——应当建立一个新的法律制度,这一制度应当包括清晰、具体和简单的规则,规定如何组织开发外空资源,提供许可并且监督获得许可者是否遵守许可规则及法律条款的规定。

——决定做出机制应当保证国家对于做出决定的影响与其投资和开发的活动相适应。

——应当制定一个授予许可的过程的精确时间表。

——授予开发规制外空资源的许可并不意味许可持有人对此持有特权。许可所授予持有人的权利应当是在许可持续的时间里,商业开发和利用位于月球和其他天体上的资源。一旦这个时间段届满,这个开发地点在理论上应重新被送入市场,对以后的使用者开放。显然,不能排除先前获得许可的经营者申请继续经营这一开发地点的权利。

——经济鼓励可以使外空资源的开发更有效地进行,所以应当设立这样一个机制鼓励公共和私人投资。

——应当建立一个规制外层空间资源开发强制性的争端解决机制。这个机制的出现有利于增强法律的效力。因为如果规则被违反,可以通过这一机制强制执行。

——应当允许并鼓励国际参与者参与开发活动,为他们提供灵活并具体的机会。

——应当设置保障外空资源的开发不仅仅是为了直接参与者获益,而是为了全人类的利益机制。当然,这并不是要求强制平分所得利益,对于这一理念的执行不仅要求对于法律的整体接受(尤其是发展中国家),也要求遵守外层空间的几个基本原则。例如《外空条约》第一条规定的:"要求对外层空间的开发和利用为了全人类利益而进行"。

如果规制月球和其他天体开发的法律制度按照上述的方式建立,则一方面,在很大程度上它可能会被主要的国家认可;另一方面,也可以保障开发活动的安全,有益和成功进行。

结论

在月球表面建立人类的永久站点以及商业开发和利用月球资源是21世纪带来令人神往和引人注目的事件。如此重要的事件需要在一个安全的和适当的法律环境中进行。由于现有的国际空间法之中不存在任何详细的处理外空资源开发的规则,所以,需要建立一个专门的法律制度。

规制非国家管辖的深海海床资源利用的法律框架、南极矿物开发活动的法律框架以及地球静止轨道资源的法律框架,为月球和其他天体资源开发将提供可以引用的参考要素。如果对这些要素加以借鉴,则有可能建立一个可以保证外空自然资源有秩序和安全开发的法律制度。

The Exploitation of the Resources of the Deep Seabed, Antarctica and the Allocation of the Geostationary Orbit: Valuable Lessons for the Management and Commercial Use of the Natural Resources of the Moon and other Celestial Bodies?

Fabio Tronchetti[①]

Abstract: The exploitation of the natural resources of the Moon and other celestial bodies represents one of the most exciting future developments in the field of space law and space activities. The establishment of a manned basis on the surface of the Moon and the mining and use of lunar resources are all events which catch fascination of the international community. Despite its fascinating character, the possibility to exploit extraterrestrial natural resources for commercial purposes raises concerns related to the ability of the existing international space law to ensure the safe and orderly carrying out of such exploitation. Currently, no rules specifically dealing with such a hypothesis exist. This ab-

---

① Fabio Tronchetti, Associate Director of the Space Law Research Institute, Harbin Institute of Technology, People's Republic of China. email: fabio. tronchetti@ yahoo. com.

sence generates uncertainty on the legal regime applicable to extraterrestrial mining activities and discourages investors in investing into it. Hence, a new legal framework to regulate the exploitation of the natural resources of the Moon and other celestial bodies should be created.

In this respect, the legal regimes governing mining activities of the deep seabed resources, mineral operations in Antarctica and the allocation and use of the geostationary orbit provide valuable solutions and examples to be used for the establishment of such legal framework.

The present paper will make a comparative analysis of these three legal regime aimed at demonstrating their potential impact on the regulation of extraterrestrial mining activities.

Introduction

The beginning of the 21st century has been characterized by a new and exciting era of exploration and use of outer space. Several notable developments and projects, such as private sub-orbital space flights[1] and the first manned mission to Mars[2], are on their way to become a reality in the not-too-distant future.

Among these developments there is one which is increasingly catching attention and fascination of the general public and the legal community: the exploitation of the natural resources of the Moon and other celestial bodies. The possibility to mine and use for commercial purposes the resources located in the lunar and other celestial bodies' soil does no longer represent a dream or a topic for a science fiction novel but it is gradually emerging as a feasible and concrete

---

[1] The private company Virgin Galactic has announced its intention to start providing sub-orbital flights to paying customers by 2012. For information see: www.virgingalactic.com.

[2] American President Obama is expected to request the US Congress to fund the construction of a new heavy-lift launcher the main purpose of which will be to carry astronauts to the Moon and Mars. See in this respect: http://blogs.sciencemag.org/scienceinsider/2009/12/exclusiveobama.html.

option. States as well as private operators are, indeed, showing a growing interest towards exploiting extraterrestrial resources. The interest of States is clearly demonstrated by the fact that in recent years some of the major space powers, such as the United States[①], China[②], India[③]

---

① On June 18, 2009, the United States has launched the Lunar Reconnaissance Orbiter (LRO) mission, the main purpose of which is to study the physical composition of the Moon by focusing particular attention on the Polar Regions (see: http://lunar.gsfc.nasa.gov/). The LRO mission represents the first step in the realization of the Vision for Future Space Exploration, which was proposed by the former US President George W. Bush in 2004. The Vision foresees the return of astronauts on the Moon by 2020, the establishment of a permanent manned basis on the lunar surface and the use of the Moon as a basis for future space exploration. For further information on the Vision for Future Space Exploration see: http://www.nasa.gov/externalflash/Vision/index.html.

② China is probably the most active State in the field of exploration of the Moon and analysis of lunar resources. China's Moon exploration program pursue the following objectives: 1) analysis of the Moon's composition by satellite; 2) the launch of a rover on the Moon's surface by 2012; 3) a manned mission by 2017. On October 24, 2007, the first spacecraft of the programme, Chang'e-1, was launched. Its purpose was to study the composition and quality of the lunar resources. See in this regard: http://www.spacedaily.com/reports/China_Moon_Mission_ChangE_1_In_Good_Condition_999.html. According to the State Administration of Science and Technolgy and Industry for National Defense Chang'e-2, China's second lunar prob, will be launched at the end of 2010 with the purpose of testing key technologies for Chang'e-3 and provide high resoultions images of landing areas. See: http://luna-ci.com/2009/11/30/china-announces-change-2-launch-date-and-change-3-lander-details.

③ India launched its first mission to the Moon, Chandrayaan 1, on 22 October 2008. The mission was aimed at mapping the entire lunar surface, both on the near and far side, in order to get a better knowledge of the minerals contained on the Moon and to facilitate the future presence of human beings on its surface. The mission ended prematurely on 29 August 2009, fourteen months before its expected end, due to an abrupt malfunctioning. See: http://www.isro.org/Chandrayaan/htmls/home.htm.

and Japan①, have launched robotic missions with the aim of mapping the mineral composition of the Moon and locating the most appropriate location for the building of a permanent lunar basis. In this respect, the United States and China have set out the most ambitious goals: while the former has declared its intention to bring back men to the Moon by 2020, the latter has planned to send its first manned lunar missions by 2017.

This global attention in the Moon and other celestial bodies is mainly driven by the high economic value of the natural resources contained therein. The Moon is rich in minerals distributed uniformly across its surface and subsurface. Several lunar missions have confirmed the presence of vast amount of silicon, iron, aluminum, oxygen, hydrogen, chromium, manganese and other minerals. These substances can be either brought back to Earth or used in situ for life support of a permanent lunar basis or as a rocket propellant②. The most valuable lunar resource is, however, Helium-3. Helium-3 is an isotope hardly present

---

① On 14 September 2007 Japan launched the Selene mission whose purpose was to analyze the Moon's history and its physical composition. See: http://www.jaxa.jp/projects/sat/selene/index_e.html.

② See: http://www.technologyreview.com/Energy/19296/; http://www.popularmechanism.com/science/air/. A very recent NASA mission, the Lunar Crater Observation and Sensing Satellite (LCROSS) mission, has also confirmed the presence of water-ice at the south pole of the Moon. The mission consisted of a rocket and a probe smashing into a lunar crater, the Cabeus crater, on 9 October 2009. This impact was supposed to generate a plum of debris visible by Earth telescopes which could confirm the presence of ice. Although the debris cloud was smaller than expected, it provided the evidences scientists were looking for. In addition, the work of the probe, which followed the rocket into the lunar crater, proved to be highly successful. It detected vast amounts of water-ice and water vapour. For information about the LCROSS mission and its result see: http://news.bbc.co.uk/2/hi/8359744.stm; http://www.nasa.gov/mission_pages/LCROSS/main/prelim_water_results.html; http://www.space.com/scienceastronomy/090923-moon-water-discovery.html.

on Earth but abundant on the Moon which combined with other materials, such as deuterium, can be used as fuel in fusion power reactors. The importance of Helium-3 is that it can produce nuclear power and, as a result, energy in a clean way, through a process of nuclear fusion which does not generate toxic waste. Thanks to these special characteristics the mining of Helium-3 may have a tremendous impact on the way energy is produced and made available on Earth. Helium-3, indeed, could replace fossil fuels and other substances as primary source of energy on Earth[1]. The celestial bodies other than the Moon contain vast deposits of natural resources too. This is particularly true with regard to the around 1400 Near Earth asteroids which cross the Earth's orbit around the Sun. These asteroids are particularly rich in iron and water.

While, on one side, the exploitation of extraterrestrial resources is expected to benefit not only those directly involved in it but also the majority of people on Earth, especially when taking into consideration the positive impact of the use of Helium-3, on the other side, it raises concerns about the ability of the current space law regime to ensure its orderly, profitable and safe development. Currently, a specific set of internationally agreed rules establishing how the commercial use of extraterrestrial resources has to be carried out does not exist. The two most relevant legal instruments in this respect, namely the 1967 Outer Space Treaty[2] and the 1979 Moon Agreement[3] fail, indeed, to set out a clear and detailed legal framework

---

[1] For instance, a study has demonstrated that 25 tonnes of Helium-3 can provide all the power that the United States needs in a year. See in this respect: See: Sci/Tech. Moon map aids discovery, http://news.bbc.co.uk/1/hi/sci/tech/226053.stm.

[2] Treaty on Principles Governing the Activities of States in the Exploration and Use of Outer Space, Including the Moon and Other Celestial Bodies, 27 January 1967, 610 U.N.T.S. 205, 18 U.S.T.,2410, T.I.A.S. No. 6347, 6 I.L.M. 386 (hereinafter Outer Space Treaty).

[3] Agreement Governing the Activities of States on the Moon and other Celestial Bodies, 5 December 1979, 1363 U.N.T.S. 3, 18 I.L.M. 1434 (hereinafter Moon Agreement).

dealing with it.

The absence of such a legal framework not only may cause the exploitation of extraterrestrial materials to be a risky and unpredictable business but also may prevent it from actually ever taking place. First of all, due to the lack of specific rules indicating under which conditions exploitative activities may be performed and what are the rights and duties of the subjects involved, it would be very difficult to envisage the results of such activities and, in particular, of the financial benefits to be generated therein. Because of this uncertainty, States and private companies would be discouraged from investing in it. It has always to be kept in mind that mining and using resources located in a celestial body is a risky and expensive activity. Hence, no one would invest in such an activity without the presence of a stable legal regime which, on one hand, protects the financial and technical investments made and, on the other hand, creates the possibility to make a profit from it. Secondly, the absence of an appropriate legal framework is likely to generate tensions and conflicts among those carrying out extraterrestrial exploitative activities. In case, for example, two or more subjects were interested in the same lunar site how this situation would be solved? Under which legal basis one subject would be authorized to exploit that site while the others would be excluded from doing so? Under a first come, first served approach? Clearly, a similar solution has to be avoided as space operators would start competing to get the most favorable site by increasing, thus, the risk of tensions among them and by endangering the peaceful nature of outer space. Thirdly, some States and private operators could try to take advantage of the uncertain rules regulating the exploitation of extraterrestrial materials by performing such exploitation in a greedy and merely profit oriented manner, regardless of the respect for the space environment and for the basic space law principles. This scenario would be disgraceful as it would threaten the delicate environmental balance of outer space as well as the existence and proper functioning of the space law regime.

Having, thus, explained the need for setting forth a legal regime to govern the exploitation of extraterrestrial resources, the question is: How this regime should be created? What principles should it contain? In this respect, it is important to point out that when developing a new legal regime the preliminary step is to verify whether existing legal framework regulating international areas or international resources may be used as a model. In this case, the answer is positive. The legal regimes managing the exploitation of the mineral resources located in the deep seabed and the ocean floor beyond national jurisdiction, as defined in the 1994 Amendment to Part XI of the Law of the Sea Convention[①], mining activities in Antarctica, as contained in the 1988 Wellington Convention[②], and the allocation and use of the geostationary orbit provide valuable solutions to be used in developing a legal framework to manage the exploitation of extraterrestrial resources.

After describing the inability of the existing space law regime to provide an adequate legal structure to govern the exploitation of the natural resources of the Moon and other celestial bodies, the paper will make a comparative analysis of the three above mentioned legal regimes aimed at demonstrating their positive impact on the regulation of such exploitation. In addition, the main problems and limits of these regimes will be discussed so as to avoid the emerging of similar difficulties in relation with the commercial use of extraterrestrial materials.

The last section of the paper will describe the main principles which

---

① Agreement Relating to the Implementation of Part XI of the Law of the Sea Convention (1994), 33 ILM 1309 (1994), SopS 49-50/1996.

② Convention on the Regulation of Antarctic Mineral Resource Activities (usually referred as Wellington Convention), June 2, 1988, 27 ILM (1988) 868.

should be included in a legal framework governing the exploitation of extraterrestrial natural resources.

Ⅰ. Space law and the exploitation of the natural resources of the Moon and other celestial bodies: the need for a legal regime

As already mentioned in the introduction, the existing space law framework does not provide an appropriate legal regime to regulate the exploitation of the natural resources of the Moon and other celestial bodies. The provisions of two international treaties, the Outer Space Treaty and the Moon Agreement, must be analyzed in order to understand why new rules to govern such exploitation need to be established. The Outer Space Treaty is the main instrument regulating activities in outer space[①]. Its provisions provide guidance and directions to all the operations taking place in the space environment. Its importance is demonstrated by the fact that 99 States, including the major space powers, are parties to it.

Several principles laid down in the Outer Space Treaty are of primary importance for the exploitation of extraterrestrial resources. In particular, the idea that the exploration and use of outer space should be car-

---

① For an analysis of the provisions of the Outer Space Treaty see: P. G. Dembling & D. M. Arons, "The evolution of the Outer Space Treaty", J. Air & L. Comm. 33 (1967), p. 419; H. Qizhi, "The Outer Space in Perspective", Proceedings of Fortieth Colloquium on the Law of Outer Space (1997), p. 52; C. Q. Christol, The Modern International Law of Outer Space (1982) New York, p. 21 ss; B. Cheng, Studies in International Space Law, p. 215 ss; M. N. Andem, International Legal Problems in the Peaceful Exploration and Use of Outer Space (1992), Rovaniemi, p. 30 ss.; I. H. Ph. Diederikis Verschoor, An Introduction to Space Law, The Netherlands, (2008), p. 24 ss.

ried out for the benefit and in the interest of all countries (Article I, par. 1), the freedom of exploration and use of outer space (Article I, par. 2), the non-appropriative nature of outer space (Article 2), the responsibility of States for private space activities (Article VI) and the jurisdiction of the State of registry over its space objects (Article 8).

The problem with the provisions of the Outer Space Treaty is that they are of very general character and they do not provide an explanation of the terms used. For instance, how the word "benefit" should be interpreted? How the use of outer space can be carried out for the benefit and in the interest of all countries in practical terms, especially when exploiting extraterrestrial resources? Additionally, while it is clear that the Treaty prohibits the appropriation of outer space, it is doubtful whether this prohibition covers also the resources located in the Moon and other celestial bodies. In this respect, some authors express the view that the restriction in Article II applies equally to outer space and its resources[1], whereas others claim that analogy with the rules regulating the freedom of the high seas, the appropriation of space resources merely forms part of the freedom of exploration and use of outer space[2].

The point is that due to the uncertain and vague nature of the principles of the Outer Space Treaty the exploitation of the natural resources of the

---

[1] See: for instance, S. Gorove, "Interpreting Article II of the Outer Space Treaty", in Proceedings of the Eleventh Colloquium on the Law of Outer Space, (1968), p. 40; A. A. Cocca, Report of the 54th International Law Association, (1970), p. 434; N. Markov, ibid, p. 411.

[2] D. Goedhuis, "Some Recent Trends in the Interpretation and the Implementation of the Rules of International Space Law", 19 Columbia J. of Transnational L. 213, 219 (1981); C. Q. Christol, "Article II of the Outer Space Treaty Revisited", 9 Annals of Air & Space L. 217 (1984).

Moon and other celestial bodies cannot be based upon these principles only. In order for this exploitation to be successful and properly organized, what is needed is the presence of clear rules addressing the specific legal issues which may arise in the course of this exploitation, such as those related to the duration of mining activities and to property rights over the extracted materials, and indicating what is allowed and what is not. Therefore, a new set of legal rules which supplement and extend those of the Outer Space Treaty need to created.

The inability of the Outer Space Treaty to provide an adequate legal regime to regulate the exploitation of extraterrestrial natural resources is also demonstrated by the fact that shortly after the successful completion of the first manned lunar mission[1], States decided to enter into negotiation on a new treaty specifically dealing with activities on the Moon and other celestial bodies. The result of this negotiation, which lasted from 1971 to 1979, was the Agreement Governing the Activities of States on the Moon and Other Celestial Bodies, better know as Moon Agreement[2]. The Moon Agreement was opened for signature on 18 December 1979 and entered into force on 11 July 1984, when the fifth instrument of ratification was deposited. The main purpose of the Agree-

---

[1] On 20 July 1969, the two American astronauts Niel Armstrong and Edwin Aldrin were the first human beings ever to make a step on the lunar surface.

[2] For an analysis of the Moon Agreement see: G. Zhukov & Y. Kolosov, International Space Law, (1984), Novosti Press Agency, Moscow, p. 173; B. Cheng, supra, footnote 11, p. 246; H. W. Bashor Jr. , The Moon Treaty Paradox (2004), Libris Corporation; C. Q. Christol, The Modern International Law of Outer Space, (1982), New York ; L. Vikkari, From Manganese Nodules to Lunar Regolith: a Comparative Legal Study of the Utilisation of Natural Resources in the Deep Seabed and Outer Space, (2002), Rovaniemi; H. A. Wassenbergh, Principles of Outer Space in Hindsight, (1991), p. 39; N. Jasentuliyana & R. S. K. Lee, Manual of Space Law, New York, (1979), Vol. I, p. 253.

ment was to set out legal rules to govern manned activities on the lunar and other celestial bodies' surface, particularly those aimed at exploiting the natural resources contained therein.

Unfortunately, unlike the Outer Space Treaty, the Moon Agreement has not encountered success. At the moment only 13 States, not including the major space powers, have ratified it[①]. The main reasons behind its failure is to be found in the provisions of its Article 11, which declares the Moon and its natural resources to be "the common heritage of mankind" and applies the common heritage of mankind concept to the exploitation of such resources[②].

Briefly, the common heritage of mankind concept is based on the assumption that all human beings are members of the human race irrespectively of which part of the world they live and that all of them should be given the same opportunity for improving their economic and

---

① The thirteen States which have ratified the Moon Agreement are: Australia, Austria, Chile, Mexico, Morocco, the Netherlands, Pakistan, the Philippines, Uruguay, Kazakhstan, Belgium, Peru and Lebanon.

② For an analysis of the meaning of Article 11 of the Moon Agreement see : B. Rosenfield, "Article XI of the Draft Moon Agreement", in Proceedings of the 22th Colloquium on the Law of Outer Space, (1980), p. 209; R. J. Lee, "Creating an International Regime for Property Rights Under the Moon Agreement", in Proceedings of the Forty-Second Colloquium on the Law of Outer Space, (1999), p. 409; K. V. Cook, "The Discover of Lunar Water: An Opportunity to Develop a Workable Moon Treaty", (1994), 11 Geo. Int'l Envtl. L. Rev., p. 647; S. Hobe, "Common Heritage of Mankind-An Outdated Concept in International Space Law", in Proceedings of the Forty-first Colloquium on the Law of Outer Space, (1998), p. 271.

living conditions①. Starting from this assumption, it holds that all States acting together on behalf of mankind as a whole, should share in the management of certain areas that, due to the economic and scientific value of the resources contained there, are considered to be the common heritage of mankind. In particular, this concept requires that all activities within the common heritage of mankind area, particularly those aimed at exploiting the area's resources, must be carried out only in accordance with the rules set forth by an international regime, whose primary purpose is the orderly management of the area and the equitable sharing by all States of the benefits generated thereof, taking into particular account the needs of developing States irrespectively of their degree of involvement in those activities. The common heritage of mankind includes some further elements, such as the preservation of the area's environment, the peaceful nature of the activities carried out in the area and the freedom of scientific investigation.

The problem with the common heritage of mankind concept is that developing and developed States hold opposite views about its interpretation and application. The former group advances a "common property" interpretation of the common heritage of mankind concept for areas be-

---

① For a broad explanation of the common heritage of mankind concept see: C. C. Joyner, "Legal Implications of the Concept of the Common Heritage of Mankind", in 35 Int'l & Comp. L. Q. 190, (1986); S. Gorove, "The Concept of the Common Heritage of Mankind: A Political, Moral or Legal Innovation?", 9 San Diego L. Rev. 390, (1972); G. M. Danilenko, "The Concept of the Common Heritage of Mankind in International Law", 13 Annals Air & Space L. 247; C. Q. Christol, "The Common Heritage of Mankind Provisions in the 1979 Agreement Governing the Activities of States on the Moon and Other Celestial Bodies", in 14 International Law 429, (1980); V. Kopal, "Outer Space as a Global Common", in Proceedings of the Fortieth Colloquium on the Law of Outer Space, p. 108, (1997).

yond national jurisdiction. This common property approach requires common management of such areas, common sharing by all States of the mined resources and the benefits generated therein, regardless of the level of participation in the exploitative activities and mandatory transfer of technology from developed to developing States.

The latter group of States, particularly the United States, refuses the interpretation of the common heritage of mankind concept proposed by the developing countries by claiming it to be detrimental to the interests of those engaged in exploitative activities and no-market oriented. In their view, the concept should be interpreted in such a way as to exclude changes in the existing conditions for access to international resources. In particular, the concept should not lead to a modification of the traditional freedom of the high sea, which provides States with freedom of exploration and use. Accordingly, developed States only recognize that the common heritage of mankind may contribute to certain improvement in the distribution of financial and other benefits derived from the exploitation of the resources located in the common heritage of mankind area. In this respect, the special needs of developing States should be taken into consideration. However, only the States exploiting the resources are entitled to decide how to share them and what is equitable.

The impossibility to reach a common understanding on how to interpret the common heritage concept and, as a result, on how to apply it to the exploitation of lunar and other celestial bodies' resources, led both developed and developing States to the refusal to ratify the Moon Agreement.

One could wonder whether the Agreement has any chance to become successful in the future, particularly taking into consideration the fact that in the last five years 4 States have become parties to it[①]. Despite these recent ratifications it is very unlikely that many other States, particularly the developed ones, would decide to join it. The United States, for instance, has declared not to be interested in entering into the Moon Agreement. This limited acceptance of the Agreement makes it little or no relevant for future extraterrestrial exploitative activities.

Thus, being the Moon Agreement's provisions inapplicable, the only existing space law principles relevant to the exploitation of extraterrestrial natural resources are those contained in the Outer Space Treaty. However, as previously explained, these principle are not detailed enough to ensure the safe and proper development of such exploitation. Therefore, a new legal framework to regulate the commercial use of the natural resources of the Moon and other celestial bodies is required. The rules governing mineral activities in the high seas, in Antarctica and the use of the geostationary orbit may be taken as examples to set up such legal framework.

II. The Law of the Sea Convention and the Exploitation of the Seabed Resources Located Beyond National Jurisdiction: the Impact of the 1994 Implementation Agreement

1982 ~ 1994: the Road towards the 1994 Implementation Agreement of Part XI of the Law of the Sea Convention

Exploitative activities of the mineral resources located in the seabed and ocean floor beyond the limits of national jurisdiction are governed by

---

① These four States are: Kazakhstan in 2001, Belgium in 2004, Peru in 2005 and Lebanon in 2007.

Part XI of the 1982 United Nations Law of the Sea Convention[①], as amended by the 1994 Implementation Agreement of Part XI of the Law of the Sea Convention. The provisions of the 1994 Implementation Agreement represent the most valuable instrument for the establishment of a legal regime aimed at regulating the exploitation of extraterrestrial resources, as they provide a new interpretation of the common heritage of mankind concept as well as rules to govern the commercial use of resources located in international areas which have been accepted by both developed and developing States. In order to proper understand the importance of the 1994 Implementation Agreement it is necessary to analyze the process which led to its adoption.

In the beginning of the 1970's, there was a general consensus among States on the need for a new global treaty regulating activities in the sea. The negotiations of this new treaty, which were carried out within the United Nations framework, began in 1973 and ended on 10 December 1982 when the United Nations Law of the Sea Convention was open for signature[②].

During the negotiation process, one of the most debated topics was the establishment of a legal framework regulating explorative and exploitative activities of the resources contained in the deep seabed outside national jurisdiction, as developed and developing States held opposite views on how such legal framework should be organized. Taking advantage of their numeric majority and of the voting system within the Unit-

---

① United Nations Convention on the Law of the Sea (1982), 21 ILM 1245 (1982), SopS 49-50/1996.

② For an analysis of the Negotiations of the Law of the Sea Convention, see: Churchill R. R., A. W. Lowe, The Law of the Sea, 3ed., (1999) Manchester Univ. Press, p. 223; J. T. Swing, "Who Will Own the Oceans"?, 54 Foreign Aff. 527, (1975~1976); B. H. Oxman, "The Third United Nations Conference on the Law of the Sea: the Tenth Session", in 76 A. J. I. L. 1, (1982).

ed Nations General Assembly, which gives each State one vote, the developing States were able to insert into the final text of the Law of the Sea Convention and, in particular, in its Part XI, rules governing deep seabed mining operations which reflected their position and requests.

Part XI of the Law of the Sea Convention declared the seabed and its resources "the common heritage of mankind". It set up a complex mechanism for the management and exploitation of the common heritage of mankind area and its resources. An International Seabed Authority empowered to authorize, control and manage the exploitation of the deep seabed resources was established. Levies on mining activities were to be distributed among all States parties to the Convention in accordance with the common heritage of mankind redistributive approach. The Authority itself was to engage in seabed exploitation through its mining company, the Enterprise. Mining companies wishing to operate within the common heritage of mankind area were obliged to make to the Authority an application for two sites of equal value. The Authority would have chosen one for which it would have given approval and would have kept the other, which the Authority itself would have used, either through the Enterprise or in collaboration with developing States (the so-called "parallel system"). The Authority could force developed States to transfer, on fair commercial terms, mining technology that could not be obtained on the open market, to developing States, in order to enable them to engage in seabed mining activities. In addition, decisions of the Authority, whose main organs were the Council and the Assembly, were to be taken on a one State, one vote basis, thus resulting in the Authority being directed and influenced by the developing States in most of its decision making processes.

When the Law of the Sea Convention was opened for signature in 1982 it was clear that developed States were not ready to accept the provisions of its Part XI. In their opinion, these provisions were detrimental to their political and economical interests and an obstacle to the development of seabed resources. The main criticisms leveled by the developed States to the mechanism created to regulate deep seabed mining were the following: 1) a decision making system which did not give industrialized States influence commensurate with their activities or investments; 2) mandatory transfer of technology; 3) economic principles that were inconsistent with free market philosophy and that discouraged deep seabed resources mining. Because of these reasons developed States refrained from singing or ratifying the Law of the Sea Convention.

While, on one side, developed States refused to accept Part XI of the Law of the Sea Convention, on the other side, most of them recognized the need for establishing a workable legal regime to regulate deep-sea mining. Hence, a group of western States decided to set up an interim regime to allow and manage mining activities before the entering into force of the Convention, in order to protect their domestic companies which had already invested hundreds of millions of dollars in preparation for seabed mining. According to this regime, which was called "Reciprocating States Regime", each State had to adopt similar national legislation to regulate deep seabed mining. The United States opened the way with its Deep Sea Bed Hard Mineral Resources Act of 1980[1], followed by the Federal Republic of Germany's Act on the Interim Regulation of Deep Sea Bed Mining in the same year. Later, Britain, France, Japan and Italy adopted similar acts[2]. In 1982 the Federal Republic of Germany, the UK, France and the United States signed an

---

① Deep Seabed Hard Mineral Resources Act, 30 USC 1401 et seq, (1980).

② The legislation has been reproduced as follows: Federal Republic of Germany, 20 (International Legal Materials) ILM 393 (1981), 21 ILM 832 (1982); France, 21 ILM 808 (1982); United Kingdom, 20 ILM 1219 (1981); Japan, 22 ILM 102 (1983); Italy, 24 ILM 983 (1985).

Interim Agreement relating to Polymetallic Nodules of the Deep Sea Bed. Under this Agreement citizens of, and companies incorporated in, the States concerned were prohibited from engaging in exploration or exploitation of deep-seabed resources unless they were licensed by that State or by one of the other States. Licensees were also obliged to pay a levy, which would be transferred to the International Sea Bed Authority if and when the Law of the Sea Convention had entered into force for them. The Agreement's provisions significantly differed from those of Part XI of the Law of the Sea Convention. The levy was only half of that envisaged in the Convention: no provisions requiring applicants to reserve two sites for exploitation, one of which for eventual use by the Enterprise, and obliging developed States to transfer technology to developing States were present[①].

However, the Reciprocating States Regime was only meant to be an interim regime before the Law of the Sea Convention entered into force. In the late 1980's, growing understanding spread among developed States on the need for incorporating the amendments to Part XI set up in that Regime into the body of the Law of the Sea Convention. Developed States, indeed, agreed on the usefulness of having one universal system governing deep seabed mining beyond national jurisdiction. This view encountered the favor of most of the developing States as well. The broad acceptance of this view, particularly on the side of the de-

---

[①] In the following years, the States belonging to the Reciprocating States Regime signed several additional instruments dealing with issues like conflicting claims and licensing schemes, such as the 1994 Draft Memorandum of Understanding on the Settlement of Conflicting Claims with Respect to Seabed Areas, reproduced in Law of the Sea Bulletin (LOSB) 37 (1984), the 1994 Provisional Understanding Regarding Deep Seabed Matters, reproduced in 4 LOSB 101 (1985); 23 ILM 1365 (1984) and 1996 New York Understanding, reproduced in 8 LOSB 38 ~ 39 (1986).

veloping States, can be explained if we take into consideration the fact that several factors which affected the negotiations of the Law of the Sea Conventions were no longer present in the late 80's. First of all, developing States were not able to act as a cohesive group capable of influencing decisions within the United Nations anymore. Secondly, developing States which were already parties to the Law of the Sea Convention became increasingly worried about the financial implications of it, as the number of ratifications of it approached the number of sixty needed to bring it into force. In the absence of major contributors such as the United States, Germany and the United Kingdom, they would have the burden to financially support the Authority and the functioning of the system created by the Convention to manage seabed activities. In addition, most of the developed States, while rejecting the original Part XI of the Law of the Sea Convention unacceptable, considered the remaining sections of the Convention to be well structured and potentially very useful.

Thus, in 1990 developed and developing States engaged in a process aimed at amending Part XI of UNCLOS and began informal consultations under the auspices of the UN Secretary General. The result of this process was the adoption by the UN General Assembly of the "Agreement Relating to the Implementation of Part XI of the United Nations Convention on the Law of the Sea of 10 December 1982" on July 28, 1994. The Agreement was opened for signature on July 29 and was promptly signed by fifty States, including eighteen developing and eighteen developed States. The United States agreed to apply it provisionally. Thanks to the success of the Implementation Agreement, the Law of the Sea Convention could enter into force in November 1994. The Implementation Agreement entered into force, with the provisional participation of the US, in 1996.

The 1994 Implementation Agreement

The Implementation Agreement significantly amends Part XI of the Law of the Sea Convention[①]. Its provisions resolve the criticisms leveled by the developed States to the original Part XI and apply a free-market approach to the management of the Area and its resources. In doing so, the Implementation Agreement introduces a new version of the common heritage of mankind concept in which the rigid political and economic requirements have been significantly softened.

The following are the main amendments made by the Implementation Agreement to Part XI:

(1) Decision making[②]: The former system of decision-making in the Council has been modified so as to give the United States, and other States with major economic interests, a stronger impact on the decision-making mechanism proportionate with their interests and importance. Decisions have to be taken by consensus. When consensus is not possible to be reached and when questions of substance are discussed, decisions shall be taken by two-thirds majority of members present and voting. The Council consists of thirty six members distributed as follow: four members from the largest consumers or importers of mineral products; four members from among the largest exporters of mineral products, four members from among those States which have made the largest investments in preparation for and in the conduct of activities in the Area; six members from developing States; and the remaining

---

① For an analysis of the 1994 Implementation Agreement, see: C. B. Thompson, "International Law of the Sea/Seed: Public Domain versus Private Commodity", in 44 Nat. Resources J. 843, (2004); A. De Marffy-Mantuano, "Current Development: The Procedural Framework of the Agreement Implementing the 1982 United Nations Convention on the Law of the Sea", in 89 A. J. I. L. 814, (1995).

② Annex, Section III, 1994 Implementation Agreement.

eighteen members selected to achieve equitable geographic distribution. This means that the United States and other developed States acting in concert may block decisions on issues of major significance, such as financial matters.

(2) Transfer of technology[①]: The requirement of mandatory transfer of technology has been abolished. According to the new approach developing States should obtain deep seabed mining technology on the open market, at a fair and reasonable price, or through joint venture with industrialized States. States Parties shall promote international technical and scientific cooperation with regard to the activities of the Area and undertake to cooperate with the Authority in facilitating the acquisition of technology by the Enterprise or developing States.

(3) Production Policy[②]: deep seabed mining shall be carried out in accordance with sound commercial principles, and there shall be no subsidization or discriminatory practices in favor of some particular States or producers.

(4) Exploration Procedures[③]: New procedures specifying timetables for the approval of proposed exploration work plans are established. Each plan is approved for a period of fifteen years and may be extended for periods of not more that five years each. Such procedures provide economic certainty for investors in such projects.

(5) Parallel system: The parallel system of fields to be presented to the Authority has been abandoned. The Agreement, indeed, removes the requirement that each State Party fund one mine site of the Enterprise.

The 1994 Implementation Agreement: a Valuable Lesson for Extraterrestrial Mining

The analysis of the provisions of the 1994 Implementation Agreement

---

① Annex, Section V, 1994 Implementation Agreement.
② Annex, Section VI, 1994 Implementation Agreement.
③ Annex, Section I, 1994 Implementation Agreement.

and of the process which led to their adoption teaches us several important lessons to be kept in mind when developing a legal framework to regulate the exploitation of extraterrestrial natural resources.

The first lesson is the following: the most appropriate solution to manage exploitative activities of resources located in international areas is the establishment of an international regime. While some could argue that it would be preferable not to create any regime and to leave States free to act independently and in accordance with their own national rules only, the evolution of the Implementation Agreement shows that this is not the way to be followed. After enacting national acts to govern deep seabed mining, in the late 1980's the developed States felt the need for transferring the legal solutions created at national level into the framework of the Law of the Sea Convention, so as to establish a single, universal and coherent legal regime to govern mineral activities in the seabed beyond national jurisdiction. This was considered to be the best choice to guarantee the safe, coordinate and profitable development of such activities.

The Implementation Agreement also shows how a legal regime governing the exploitation of international resources should be created and what elements it should contain. The key to its success is represented by the creation of a balance between the interests of developing and developed States. One of the main reasons of the failure of the original version of Part XI was its inability to create such a balance and its being too developing countries oriented. When setting up an international legal framework is, thus, necessary to make sure that, while the special needs of the developing States are recognized and protected, economic incentives aimed at encouraging developed States to accept and participate in such a framework are established. It has always to be kept in mind that only developed States have the financial and technological capabilities to exploit international resources, either located in the high sea or in space. Without the active contribution of these States this exploitation will never take place. Therefore, it is of fundamental importance that an international legal framework is able to create the conditions to make exploitative activities a profitable business.

Another important element provided by the Implementation Agreement is to guarantee that the States which contribute the most to the exploitation of resources situated in an international area have an adequate impact over the decision-making mechanism of the legal regime regulating such exploitation. One of the biggest criticisms put forward against the original text of Part XI was the fact that the decisions of the International Seabed Authority had to be taken on a one State, one vote basis, by giving developing States the power to control and even block any decision of the Authority. The Implementation Agreement solved this problem by providing the States with the major economic interests in the seabed resources an appropriate voice in the decision – making system of the Authority. A similar solution must be adopted with regard to the legal regime to regulate the exploitation of the natural resources of the Moon and other celestial bodies.

In addition, the Implementation Agreement offers useful solutions relating to the mechanism to regulate the granting and the duration of the licenses to explore and exploit mineral resources located beyond national borders. The Agreement specifies the timetable for the approval of explorative working plans of seabed sites and the duration of each approved plan. This system has a very positive impact because it contributes to generate certainty among those who intend to invest money in seabed mining. A similar solution should be adopted with regard to the concession and the duration of licenses to exploit extraterrestrial natural resources. Indeed, a mechanism which clearly states how long a subject who has applied for a license should wait before being granted such a license and which indicates the maximum duration of the licensed exploitative activities, would generate a stable and certain legal environment likely to stimulate investors to devote their resources to the exploitation of extraterrestrial materials.

To summarize the following elements of the Implementation Agreement should be transferred and applied to the exploitation of extraterrestrial resources:

(a) The establishment of a legal framework to regulate such exploitation;

(b) The creation of a balance between the interests and needs of developed and developing States;

(c) The presence of economic incentives which make the exploitation of extraterrestrial resources a profitable business;

(d) A decision-making mechanism which give States an importance appropriate to their impact on the exploitative activities;

(e) A timeframe for the concession and the duration of licenses.

III. Mineral activities in Antarctica: the 1988 Wellington Convention

Activities in Antarctica are regulated by the so called "Antarctic Treaty System", a conventional regime consisting of several international agreements[1]. The Antarctic Treaty System is to be considered one the

---

[1] The Antarctic Treaty System comprises: the Antarctic Treaty, December 1959, 12 UST 794, TIAS No. 4780, 402 UNTS 71 (entered into force on 23 June 1961); the Convention on the Conservation of Antarctic Seals, June 1, 1972, 27 UST 441, TIAS NO. 8826, ILM 11 (entered into force March 11, 1978); the Convention on the Conservation of Antarctic Marine Living Resources, May 20, 1980, TIAS 10240, ILM 19 (1980), 841~859 (entered into force April 7, 1982); the Convention on the Regulation of Antarctic Mineral Resource Activities, June 2, 1988, 27 ILM (1988) 868, (not in force); the Protocol on Environmental Protection to the Antarctic Treaty, 1991, 30 ILM (1991) 1455, (entered into force on 14 January 1998).

most successful legal structures ever created to govern operations in an international area, as it has allowed more than 50 years of peaceful scientific investigation and environmental protection of the Antarctic area. The Antarctic Treaty System is based upon the 1959 Antarctic Treaty①. Indeed, the provisions of the Antarctic Treaty, such as those indicating that Antarctica shall be used exclusively for peaceful purposes and providing State parties with freedom of scientific investigation of the Antarctic region, provide direction and guidance for all activities to be carried out in Antarctica. Among the provisions of the Antarctic Treaty those laid down in its Article IV are of special importance, as they deal with territorial claims over Antarctica's areas. The legal status of Antarctica is rather complicated. Before the entry into force of the 1959 Antarctic Treaty several States successfully carried out explorative missions of some Antarctic regions. As a result of these missions, there were: a) States which claimed sovereignty over the parts of the Antarc-

---

① For an analysis of the Antarctic Treaty, see: J. Hanessian, "The 1959 Antarctic Treaty", 9 Int & Comp. L. Quart. 436, (1960); A. Watts, Internatonal Law and the Antarctic Treaty System, (1992 Cambridge); C. Joyner – S. K. Chopra (Eds.), The Antarctic Legal Regime, (1988 Martinus Nijhoff Publishers); R. Sattler, "Symposium: Issues in Space Law: Transporting a Legal System for Property Rights from the Earth to the Stars", 6 Chi. j. Int'l L. 23, (2005); J. Couratier, Le Systeme Antarctique, (1991) Bruxelles, Etablissement Emile Bruylant. The Antarctic Treaty now has 45 States Parties. 28 are Consultative Parties on the basis of being original signatories or by conducting substantial research. These States have the right to participate in decision-making at the Antarctic Consultative Parties Meetings. The other States Parties to the Treaty are only allowed to attend such Meetings.

tic continent they had explored[①]; b) States which, in spite of having played a crucial role in discovering Antarctica, did not claim any territorial rights and, at the same time, refuse to recognize claims made by other States. Nevertheless, these States reserved the right to make territorial claims in the future[②]; c) States which did not put forward any claim, did not reserve themselves any right to make claims in the future and refused to accept the claims made by others[③]. These States called for international management of the Antarctica area.

These diverging views made the legal status of Antarctica the most debated point during the negotiations of the Antarctic Treaty. The solution adopted by Article IV of the Treaty was to put territorial and sovereignty claims in abeyance; in simple terms, it froze the claims and the oppo-

---

① The first claim was made by the United Kingdom on 21 July 1908 and covered the sector between 80° West Meridian and 20° West Meridian. New Zealand, on 30 July 1923, fixed the boundaries of a sector ranging from 150 West Meridian to 160° East Meridian. On 27 March 1924, France claimed sovereignty over an area going from 136° East Meridian to 142° East Meridian. Australia, on 7 February 1933, claimed two sectors going from 45 to 136 East Meridian and from 142° to 160° East Meridian. Norway made its claim for 20 West Meridian to 45 East Meridian on 14 January 1939. Argentina, on 16 July 1939, sets its from 25° to 75° West Meridian, while Chile, on 6 November 1940, asserted its rights from 53° to 90° West Meridian. It is interesting to note that Argentina's and Chile's claims were located entirely or partially in the zone claimed by the United Kingdom.

② These States were the United States, whose claims could have been based on the explorations of Palmer in 1818 and Wilkes in 1840 and the Soviet Union, which could have taken advantage of the first circumnavigation of Antarctica by Adm. Bellingshausen between 1819 and 1821.

③ Among these States there were Germany and Italy.

sitions to the claims over Antarctica as they were in 1959[1]. Article IV was of crucial importance because it allowed States to put aside their contrast and to cooperate in the peaceful exploration and study of Antarctica. While the Antarctic Treaty defines and regulates the legal status of Antarctica, it does not address the issue of recovery and exploitation of the mineral resources contained therein. This is in large part due to the fact the when the Treaty was under negotiation there were insufficient geological data which could demonstrate the presence and the value of mineral resources in the Antarctic region. However, when in the beginning of the 1970's scientific reports showed the potential economic value of the Antarctic mineral resources, the Parties to the Antarctic Treaty felt that leaving the legal status of these resources unresolved could represent a threat to the peaceful nature of Antarctica, as States could start competing to obtain sovereignty over the most valuable Antarctic areas and the resources located therein. Thus, they decided to begin discussing how to manage mineral activities in Antarctica.

The negotiations of the Convention on the Regulation of Antarctic Mineral Resources officially began in 1982[2]. These negotiations toke place

---

[1] Article IV thus declares that its provisions shall be interpreted neither as "a renunciation by any Contracting Parties of previously asserted rights of or claims to territorial sovereignty in Antarctica" nor as "a renunciation or diminution by any Contracting Parties of any basis of claim to territorial sovereignty in Antarctica which they may have whether as a result of its activities or those of its nationals".

[2] For an analysis of the negotiations of the Convention on the Regulation of Antarctic Mineral Resources, see: C. C. Joyner, "The Antarctic Minerals Negotiating Process", 81 AJIL 888, (1987); A. Watts, "Lesson to be learned from the Mineral Resources Negotiations", in R. Wolfrum(ed.), Antarctic Challenge III, p. 319~331, (Berlin 1988); F. Francioni, "Legal Aspects of Mineral Exploitation in Antarctica", 19 Cornell Int'l L. J. 163, (1986); G. D. Triggs, "Negotiations of a Mineral Regime", in G. D. Triggs (ed.), The Antarctic Treaty Regime. Law, Environment and Resources, p. 182~195, (Cambridge 1987).

among the so called Consultative parties to the Antarctic Treaty. It has to be explained that while each State could adhere to the Treaty, only those States undertaking "substantial research activity" could gain the status of Consultative Party. As the majority of developing States lacked the financial capability to carry out this type of activity, Consultative Parties were mainly composed of developed States.

The negotiation process ended on 2 June, 1988, when the Convention on the Regulation of Antarctic Mineral Resources was adopted in Wellington (hence the name Wellington Convention). According to Article 62, in order to enter into force the Convention had to be ratified by all Consultative Parties which had participated to the negotiations. When France and Australia withdrew their support to the Convention, the entire ratification process collapsed. These two States justified their choice by declaring that the exploitation of mineral resources of Antarctica would be detrimental to the Antarctic environment. Attempts made by other Consultative Parties to convince France and Australia of the good nature of the Wellington Convention failed. Thus, at the end no State ratified it.

Three years after the failure of the Wellington Convention a new instrument, the Protocol on Environmental Protection to the Antarctic Treaty, the so-called Madrid Protocol, was adopted①. The 1991 Madrid Protocol put an end to the possibility to mine and use Antarctica's mineral

---

① For an analysis of the Protocol see, L. Pineschi, "The Madrid Protocol on the Protection of the Antarctic Environment and its Effectiveness", in F. Francioni and T. Scovazzi (eds.), International Law for Antarctica p. 377 (2nd ed. 1996); C. Redgwell, "Environmental Protection in Antarctica: the 1991 Madrid Protocol", 43 ICLQ 599, (1994); D. Vidas, "The Protocol on Environmental Protection to the Antarctic Treaty: A Ten-Year Review", Yearbook of International Co-operation on Environment and Development 51, (2002/2003).

resources for commercial reasons by declaring that: "Any activity relating to mineral resources, other than scientific research, shall be prohibited".

Although no State Parties to the Antarctic Treaty System has ratified the Wellington Convention, it is still worth analyzing its provisions due to their potential impact on the development of a legal regime to regulate the exploitation of the natural resources of the Moon and other celestial bodies.

The Convention on the Regulation of Antarctic Mineral Resources (The Wellington Convention)

The main purpose of the Wellington Convention is to set up a legal framework to regulate explorative and exploitative activities of the Antarctic mineral resources[1]. The Convention makes clear that these activities shall not endanger the peaceful nature and the environmental balance of Antarctica. In addition, mineral activities shall not be monopolized by one or two States but open to all States on fair terms and shall be carried out by taking into consideration the interests of the international community. Ensuring the protection of the Antarctic environment is one of the primary concerns of the Convention[2]. All mineral resource operations are subject to a preventive assessment aimed at verifying

---

[1] For an explanation of the provisions of the Convention see, for instance, C. Joyner, "The Evolving Antarctic Minerals Regime", 19 Ocean Dev. & Int'l L. 73 (1988); J. G. Starke, "International Legal Notes", 62 Austl. L. J. 956, (1988); Note, "Death of a Treaty: the Decline and Fall of the Antarctic Minerals Convention", 22 Vand. J. Transnat'l L. 631, (1989); B. H. Heim, "Exploring the last frontier for mineral resources: a comparison of international law regarding the deep seabed, outer space and Antarctica", 23 Vand. J. Transnat'l L. 819, (1990).

[2] See Art. 2, 3 and 4, Convention on the Regulation of Antarctic Mineral Resources.

their potential environmental impact. These operations shall not be authorized and shall be stopped in case they represent a threat to the Antarctic ecosystem.

On the institutional level the Convention creates an Antarctic Mineral Resource Commission, a Regulatory Committee, a Special Meeting of Parties and a Scientific, Technical and Environmental Committee.

The Commission, which is composed by the Consultative Parties which possessed this status when the Convention was open for signature[①], adopts decisions concerning: the protection and conservation of the Antarctic environment; the designation of protected areas; the identification of areas for possible exploration and development, and the review of action by the Regulatory Committee. Decisions are generally taken by a three-quarter majority although those relating to the submission of exploration and development applications are adopted by consensus[②].

A Regulatory Committee is established for each designated area. Its main functions are: to look upon applications for exploration and development permits; to approve management scheme and to monitor exploration and development[③].

The Scientific, Technical and Environmental Advisory Committee consist of scientists of all Parties to the Convention[④]. Its function is not only to give scientific or technical advices but also to provide for a sort of

---

① See Art. 21, Convention on the Regulation of Antarctic Mineral Resources.

② See Art. 41 (2), Convention on the Regulation of Antarctic Mineral Resources.

③ See Art. 29, Convention on the Regulation of Antarctic Mineral Resources.

④ See Art. 23, Convention on the Regulation of Antarctic Mineral Resources.

participation in the decision-making by all the Parties which are not represented in the Commission.

The Special Meeting of Parties is open to all members[①]. It represents a forum where the non-consultative Parties may try to accommodate their interests.

Mineral activities are supposed to take place in a three stage process: processing, exploration and development. Prospecting is defined as an activity "aimed at identifying areas of mineral resources potential for possible exploration and development"[②]. Article 37 (1 and 2) establishes that prospecting does not provide the operator with any right to resources and prospecting does not require authorization from the institutions of the Convention. The sponsoring State has the duty to notify the Commission at least nine months before the commencement of planned prospecting. Such notification must contain the identification of the area, the description of the methods to be used and an evaluation of possible environmental impacts.

The rules regulating exploration and development are more complex. The beginning of exploration and development activities is subordinated to prior evaluation and assessment by the institutions of the regime. After the decision concerning the initiation of the activities has been made, a sequence of further actions of the institutions may lead to the concession of a permit to carry out minerals exploration and, possibly, development.

This sequence includes three different phases: a preparatory phase (identification of an area), the concession of an exploration permit (application, preparation of the Management Scheme, its approval and issuance of the exploration permit) and the granting of a development

---

① Art. 28, Convention on the Regulation of Antarctic Mineral Resources.

② Art. 1 (8), Convention on the Regulation of Antarctic Mineral Resources.

permit (application, modification of the Management Scheme, approval, issuance of the development permit).

The preparatory phase consists of a request of a party to the Commission to "identify an area for possible exploration and development of a particular mineral resource or resources"①. Such request, accompanied by the necessary information②, shall be transmitted to all Parties. The Commission, giving "special weight to the conclusion reached by the Special Meeting and the Advisory Committee on the request", shall decide by consensus whether or not such identification is consistent with the Convention. This means that each member of the Commission can block any activity.

After an area is identified, the respective Regulatory Committee is set up by the Commission. The Committee shall divide the area into blocks and indicate periods in which an application may be submitted. After the Regulatory Committee has completed its preparatory work, an application for a permit may be filed by any Parties on behalf of its operator. Such application must include information on the planned activity and must be submitted together with a certification of the sponsoring State that the operator has the capacity to comply with the Convention requirements, and that it has the financial and technical capabilities to undertake the planned activities③. After the application has been submitted the Regulatory Committee has two options: 1) to reject it for reason of its failure to meet the legal requirements; 2) to enter into the

---

① Art. 39, para. 1, Convention on the Regulation of Antarctic Mineral Resources.

② Art. 39, para 2, Convention on the Regulation of Antarctic Mineral Resources.

③ Art. 44, Convention on the Regulation of Antarctic Mineral Resources.

preparation of a Management Scheme①.

The Management Scheme is the instrument governing exploration and development activities. Article 47 provides a non-exclusive list of issues that a Management Scheme has to cover②. The approval of the Management Scheme represents the authorization for the concession without any further delay of an exploration permit by the Regulatory Committee, by which the operator is provided with exclusive rights to explore the resources located in the assigned block in accordance with the management Scheme's provisions③.

The procedure dealing with the application for a development permit in general follows the system used to take a decision on an application for an exploration permit with the exception that no new Management Scheme is established. Instead, the Regulatory Committee may decide if a modification of the Scheme is required.

An approved Management Scheme and the respective permit may be modified and suspended if the activities are likely to generate or have provoked unacceptable impacts over Antarctica' environment or may be cancelled if such impacts may not be avoided. In addition, the Regula-

---

① Art. 51 (3), Convention on the Regulation of Antarctic Mineral Resources.

② For instance, performance requirements, financial obligations, enforcement of the Management Scheme or applicable law, etc.

③ The Management Scheme is approved if accepted by a two-thirds majority, which majority shall include a simple majority of the group of claimant States and a simple majority of non-claimant States. Thus, a Management Scheme needs the affirmative vote of seven members of a ten-members Regulatory Committee, which must include at least two from the group of claimant States and three from the group of non-claimant States. As a consequence, it is beyond the power of a single claimant State to provide for or even to block the approval of a Management Scheme.

tory Committee may modify, suspend and cancel the Management Scheme and the permit if the operator has failed to comply with the Convention requirements. Monetary sanctions can be imposed upon the operator as well.

The Convention on the Regulation of Antarctic Mineral Resources: Which Impact on the Extraterrestrial Resources' Regime?

This Convention on the Regulation of Antarctic Mineral Resources represents a useful instrument to be used as a model to set up a legal regime to govern the exploitation of extraterrestrial resources. The Convention, in fact, not only contains several elements which can be inserted into such a legal regime but it also shows what mistakes must be avoided when establishing a legal framework to manage the activities within an international area.

In this respect, the first step is to understand why the Convention failed. While the official reason was the refusal of France and Australia to ratify it due to environmental concerns, other causes may be indicated. Such causes were of economic and political nature, finding their origin in some controversial features of the Convention's provisions.

First of all, the Convention lacks economic incentives for mining operators. The system created by the Convention to govern mineral activities, indeed, contains a certain level of uncertainty that may cause mining operations to be a non-profitable business. In this regard, the fact that the Commission's decisions relating to the identification of an area for possible exploration and development are to be taken by consensus may halt the success of a mineral activity since its beginning. In particular, the fact that a similar request may be rejected due to the refusal of one State member of the Commission only, regardless of the fact that the applicant may have successfully carried out the prospecting phase in the full respect of environmental requirements and that he may have already devoted huge financial and technical resources to it, constitutes a tremendous disincentive from an economic point of view. Because of this possibility, indeed, no operator would be encouraged to invest in mineral resource activities in Antarctica. On the contrary, if an operator has proven to be trustworthy during the prospecting operations undertaken within a certain area, he should be granted a priority right to explore and develop such area.

Secondly, another problem of the system governing Antarctic mineral resource activities concerns its timeframe. The three-stage process which leads to the concession of an authorization to operate is extremely slow and plays a discouraging effect on potential investors.

Thirdly, additional troubles are caused by the institutional framework established by the Convention. This framework is not only complicated but also inefficient, as the voting procedures are complex and the powers of the institutions tend to overlap.

Fourthly, while the Convention declares one of its main objectives to be the creation of fair opportunities to participate in mineral activities, in practical terms such opportunities are not created and the special interests of developing countries are not protected.

Thus, taking into consideration the causes of the failure of the Convention, it is possible to affirm that a legal instrument governing mineral activities within an international area should contain the following elements:

(a) Economic incentives for operators and certainty of the legal regime governing mineral activities;

(b) A reasonable timetable to provide the operator with the authorization to proceed in mineral activities;

(c) A simple institutional framework in which each institution has a clear and distinct function;

(d) Efficient and fair voting procedures;

(e) Mechanisms to ensure international participation in mineral activities.

Nevertheless, despite its limits, the Convention provides some useful elements to be inserted in the regime governing future exploitation of extraterrestrial resources.

Firstly, reference can be made to the Convention's provisions aimed at protecting the Antarctic environment. Such provisions set up environmental parameters and requirements to be respected when prospecting and exploring Antarctica. Similar rules should be applied to extraterrestrial mineral activities too. Indeed, the respect and preservation of the lunar and other celestial bodies' environment is to be considered a prerequisite for exploitative operation to be carried out. This not only for ethical reasons but also because a detrimental management of extraterrestrial sites would prevent them from being used on a permanent basis, by reducing, thus, their potential economic value.

Secondly, the Convention sets up a mechanism to settle disputes among mining operators. A similar mechanism should be included in the legal regime regulating mineral activities in outer space. Indeed, an international regime is more likely to be successful if it contains a procedure to settle controversies among the participating Parties.

Ⅳ. The allocation and use of the geostationary orbit

The geostationary orbit as a limited natural resource

The term geostationary orbit refers to the circular orbit 35,757 km above the equator where a satellite rotates around the Earth in 23 hours 56 minutes and 4 seconds[①]. As this period is synchronous with the time the Earth needs to rotate around its axis, a satellite launched into the geostationary orbit appears to an observer on the Earth's surface as

---

① For a description of the characteristics of the geostationary orbit see: K. U. Schrogl, "Question relating to the character and utilization of the geostationary orbit", in "International space law in the making: current issues in the United Nations Committee on the Peaceful Uses of Outer Space, (K. U. Schrogl – M. Benk?,eds.), Frontières, 1993; ; S. Cahill, "Give me my space: implications for permitting national appropriation of the geostationary orbit", 19 Wis. Int'l L. J., (2001), p. 231; F. Lyall, Law and Space Telecommunications, Dartmouth, (1989), p. 388.

being fixed, stationary over a certain point of the equator. Hence, this orbit is called "geostationary".

Considering the fact that the area visible from a satellite placed in such orbit covers one third of the Earth's surface, three satellites are in the condition to provide with their signals almost global coverage with the exclusion of the polar regions. Thanks to such features, the geostationary orbit is a strategic resource for telecommunications, broadcasting and meteorological purposes.

It is important to clarify that satellites operate through radio signals and thus use the radiofrequency spectrum to provide their services. The radiofrequency spectrum is a specific band of the electromagnetic spectrum that allows satellites to communicate with the Earth. Therefore, satellites require orbital locations and allocated frequencies for space communications services in order to operate within the geostationary orbit.

Despite being the most effective orbit for providing communication and other services, the geostationary orbit is affected by several elements that hinder its continued use. First of all, once a satellite is placed into it, due to the impact of factors like the elliptic shape of the Earth's equator, the attraction of the Moon and the Sun and the solar radiation pressure, an active station maintenance system is required to help it to stay within their desired orbit and in synchronicity with the Earth's rotation. This system is of primary importance because every modification of the satellite's location would affect its functionality and increase the risk of collision with other satellites. Secondly, because of this physical characteristic, the geostationary orbit can only accommodate a limited number of satellites. It has been estimated that with the current technology a satellite can maintain its optimal position within an accuracy of $0,1°$ of longitude. Therefore, there are only 1800 slots, each $0,2°$ wide, in the geostationary orbit where satellites may be placed without facing the risk of collision or interference. The number of satellites currently placed in that orbit is, anyway, far from this figure. Thus, contrary to common perception, the risk of physical collision among satellites, the so-called "risk of physical congestion", is relatively low. The problem concerns the possibility of radio frequency interference occurring among systems. If two different transmissions are made in the same geographic area at the same frequency, they will interfere with each other, leading to the loss or deterioration of the signal. Since only a small part of the frequency spectrum is assigned to the space services using the geostationary orbit and the number of satellites keeps growing, the congestion of the radiofrequency spectrum is not only a risk but already a reality.

Because of these impediments the geostationary orbit is considered to be a limited natural resource[①]. Such impediments, indeed, restricts the number of satellites to be placed in orbit and makes this placement risky and expensive.

The Allocation of the Geostationary Orbit

The organization responsible for international administration and allocation of geostationary slots and frequencies for satellites communication is the International Telecommunication Union (ITU)[②]. Within the ITU framework the responsibility of managing the frequency spectrum, as well as the positions of geostationary satellites is attributed to the Radio-

---

[①] The universal recognition of the geostationary orbit as a limited natural resource was made by Article 33 of the 1973 ITU Convention which attributed such title to the orbit.

[②] The International Telecommunication Union is a specialized agency of the United Nations. According to Article 1 of the 1992 ITU Convention the purposes of the Union are: a) "to maintain and extend international cooperation among all its Member States for the improvement and rational use of telecommunications of all kind"; b) "to promote and to offer technical assistance to developing States in the field of telecommunications…"; c) "to promote the development of technical facilities and their most efficient operation with a view to improving the efficiency of telecommunication services, increasing their usefulness and making them, so far as possible, generally available to the public"; and d) "to promote the use of telecommunication services with the objective of facilitating peaceful relations".

communication Sector. In accordance with Article XII of the 1992 Convention the objective of the Radiocommunication Sector is to "ensure the rational, equitable, efficient and economical use of the radio frequency spectrum by all radiocommunication services, including those using the geostationary-satellite or orbit satellite". In order to fulfil these purposes the Radiocommunication Sector ensures that the Radio Regulations, namely an intergovernmental treaty text of the ITU containing rules for the allocation of the frequency bands and technical parameters to be observed by operators, are respected.

As a consequence of the physical limitations of the geostationary orbit described above, a tension between the goal of ensuring fair and equitable access to it on the one hand and its efficient use on the other exists. Such tension finds its origin in the divergent opinions held by developed and developing States on the way of granting orbital positions and frequencies, as former support a free-market approach while the latter a dirigist one.

The main system for allocating geostationary orbital slots and frequencies is the so called "*a posteriori*" method, which is based on a first come, first served approach[1]. This system consists of several steps:

---

[1] For an analysis of the "a posteriori" method of allocation see: R. S. Jakhu, "The legal status of the geostationary orbit", in 7 Annals Air & Space L., (1982), p. 333; J. C. Thompson, "Space for rent: the International Telecommunication Union, space law, and orbit/spectrum leasing", 62 J. Air L. & Comm., (1996 ~ 97), p. 279; J. Wilson, "The International Telecommunication Union and the geostationary satellite orbit: an overview", in 23 Annals Air & Space L., (1994), p. 241; L. D. Roberts, "A lost of connection: geostationary satellite networks and the International Telecommunication Union", 15 Berk. Tech., L. J., (2000), p. 1095; F. Lyall, "Paralysis by phantom: problems of the ITU filling procedures", in Proceedings of the Thirty-Ninth Colloquium on the Law of Outer Space (1996), p. 189; O. Fernandez-A. Brital, "The legal status of the geostationary orbit and ITU recent activities", in Proceedings of the Thirty-second Colloquium on the Law of Outer Space, (1989), p. 223.

when a satellite operator wishes to develop a communication satellite system, it contacts the State member who informs the Radiocommunication Bureau of the intention to assign particular frequencies and geostationary positions to this operator. Such request is reviewed in the light of the Table of Allocation and of the Master International Frequency Register to make sure that nobody has claimed these frequencies before and that no interference with already existing systems is expected to take place. If no problems are encountered during the review process, the ITU adds the operator's notification to the frequency register and the frequencies and a geostationary slot are attributed to such operator on a temporarily basis, namely for whole period in which the satellite system is operational. It is important to stress that the operator is, thus, given a temporary right to use a certain orbital slot but it does not gain any property right over it.

The a *posteriori* procedure is clearly early-registrants oriented. The first operator to apply for a frequency is the first to be allowed to use it, obviously if the process of notification and registration is successful. Moreover, once the operator's system is using the allocated part of the orbit/spectrum resource, it is protected from interference by later users. This system is obviously favorable to developed States as they have the technological and financial resources to place and maintain a satellite into the geostationary orbit.

When the *a posteriori* procedure was established in the beginning of the 1960's, it seemed to be appropriate for managing satellites activities in the geostationary orbit given the moderate use of the orbit/spectrum resource. However, when in the 1970's and 1980's the number of satellites augmented together with the request for satellite services, developing States began increasingly concerned about the scarcity of the orbit/spectrum resource and the way it was allocated. Thus, they started criticizing the *a posteriori* system and requesting a new allocation procedure based on principles of equitable access to the geostationary orbit. In this respect, the first result that the developing States were able to achieve was the insertion in the text of the ITU Convention (Article 33) of the principle that equitable access to the geostationary orbit had to be assured "taking into account the special needs of the developing States and the geographical situation of particular States". The language of Article 33 of the ITU Convention was particularly significant because it gave full recognition of the request to the less-developed States in gaining a balance in the use and management of the orbit/spectrum resource by emphasizing that equity was to be measured not simply in terms of efficiency and economy. Lately, at the end of the 1980's, agreement was reached on a new way of assigning the orbit/spectrum resource, which was called "a dual system of allocation" or the "*a priori*" method[1]. Under this system, which applied only to the Fixed Satellite Services (FSS)[2], and within that service, only to the so defined "expansion band", each ITU member was entitled to an orbital posi-

---

[1] For a description of the "a priori" method and of the process leading to its adoption see: C. Q. Christol, "The legal status of the geostationary orbit in the light of the 1895~1988 activities of the ITU", in Proceeding of the Thirty-Second Colloquium on the Law of Outer Space, (1989), p. 215; S. Ospina, "The ITU and WARC-ORB: will the revised radio regulations result in a sui-generis legal regime for the GSO?", in Proceeding of the Thirty-Second Colloquium on the Law of Outer Space, (1989), p. 247; T. Lozanova, "Legal status of the geostationary orbit in the light of the recent activities of ITU", in Proceeding of the Thirty-Second Colloquium on the Law of Outer Space, (1989), p. 233; S. Wiessner, "Access to a res publica internationalis: the case of the geostationary orbit", in Proceedings of the Twenty-Ninth Colloquium on the Law of Outer Space, (1986), p. 147.

[2] The 1988 WARC Final Acts defined a FSS as "a radiocommunication service between Earth stations at given positions, when one or more satellites are used; the given position may be a specific fixed point with specified areas; in some cases this service includes satellite-to satellite links, which may be also be operated in the inter-satellite service; the fixed-satellite service may also include feeder links for other space radiocommunication services", see: Final Acts, 1988, Article I, Mod. 22.

tion, within a predetermined arc and a predetermined band. Thus, by means of an *a priori* allotment plan each State received at least an orbital slot and one frequency to be used for communication purposes. Since all States, including the late arrivals, were subjected to the allotment plan and this plan did not require a State to prove its ability to use the allocated resource at any given time, this new *a priori* procedure largely favored the developing States.

The ITU system of allocation of the orbit/spectrum resource: a useful example for extraterrestrial mining legal regime?

The preliminary consideration is that both the geostationary orbit and the minerals present on the surface and the subsurface of the Moon and other celestial bodies, are "limited natural resources". Both these resources share the need for being properly managed and allocated in order to prevent their wasteful use and to maximize their value. Therefore, the analysis of how the geostationary orbit is administered may provide useful and practical elements to be applied to extraterrestrial mining.

First of all, the legal framework governing the orbit/spectrum resource includes the concepts of equitable access and efficiency. Although their application to the system allocating orbital slots and frequencies has caused several problems and disputes between the developed and developing States, these two concepts should become part of the future lunar and other celestial bodies' legal regime. Their presence is necessary to allow such regime to strike a balance between the requests and interests of both developed and less developed States and to comply with Article I of the Outer Space Treaty, requiring States to explore and use outer space without discrimination and for the benefit and interest of all States.

Secondly, the system of allocation of orbital slots is based on the idea that the use of positions and frequencies is limited in time. No entity, indeed, is provided with a permanent title to the geostationary resources. This aspect is of fundamental relevance for the future lunar and other celestial bodies' regime. One crucial aspect of such regime should be that entities are allowed to exploit extraterrestrial sites only for a limited and pre-determined, although renewable, period of time, without gaining any permanent proprietary title to those sites. A similar provision would ensure compliance with Article II of the Outer Space Treaty, declaring outer space, including the Moon and other celestial bodies, as non-appropriable.

However, there are some other elements of the allocation system of orbital slots that should not be introduced into the legal regime regulating the exploitation of extraterrestrial mineral resources. One of the two procedures for the allocation of orbital positions and frequencies, namely the a posteriori one, is based on the first come, first served approach. Such approach should not constitute the basis for the regulation of extraterrestrial exploitative operations. A legal regime built on such an approach, indeed, would advantage the industrialized States only, since only these States have the technological and financial requirements to carry out this type of activities. On the contrary, developing States would be basically excluded from exploiting extraterrestrial resources and from enjoying the benefits derived therein. Additionally, it has to be taken into consideration the different nature of the geostationary orbit and the lunar resources, the former non-exhaustible, the latter exhaustible. The application of the first come, first served approach to the exploitation of extraterrestrial mineral resources would likely result in the quick exhaustion of these resources and in the contamination of the lunar and other celestial bodies' environment.

It may also be added that even the other procedure to allocate orbital slots, the a priori procedure, is not suitable for the future lunar exploitative regime. As previously described, such procedure guarantees all

States with at least one portion of the orbit/spectrum resource without requiring them to prove their need or their technical capability to use the assigned resource. The a priori system, while being fair and appreciable from an ethical point of view, tends to cause inefficiency and the waste of a limited natural resource, due to the fact that the larger part of the developing States is not in the position to make use of their assignments. A similar approach is not acceptable to the future regime regulating the exploitation of the extraterrestrial mineral resources. Considering the great level of risk and the huge amount of money connected with such exploitative activities, the a priori setting up of a system of rules that is likely to generate inefficiency and waste is to be prevented. Imagine a hypothetical situation where the a priori procedure used in the ITU system is transposed and applied to the exploitation of the minerals substances of the Moon. In this case, certain lunar sites, containing valuable resources, would be equitably allocated to all States irrespectively of their stage of technological advancement. The end of this process would be that the majority of lunar sites would remain unused and, as a consequence, an unproductive situation would result.

Therefore, the future legal regime regulating exploitative activities over the Moon and other celestial bodies needs to find alternative and more productive methods for ensuring efficiency and equitable opportunities for all States than those currently existing in the ITU regime.

V. A legal regime to govern the exploitation of the natural resources of the Moon and other celestial bodies

The comparative analysis of the legal regimes regulating the extraction and use of deep seabed resources, mineral activities in Antarctica and the allocation and utilization of the geostationary orbit has revealed the possible impacts of these regimes on the future exploitation of extraterrestrial resources. Taking into consideration the elements emerged by such analysis, this exploitation should be organized in the following way:

—A new legal regime should be established. This regime should include clear, detailed and simple rules indicating how the exploitation of extraterrestrial natural resources should be organized and the rights and duties of the parties involved.

—The exploitative activities should be directed and managed by an International Space Authority. The main purpose of the Authority should be to provide licenses to mine and commercially use the resources of an extraterrestrial site and to control whether the licensees comply with the terms of the license and the provisions of the legal regime.

—The decision – making mechanism of the Authority should give States a power to influence decisions proportionate with their impact on and investments in exploitative activities.

—A precise and fixed timetable should regulate the process leading to the concession of a license.

—A license to exploit the resources of an extraterrestrial site does not give the licensee any proprietary title over that site. The license would entitle a subject to mine and use for commercial purposes the resources located in a lunar or other celestial bodies' site for the period of the duration of the license. When this period is over that site would be theoretically put on the market again and open for follower users. Clearly, the possibility for the former licensee to apply for continuing operations over that site would not be precluded.

—Economic incentives able to make the exploitation of extraterrestrial resources a profitable business should be created so as to stimulate public and private investments in it.

—A mandatory dispute settlement mechanism regulating disputes arising from the exploitation of space resources should be created. The presence of such mechanism would contribute to strengthen the legal regime as the rules of the latter could be enforced in case a subject has failed to comply with them.

—Feasible and concrete opportunities allowing and stimulating international participation in exploitative activities should be laid down.

—Mechanisms and practical solutions aimed at ensuring that the exploitation of extraterrestrial resources is beneficial not only to those directly involved in it but also to all mankind should be set out. While no mandatory sharing of benefits should be required, the implementation of this concept would be necessary not only to guarantee the general acceptance of such a legal regime, particularly by the developing States, but also to comply with some of the fundamental principles of the space law system, such as that laid down in Article I of the Outer Space Treaty requiring the exploration and use of outer space to be carried out for the benefit and in the interests of all countries.

If a legal regime to regulate the exploitation of the natural resources of the Moon and other celestial bodies would be established in a similar way there is a high chance that not only it would be positively received by the majority of States but that it would be able to ensure the safe, profitable and successful development of such exploitation.

Conclusion

The establishment of a permanent manned basis on the surface of the Moon and the extraction and commercial utilization of the resources contained therein would probably represent some of the most fascinating and remarkable events of the 21st century. Events of such an importance would need to be carried out in a safe and proper legal environment. Considering the fact that international space law does not contain any specific rule dealing with the exploitation of extraterrestrial resources a dedicated legal regime should be created.

The legal frameworks governing the use of the resources located in the deep seabed beyond national jurisdiction, mineral activities in Antarctica and the allocation of the geostationary orbit provide valid elements to be applied to the exploitation of the lunar and other celestial bodies' resources. If these elements would be taken into consideration, indeed, it would be possible to establish a legal regime able to guarantee the orderly and safe development of extraterrestrial natural resources.

Impact Assessment Processes in the Mitigation of Space Debris

Lotta Viikari[①]

Abstract[②]: It is not always easy to establish liability pursuant to space law, yet damages can be considerable. The damaging potential of space activities can exceed the capacity of any single spacefaring entity to make reparation. Absolute and unlimited liability could render the highly hazardous activities uninsurable. Complex causation questions may complicate the situation further. The mere determination of the liable entity can be a problem.

Accordingly, allocation of losses within a larger community of relevant entities to balance the competing concerns would seem useful. It could better retain the economic viability of the space sector, yet still secure adequate indemnification for damages. Compensation claims for damage resulting from particularly risky activities should be facilitated, but op-

---

① Lotta Viikari, Professor of Public International Law, Director of Institute of Air and Space Law, University of Lapland, Rovaniemi, Finland. Email: Lotta. Viikari@ ulapland. fi.

② This article is based on a presentation given in the 60th International Astronautical Congress, 12 ~ 16 October 2009, Daejeon, South Korea.

erators of activities that are deemed necessary yet entail high risks should be shielded from excessive claims.

The setting in the space sector seems in many respects similar to that in the use of nuclear power, which also entails significant risks. There the solutions adopted include, i. a., a three-tiered system of compensation with absolute but limited liability of the operator of a nuclear installation, coupled with limited liability of the state in which the installation is located, and an international compensation fund. There are also certain other examples of international trust fund mechanisms serving very similar purposes which the space sector could draw inspiration from.

1. Introduction

Environmental impact assessment (EIA) is a procedure for evaluating the likely impact of a proposed activity on the environment[①]. It is "an environmental management tool whose objective is to identify, predict and evaluate the potential biological, physical, social and health effects of a proposed action and to communicate the findings in a way which encourages environmental concerns to be adequately addressed by stakeholders, including decision-makers and communities prior to development decisions being made"[②].

EIA seems particularly suitable for the space sector, where it is extremely difficult to amend any environmental adversities once they have been created, yet demand for the use of space resources is already high and increas-

---

① See Art 1. vi, Espoo Convention on Environmental Impact Assessment in a Transboundary Context (Espoo Convention), done 25 February 1991, in force 10 September 1997, 30 ILM 800 (1991), < http://www. unece. org/env/eia/eia. htm > [31.3.2010]. All the websites referred to below were last accessed on 31 March 2010.

② D. O. Harrop-J. A. Nixon, Environmental Assessment in Practice (1999), Routledge: London, p. 2.

ing fast. However, there are various problems related to the quality of information, as well as economic and political considerations which pose serious constraints on the development of the use of EIA in space activities. In principle, prospects for wider acceptance of the EIA among the international space community appear relatively promising, as requirements to conduct impact assessment procedures are increasingly common in national legislation-in environmental legislation obviously, but also in national laws governing space activities and in the regulations of space agencies. The recent developments in this respect within the European space sector are particularly promising. EIA is a common tool also in international environmental instruments[①].

Nevertheless, environmental impact assessment is still not a well-established tool in the international law of outer space. This is not surprising, however, considering the role of EIA as a tool for preventing transboundary impacts in particular. Obligations regarding transboundary impacts obviously are not particularly pertinent to the space sector, because of the inherently international nature of the activities, which mostly take place in global commons. Despite the introduction of some international obligations to conduct EIAs for activities that are proposed to take place in areas beyond the limits of national jurisdiction, such obligations have not been adopted for the space sector yet.

2. EIA in the Space Sector

2.1 UN Space Law

As the UN space treaties were drafted at a time when environmental

---

[①] For a more detailed treatment of the history, status, procedure and goals of EIA, see, L. Viikari, The Environmental Element in Space Law: assessing the present and charting the future (2008), Studies in Space Law, Vol. 3, Martinus Nijhoff Publishers: Leiden, Boston, pp. 261~271.

considerations were not central (in the 1960s and 1970s), their content in this respect is modest: the treaties lack provisions regarding environmental impact assessment, for instance. The nearest equivalent to any environmental assessment is contained in Article IX of the Outer Space Treaty①, which requires prior consultations in the case of a planned space activity or experiment that might cause "potentially harmful interference" with the space activities of other states parties. This, however, is an illustrative example of a futile duty to undertake consultations, for it is not coupled with any obligation whatsoever to take account of the outcome of such consultations.

Another instrument produced by the United Nations, the UN General Assembly resolution "Principles Relevant to the Use of Nuclear Power Sources in Outer Space" (NPS Principles) ②, is more explicit as concerns the prior assessment of potential impacts of space missions. Principle 4.1 requires that a state launching a space object must ensure that "a thorough and comprehensive safety assessment" is conducted prior to the launch. Where relevant, this assessment should be done in cooperation with those who have "designed, constructed or manufactured the nuclear power source, or will operate the space object, or from whose territory or facility such an object will be launched". The assessment is to cover all relevant phases of the mission and shall deal with all systems involved, including the means of launching, the space

---

① Treaty on Principles Governing the Activities of States in the Exploration and Use of Outer Space, including the Moon and other Celestial Bodies, adopted 27 January 1967 by UNGA Res. 2222(XXI), in force 10 October 1967, 610 UNTS 205, < http://www.unoosa.org/pdf/publications/STSPACE11E.pdf >.

② UN Doc. A/RES/47/68, 14 December 1992, GAOR, 47th sess., Suppl. no. 49, < http://www.unoosa.org/pdf/publications/STSPACE11E.pdf >.

platform, the nuclear power source and its equipment and the means of control and communication between ground and space". Furthermore, "[t]he results of this safety assessment (...) shall be made publicly available prior to each launch, and the [UN] Secretary-General (...) shall be informed on how States may obtain such results of the safety assessment as soon as possible prior to each launch" (Principle 4.3).

The NPS Principles are, however, a recommendatory, legally non-binding document only. Moreover, their focus is nuclear safety rather than environmental concerns in general.

2.2 National Legislation

The situation is somewhat better at the domestic level. The national legislation of certain spacefaring countries and the regulations of national space agencies at least prescribe that states should provide some kind of information assessing the possible environmental consequences of their proposed space activities. For instance, the US National Environmental Policy Act (NEPA)[①] is relevant for the space sector as well, given, in particular, the focal role of the US in space activities. Pursuant to NEPA, every "major Federal act" requires environmental impact assessment (Sect. 102). Also, space launches are subject to the NEPA process.

Although the EIAs for space missions focus primarily on impacts concerning the immediate surroundings of the launch site, global impacts and impacts to the space environment are also assessed to an extent. Furthermore, as regards threats related to the currently most severe form of space pollution, space debris, an instrument called "NASA

---

① National Environmental Policy Act of 1969 (as amended), 42 USC 4321 – 4347, < http://ceq.eh.doe.gov/nepa/regs/nepa/nepaeqia.htm >.

Procedural Requirements for Limiting Orbital Debris"[1] requires "each program and project to conduct formal assessments and plans for the disposition of spacecraft anticipated to reach the orbit or the surface of the Moon" (Sect. 1.1.4) in accordance with NASA Safety Standard 1740.14[2] or NASA Technical Standard 8719.14[3]. The Standards provide NASA programs with specific guidelines and assessment methods covering debris released during normal operations[4], debris generated by explosions and intentional breakups[5], debris generated by on-orbit collisions[6], post-mission disposal[7] and survival of re-entering space system components[8].

In addition to the process based on NEPA and NASA policy and procedures, there is a separate interagency process for evaluating the nuclear safety of space missions: where nuclear power sources are used, a special nuclear risk assessment has to be made by the US Department of Energy. Moreover, for any space mission involving the use of nuclear energy (for heating or electrical power), launch approval must be ob-

---

[1] NPR 8715.6A, effective Date: May 14, 2009, < http://nodis3.gsfc.nasa.gov/displayDir.cfm? Internal_ID = N_PR_8715_006A_&page_name = Chapter2 >.

[2] NASA – NSS – 1740.14, effective 1 August 1995, < http://www.orbitaldebris.jsc.nasa.gov/mitigate/safetystandard.html >.

[3] NASA – STD – 8719.14. Process for Limiting Orbital Debris. Approved 2007 – 08 – 28, with change 4 of 2009 – 9 – 14. < http://www.hq.nasa.gov/office/codeq/doctree/871914.pdf >.

[4] NSS – 1740.12, Chapter 3 / STD – 8719, 14 Sect. 4.3.

[5] NSS – 1740.12, Chapter 4 / Sect. 4.3.

[6] NSS – 1740.12, Chapter 5 / Sect. 4.5.

[7] NSS – 1740.12, Chapter 6 / Sect. 4.6.

[8] NSS – 1740.12, Chapter 7 / Sect. 4.7.

tained from the Office of the President①. Also, applicants for a commercial launch license must provide assurance that the proposed launch does not pose unacceptable danger to the environment②.

An example from another major spacefaring country of national environmental assessment requirements in regard to space activities is the Russian Statute on Licensing Space Operations③, which provides that in order to obtain a license for space operations in the Russian Federation, the applicant has to supply, i. a. , "documents confirming the safety of space operations (including ecological, fire and explosion safety) and the reliability of space equipment" (Art. 5h). In the same vein (but in a more pronounced manner), Australian legislation places the applicant for a launch permit under an obligation to present an environmen-

---

① See Presidential Directive/National Security Council Memorandum 25, Scientific or Technological Experiments with Possible Large – Scale Adverse Environmental Effects and Launch of Nuclear Systems Into Space, 14 December 1977 (revised 8 May 1996). For an example of the assessment of impacts of a NASA space mission using NPS, see the environmental assessment documentation concerning the "New Horizons" spacecraft, which was launched 19 January 2006, and is intended to explore Pluto and its moon Charon. The Draft Environmental Impact Statement (which contains nearly 200 pages) was released in February 2005, < http://www. pluto. jhuapl. edu/overview/deis/NH_DEIS_Full. pdf >. The subsequent Final Environmental Impact Statement (containing two volumes with over 300 pages in total) was released in July 2005, < http://spacescience. nasa. gov/admin/pubs/plutoeis/ >. As the New Horizons mission uses a radioisotope thermoelectric generator, the US Department of Energy also prepared a nuclear risk assessment to support the environmental impact statement of the mission. For more information on the mission, see the New Horizons website < http:www. pluto. jhuapl. edu >.

② See Commercial Space Launch Act (as amended by the Commercial Space Launch amendments Act of 2004), H. R. 3752, 108th Cong. (2004), < http://thomas. loc. gov/cgi – bin/query/z? c108:H. R. 3752: >.

③ Decree No. 104, 2 February 1996, < http://www. unoosa. org/oosaddb/showDocument. do? documentUid = 312&country = RUS >.

tal plan for the launch (and "any connected return") ①. Pursuant to the 1986 Outer Space Act② of UK, an applicant for a space activity license has, i. a. , to provide an assessment of the risk to public safety and property. The legislation is flexible enough to allow the assessment of proposed debris mitigation practices, for instance, when considering license applications③. Other relevant norms include the guidelines and recommendations of national space agencies, such as the French CNES (Centre National d'Etudes Spatiales) ④.

---

① Reg. 3.01, Space Activities Regulations 2001 No. 186, < http://www. austlii. edu. au/au/legis/cth/num_reg/sar20012001n186303/ >. According to Reg. 3.02(1)(g)(ii), the launches (and returns) under a launch permit have to be conducted in accordance with an environmental plan, containing the arrangements and procedures specified in Reg. 3.12. These include arrangements "for monitoring and mitigating any adverse effects of each launch, and any connected return, conducted under the launch permit on the environment; and (...) for implementing the plan; and (...) procedures (...) for reporting on the implementation of the plan; and (...) for reviewing the plan; and (...) for ensuring that each launch, and any connected return, conducted under the launch permit, is conducted in accordance with any applicable requirements under Australian law for the protection of the environment". Similar requirements apply to the operation of launch facilities. Sect. 18(b), Space Activities Act 1998 No. 123 (as amended), < http://www. austlii. edu. au/au/legis/cth/consol_act/saa1998167/ >. Space Activities Regulations 2001, Regulations 2.04(2)(e)(ii), and 2.17.

② 1986 Chapter 38, 18 July 1986, < http://www. unoosa. org/oosa/SpaceLaw/national/united_kingdom/outer_space_act_1986E. html >.

③ See R. Crowther - R. Tremayne – Smith - C. Martin, Implementing Space Debris Mitigation within the United Kingdom's Outer Space Act, Proceedings of the Fourth European Conference on Space Debris (2005), ESA/ESOC, Darmstadt/Germany, 18 ~20 April 2005, ESA SP -587, pp. 577 ~581.

④ For a comparison of the environmental assessment regulations of national space agencies, see Chapter 6 of the IADC Protection Manual, IADC - 04 - 03, Version 3.3, Revision April 04, 2004, < http://www. iadc - online. org/index. cgi? item = docs_pub >.

However, in general environmental considerations still do not appear to rank among the focal issues in national space legislation either. Even where impact assessments are regularly conducted in a thorough manner, their practical relevance in decision-making may remain less significant[①]. Partly, this is due to the lack of stringent obligations in international space treaties on states to guarantee at the domestic level that space activities are not environmentally harmful and that assessments to this end are made and taken into account in decision-making.

Neither have many states been particularly interested in environmental problems related with space activities, at least until recently. Traditionally, national space legislation has been more concerned about fulfilling the (few) concrete obligations deriving from the UN space treaties (including, i. a. , those relating to the registration of space objects) and providing the national space industry with incentives for development, for instance[②]. Such an approach is obviously not enough for ensuring effective regulation of the environmental aspects of space utilization.

2.3 International Soft Law

One additional relevant type of norms, albeit non-binding, which touch

---

① This is by no means a problem of the space sector only: the practical influence of EIAs in decision-making can be modest also in other activity areas. See R. K. Morgan, Environmental Impact Assessment: a methodological perspective (1998), Kluwer Academic Publishers: Dordrecht, Boston, London, p. 48.

② For example, one of the main aims of Australian space legislation has been to support the national launch industry by providing it with a developed legal framework. Consequently, Australia now belongs to the most advanced states globally as regards the sophistication of national space legislation. It is also one of the few states which has ratified all the UN space treaties. S. Freeland, The Australian Regulatory Regime for Space Launch Activities: out to launch?, Proceedings of the 47th Colloquium on the Law of Outer Space (2005), IISL, 4~8 October 2004 (Vancouver), AIAA, pp. 56~65, pp. 57, 63.

upon the issue of environmental assessment in the space sector are those embodied in soft law instruments created by certain international forums. Within international law, these are the most advanced norms relating to environmental assessment in space activities; they are mostly concerned with the problem of space debris.

Above all, the Inter Agency Space Debris Coordination Committee (IADC) Space Debris Mitigation Guidelines[①] recommend that "[i]n order to manage the implementation of space debris mitigation measures (...) a feasible Space Debris Mitigation Plan be established and documented for each program and project" (Part 4). This Mitigation Plan should include

(1) "management plan addressing space debris mitigation activities".

(2) "plan for the assessment and mitigation of risks related to space debris, including applicable standards".

(3) "measures minimising the hazard related to malfunctions that have a potential for generating space debris".

(4) "plan for disposal of the space system at end of mission".

(5) "[j]ustification of choice and selection when several possibilities exist".

(6) "[c]ompliance matrix addressing the recommendations of these Guidelines" (Part 4).

Although not called "environmental impact assessment", the Mitigation Plan in essence works much like an EIA.

The Technical Subcommittee of the UN Committee of the Peaceful Uses of Outer Space approved in 2007 the UN Space Debris Mitigation Guidelines[②],

---

① UNCOPUOS Scientific and Technical Subcommittee 40th session, Vienna, 17~28 February 2003, UN Doc. A/AC. 105/C. 1/L. 260.

② Annex IV (pp. 42~46), Report of the Scientific and Technical Subcommittee on its 44th session, Vienna, 12~23 February 2007, UN Doc. A/AC. 105/890.

which are based on the IADC Space Debris Mitigation Guidelines. Pursuant to the UN guidelines, they "should be considered for the mission planning, design, manufacture and operational (...) phases of spacecraft and launch vehicle orbital stages" (para. 4). Although the guidelines themselves contain no explicit reference to prior assessment of environmental impacts of space activities, the requirement to consider them also for those phases of space missions that take place before the operational phase clearly necessitates prior assessment of expected consequences.

2.4 European Regional Arrangements

A space debris document of the CNES[①] was used as a starting point for the development of a space-agency level European Space Debris Safety and Mitigation Standard[②], intended to be read in conjunction with another European document, the ESA Space Debris Mitigation Handbook[③]. The European Code of Conduct for Space Debris Mitigation[④] was completed in 2004 and signed by the five space agencies ASI, BN-

---

[①] CNES Space Debris Safety Requirements, MPM – 51 – 00 – 12, 19 April 1999.

[②] Alby et al. 2004, p. 1261. F. Alby – D. Alwes – L. Anselmo – H. Baccini – C. Bonnal – R. Crowther – W. Flury – R. Jehn – F. Klinkrad – C. Portelli – R. Tremayne–Smith, The European Space Debris Safety and Mitigation Standard, Advances in Space Research (2004), Vol. 34, Issue 5, pp. 1260 – 1263.

[③] ESA Space Debris Mitigation Handbook, Release 1.0., 7 April 1999. For a more detailed treatment, see H. Klinkrad – P. Beltrami – S. Hauptmann – C. Martin – H. Sdunnus – H. Stokes – R. Walker – J. Wilkinson, Update of the ESA Space Debris Mitigation Handbook (2002), < http://www.esa.int/gsp/completed/execsum00_N06.pdf >.

[④] 28 June 2004, Issue 1.0, < http://www.stimson.org/wos/pdf/eurocode.pdf >.

SC, CNES, DLR, and ESA by 2006. It requires a detailed "Space Debris Mitigation Plan" (Sect. 3.3) which must contain, i.a.,

(c) the management plan of space debris activities.

(d) the plan for assessment and mitigation of risks related to space debris.

(e) the measures minimising the hazard related to malfunctions which have a potential for generating space debris.

(f) the plan for the space system disposal.

(g) justification of choice and selection when several possibilities exist.

(h) contents and justifications for non-compliance with this Code of Conduct and associated consequences.

(i) the compliance matrix (...).

(j) the risk assessment analysis concerning space debris.

Later on, ESA has adopted its own "Requirements on Space Debris Mitigation for Agency Projects"[①]. This document tailors the European Code of Conduct for Space Debris Mitigation to the particular needs of ESA projects. The ESA Requirements apply to all space systems of the agency (Sect. 1). The measures for implementing and fulfilling the requirements must be documented in a "Space Debris Mitigation Document" (Sect. 4.3). Like the European Space Debris Mitigation Plan, also the ESA Space Debris Mitigation Document needs to be reviewed and updated at different stages of planning a space project.

3. Future Potential of EIA in Space Activities

Outer space is a unique arena in many ways. An obvious problem for any assessment of impacts in this sector is deficiencies in knowledge.

---

① ESA/ADMIN/IPOL(2008)2, Annex 1, 1 April 2008, < http://www.cnsa.gov.cn/n615708/n676979/n676983/n893604/appendix/200852915833.pdf >.

Space activities involve both complex natural processes and challenging technological phenomena. Predicting the behavior of complicated systems is very difficult. Since much of the relevant subject matter is poorly understood and the tools currently available remain more or less inadequate for the task of assessment, any assessment of impacts on space is likely to be expensive and time consuming. Lack of time and resources can thus pose serious constraints on the development of responsible conduct in space.

Space activities are also ultra hazardous, which diminishes the possibilities of prior evaluation of impacts. Furthermore, the modern space industry is a highly commercialized and militarized area of activity, where the stakeholders may not be very keen on distributing detailed information about their plans. Consequently, the inclusiveness of information most often leaves a great deal to be desired, and hence the outcome of proposed space activities can seldom be assessed in detail.

Quality of information is, however, of paramount importance to the effectiveness of any impact assessment system[1]. Scientists are usually expected to produce information that is as unambiguous as possible for the use of those who make the decisions about planned activities. The above limitations considerably increase uncertainty surrounding any conclusions in the space sector in this respect. In practice, the substantial gray area which thus exists between scientific resolution and political choice enables non-scientific factors to become significant components of debates regarding space missions[2].

---

[1] Morgan, see note ① on page 150.

[2] Neither can the scientific assessment of potential impacts of planned activities be deemed as truly objective; value-based judgments and hence influence of, i. a., politics cannot be eliminated. Ibid., p. 31. In fact, EIA processes have often been accused of lacking an adequate scientific basis. See ibid., p. 75~81.

Moreover, political decision-making has a focal role in space activities. Space operations often have important political and military significance, which may render environmental considerations secondary. Regardless of how scrupulously impact assessments are conducted in the space sector, other considerations may eventually seem to override environmental concerns. Hence the relevance of the principle of sustainable development[①], for instance, seems to rest on shakier ground where space activities are concerned.

Nevertheless, environmental principles are increasingly important for all space activities. The assessment of potential impacts is common practice in environmental development planning on Earth. No doubt also the space sector necessitates improved environmental protection and the application of environmentally more benign practices, including environmental assessment systems[②]. All stakeholders – even the military should have an interest in keeping outer space a safe environment for operations also in the future.

Moreover, although environmental assessment requirements may occasionally be considered as something akin to additional restrictions on the development of the space industry, they can in fact work in quite the contrary manner. The use of environmental assessment systems may in the long run even reduce project costs as well as the time needed for reaching decisions because the assessment also identifies and evaluates those potential consequences which might require expensive pollution abatement technology or potentially substantial compensation for dam-

---

① For a more detailed assessment of sustainable development and its role in the space sector, see Viikari, see note ① on page 144, pp. 129~149.

② See also M. Williamson, Space: The Fragile Frontier (2006), AIAA: Reston (VA), p. 246.

age[1]. This could (and should) make the assessment of environmental impacts increasingly appealing even to the large number of commercial entities active in the space sector.

Additionally, environmental impact assessments can give many new stakeholder groups a say in the management of space activities. Effective prior assessment of environmental impacts is of course also likely to benefit the environment itself—not least in outer space, where many environmental amenities can be considered to have a more or less unique value and can thus be compromised forever by the introduction of pollution, for instance.

Environmental assessments are already conducted for many space missions on the basis of state or space agency regulation. Also more commonly accepted practices promoting the assessment of potential impacts of proposed space activities would be needed. If we are to develop environmental impact assessment in the space sector further, we should consult the existing environmental assessment documents of national space agencies and international organs, as well as the norms of national space legislation, in order to identify beneficial practices to protect both space operations and the environment.

Some of the soft law instruments that presently exist or are being drafted are already intended for future submission to international regulatory bodies, primarily the UNCOPUOS. Eventually, they can become norms that are binding upon the entire space community. It would indeed be desirable to have a coherent set of international environmental assessment standards applicable to all space activities in order to ensure a level playing field for all actors worldwide and to minimize the hazards of human activities for the global environment of outer space as ef-

---

[1] Harrop-Nixon, see note [2] on page 143, p. 9.

ficiently as possible[①].

Additionally, democracy would seem to require enhanced public participation, or at least more open distribution of information about human enterprises in space. In principle, the effects of space activities can affect all of humanity. Hence the public involvement component of EIA can even be seen as requiring a system on the international level that would provide actors with possibilities to participate in environmental assessment. Of course, there is no realistic reason to expect any public participation mechanism of that magnitude to materialize in the near future.

Nevertheless, a more communicative approach might be becoming increasingly important for mission planners and policy makers also in practice. The present reality with its myriad groups with specialized interests in space and an increasing number of diverse space missions,

---

① It has even been proposed that some sort of "international forum or mechanism based on the cooperation between international or national, governmental or non-governmental organizazation [sic] and scientific communities should be established for the environmental assessment of certain space projects susceptible of having a harmful effect" and for research on the measures to be taken. K. Tatsuzawa, The Protection of Space Environment: its philosophy and rules, The Korean Journal of Air and Space Law (1998), Vol. 10, pp. 407~415, p. 415. In a similar manner, another author has suggested that as regards future missions to the Moon and Mars (and in particular the possible establishment of bases there), scientific studies to determine the environmental impacts of planned missions be taken and submitted to inspection by an international scientific body, which could even have the right to make a final determination of the acceptability of the missions. K. M. Weidaw, A General Convention on Space Law: legal issues encountered in establishing lunar and martial bases, Proceedings of the 47th Colloquium on the Law of Outer Space (2005), IISL, 4~8 October 2004 (Vancouver), AIAA, pp. 272~283, p. 280.

combined with laws facilitating access to courts, for instance, considerably heightens the probability that the space sector will attract opposition, even legal challenges[①]. On balance, extensive inclusion of the various stakeholders in a process which assesses the potential impacts of a proposed activity and its alternatives in a thorough and plausible manner is likely to significantly reduce complications and should thus appear attractive to all stakeholder groups.

4. More Advanced Assessment Processes

4.1 SEA

The EIA is a process applicable to 'activities' or 'projects'. Such operations do not start from scratch but can in fact be already quite well developed at the time the EIA is brought into play. 'Activities' and 'projects' are typically part of some broader policies. These policies can be written up years before the more detailed planning (and environmental impact assessment) of a particular project even begins. Yet the pre-existing policies can largely determine the practical implementation of particular projects. Hence the possibilities of an EIA process to have a real effect on the carrying out of certain activities can be relatively minor, no matter how scrupulously the EIA is done[②].

Space activities are a good example of an area where policy level planning is decisive. Strategic Environmental Assessment (SEA), as the

---

① P. M. Sterns-L. I. Tennen, Space and the Environment: public perceptions and policy considerations, Proceedings of the 37th Colloquium on the Law of Outer Space (1995), IISL, 9~14 October 1994 (Jerusalem), AIAA, pp. 268~280, pp. 268~269. Failure to anticipate such public scrutiny can lead to significant administrative delays, increased costs and missed opportunities. Ibid., p. 280.

② See Morgan, see note ① on page 150, p. 38.

next 'step' in impact assessment procedures, would thus seem to be a good option for supplementing individual space EIAs. As distinct from project EIA, SEA means carrying out EIAs of plans themselves, thereby directly addressing the environmental implications of proposed strategies and policies[①]. Accordingly, SEA is conducted much earlier in the decision-making process than EIA.

By extending the scope of assessment to cover earlier stages in planning cycles (policies, plans and programs in particular), strategic level assessments offer a way of dealing with indirect and cumulative impacts (both space-and time-crowding effects) and enable the examination of alternatives which project level assessments cannot address efficiently[②]. Although the less detailed level of information at which SEA operates is likely to entail greater uncertainty in impact predictions[③], it often re-

---

① For a more detailed account of the various different definitions and classifications of SEA, see, e. g. , SEA and Integration of the Environment into Strategic Decision-Making (2001), Final Report, Vol. 1, CEC Contract No. B4 – 3040/99/136634/MAR/B4, < http://ec. europa. eu/environment/eia/sea – studies – and – reports/sea_integration_main. pdf > , pp. 6 ~ 11. One definition given to SEA is that of the 2003 UNECE Protocol on Strategic Environmental Assessment: "the evaluation of the likely environmental, including health, effects, which comprises the determination of the scope of an environmental report and its preparation, the carrying out of public participation and consultations, and the taking into account of the environmental report and the results of the public participation and consultations in a plan or programme" (Art. 2.6; emphasis added). United Nations Economic Commission for Europe, Protocol on Strategic Environmental Assessment, < http://www. unece. org/env/eia/sea_protocol. htm > .

② Harrop-Nixon, see note ② on page 143, pp. 150 ~ 152.

③ Ibid. , p. 154.

duces the time and costs required for the subsequent project – level assessments[1].

Nevertheless, practical application of SEA is still infrequent. Governmental authorities have tended to regard SEA with suspicion, in particular because it involves public interest groups in policy-making[2]. Until recently, there has been little practical evidence suggesting the extension of the scope of assessment of environmental impacts to the treatment of plans and programs of a more general nature. The Espoo Convention on Environmental Impact Assessment in a Transboundary Context requires that EIA "shall, as a minimum requirement, be undertaken at the project level of the proposed activity", in addition to which, "to the extent appropriate, the Parties shall endeavour to apply the principles of environmental impact assessment to policies, plans and programmes" (Art. 2.7; emphasis added). According to the Espoo Convention, the assessment of environmental impacts is thus mandatory only as regards "proposed activities": the notion of activity refers to EIA, not SEA.

Nevertheless, SEA is a topical issue in the international arena, with the European countries in particular having promoted it. In 2001, a directive "on the assessment of the effects of certain plans and programmes on the environment" was adopted by the EC and the European

---

[1] M. -L. Cordonier Segger – A. Khalfan – S. Nakjavani, Weaving the Rules for Our Common Future: principles, practices and prospects for international sustainable development law (2002), Centre for International Sustainable Development Law, Faculty of Law, McGill University, Montreal, Canada, <http://www.cisdl.org/wtr/pdf/WeavingtheRulesOct2002.pdf>, p. 62.

[2] Morgan, see note [1] on page 150, p. 36.

Parliament[1]. The SEA Directive introduces a system of prior environmental assessment at the planning stage, the purpose of which is to "provide for a high level of protection of the environment and to contribute to the integration of environmental considerations into the preparation and adoption of plans and programmes with a view to promoting sustainable development" (Art. 1). The directive applies to certain plans and programmes (and their modifications) "likely to have significant environmental effects" (Arts. 2~3). It provides for the involvement of the public and environmental authorities; in the case of likely significant transboundary effects, also the potentially affected state and its public are informed and reserved an opportunity to comment on the plan (Arts. 6~7). The SEA Directive also requires subsequent monitoring of the implementation of the plans and policies adopted (Art. 10). Another relevant instrument is the Protocol on Strategic Environmental Assessment, by which the Espoo Convention was supplemented in 2003[2]. The protocol incorporates the impact assessment ideology of the

---

[1] Directive 2001/42/EC of the European Parliament and of the Council of 27 June 2001 on the assessment of the effects of certain plans and programmes on the environment (SEA Directive), OJ L 197, 21/07/2001, p. 0030~0037. The Directive supplements the EIA system for projects introduced by Council Directive 85/337/EEC on the assessment of the effects of certain public and private projects on the environment (OJ L 175, 05/07/1985, p. 0040-0048), which covers construction work and other installations or schemes, as well as other measures affecting the natural environment or landscape. EU member states have enacted national legislation in accordance with the requirements of the SEA directive, where necessary.

[2] Protocol on Strategic Environmental Assessment to the Convention on Environmental Impact Assessment in a Transboundary Context, done 21 May 2003, not yet in force, < http://www.unece.org/env/eia/sea_protocol/contents.htm >. Although negotiated under the UNECE, the SEA Protocol, too, is open to all UN member states (Arts. 21, 23.3).

Espoo Convention more firmly into the earlier level of planning: once in force, the protocol will require its parties to evaluate the environmental consequences (including effects on human health) of their official draft plans and programs①. The SEA Protocol addresses also policies and legislation, but application of SEA to these is not mandatory (Art. 13). In addition to consultations between relevant authorities, the protocol provides for extensive public participation in government decision-making, much as the Espoo Convention does in the case of EIA②. The protocol also contains an obligation to monitor the effects of implementation of the plans and programs③.

The considerable scale and magnitude of the potential adverse impacts of space activities call for an equally wide scope of assessment. The

---

① The plans and programs to which the protocol applies are specified in Art. 4 and Annexes I and II. The effects about which the protocol is concerned are defined as "any effect on the environment, including human health, flora, fauna, biodiversity, soil, climate, air, water, landscape, natural sites, material assets, cultural heritage and the interaction among these factors" (Art. 2.7). In contrast to the Espoo Convention, socio-economic conditions are not included in this list (see Espoo Convention, Art. 1. vii). Furthermore, the SEA Protocol is more concerned with the assessment of plans and programs within a state than with transboundary effects.

② Arts. 8~10. The SEA Protocol builds not only on the Espoo Convention but also on the 1998 Convention on Access to Information, Public Participation in Decision-Making and Access to Justice in Environmental Matters (Aarhus Convention), done 25 June 1998, in force 30 October 2001, 38 ILM 515 (1999), <http://www.unece.org/env/pp/documents/cep43e.pdf>. The SEA Protocol even contains explicit references to the Aarhus Convention (Art. 15 and preamble).

③ Art. 12. For more information on the SEA Protocol, see "United Nations Economic Commission for Europe, Protocol on Strategic Environmental Assessment", <http://www.unece.org/env/eia/sea_protocol.htm>.

multiple causes of deterioration of the space environment also seem to necessitate more proactive, integrated approaches than those found in conventional EIAs, which only represent a limited response to problems. The need is all the more pressing, as there are significant non-project-level factors behind individual space missions which determine the course of space activities-starting from the basic principle of international space law, namely, the freedom-of-use rule established by Article I of the Outer Space Treaty.

Within the political scene, government macro-economic and security policies often address space issues (either directly or indirectly) with modest consideration of the full scale of their impacts. The international tendency towards a profound increase in private space activities is only likely to diminish recognition of environmental and social impacts. Furthermore, SEAs can better take into account impacts which are distant from the particular project that initially causes them, 'distance' here referring to remoteness either in time or space[①], both of which are uniquely relevant to the space sector.

On balance, the cumulative assessment enabled by SEAs would thus seem to be a highly appropriate tool for supplementing individual EIAs for space missions. SEA could also appear appealing to spacefaring entities, considering the typical reduction in time and costs involved in the subsequent project-level assessments. One tentative example of an SEA-oriented approach in the space sector is provided by the IADC Space Debris Mitigation Guidelines, the idea of which is that space debris mitigation measures should be "taken into consideration from the

---

① Harrop-Nixon, see note ② on page 143, p. 151; Morgan, see note ① on page 150, p. 201.

very early phases of project planning" (emphasis added) [1]. The European SEA instruments (the directive and the protocol) could serve as models for better-defined SEA practices in the space sector.

On the other hand, the policies, plans and programs to be addressed by SEA may often be seen as requiring a level of confidentiality which makes public consultation before their approval (and sometimes even after it) impossible[2]; this could very likely be the case in many instances in the space sector. The focal role of political decision-making in space activities is likely to diminish the significance of any environmental assessment systems. Furthermore, the fundamental freedom-of-use principle and the right of every state to retain jurisdiction and control over its space mission must also be respected.

The more significant the potential international impacts of a space project, however, the more the balance should be tipped away from state discretion. This is all the more necessary when one considers that the prior assessment of environmental impacts of proposed activities can even be seen as a focal part of the general obligations of international cooperation and consultation required by the space treaties. Failure to undertake a proper environmental assessment may also constitute evidence of a breach of a due diligence obligation if reasonably foreseeable harm eventually occurs.

---

[1] P. 8, Support to the IADC Space Debris Mitigation Guidelines, IADC WG4, 5 October 2004, < http://www. iadc-online. org/index. cgi? item = docs_pub >. Pursuant to Part 4 of the Guidelines, "[d]uring an organisation's planning for and operation of a space system it should take systematic action to reduce adverse effects on the orbital environment by introducing space debris mitigation measures into the space system's lifecycle, from the mission requirement analysis and definition phases".

[2] See Harrop-Nixon, see note [2] on page 143, p. 154.

4.2 SIA

Finally, among the most recent "innovations" in the integrated impact assessment field is the introduction of what are known as Sustainability Impact Assessments (SIAs). They take into consideration environmental, social and economic factors and apply to policies, plans, programs and projects, seeking strategies which will result in long term sustainability. SIAs are increasingly concerned with processes, i. e. , with the soundness of institutional planning and management, including mechanisms for the meaningful involvement of the appropriate stakeholders. Access to information and public participation are considered essential, and efforts are made to involve public interest groups in all aspects of the SIA system.

Currently, there are still few concrete international legal obligations referring to SIAs[①]. As regards space activities, conducting impact assessment at the level of SIAs would be a substantial improvement and could, for instance, better integrate the increasingly important private sector into the assessment procedures. However, for the moment, adopting even somewhat effective environmental impact assessment and strategic environmental assessment procedures seems like a demanding enough task.

5. Conclusion

Environmental implications of space activities can no longer be ignored. Although environmentalist aspirations have not been among the most popular ones in the use of outer space, it has become quite clear that without an increasingly precautionary and sustainable approach, the space sector will continue to create environmental hazards that will

---

① See Cordonier Segger et al. , see note ① on page 160, pp. 64~65.

rapidly diminish its future prospects. Above all, the current space sector needs better debris mitigation and hence the use of improved environmental assessment systems, among other mechanisms.

Despite their success in many other areas-and the obvious need for them in space activities as well-environmental assessment procedures are still not well-established in the space sector. Partly this is because such assessments are often not quite as effective and reliable in the space sector as they tend to be in many other fields of human activity. However, many possibilities exist to amend the current deficiencies in space environmental assessments caused by lack of data, time and resources—if the will exists. Besides, the potential for damage in space activities is likely to remain at least in the foreseeable future so significant that it should never be reasonable to omit a thorough assessment of environmental and other impacts of space missions, despite the potentially high (immediate) costs and uncertainties involved.

Fortunately, the EIA appears to be slowly consolidating its role in space activities. Once environmental impact assessments are conducted regularly throughout the space sector for all missions, the establishment of strategic environmental assessment and even sustainability environmental assessment procedures for space activities will hopefully be relatively uncomplicated. The earlier in mission planning such assessments are undertaken, the more effective they are likely to be. At least in the long run, this should be beneficial for all stakeholders, as well as for the environment.

第54届国际空间法研讨会在南非开普敦举行

2011年10月3—7日,第54届国际空间法研讨会以及第62届国际宇航大会在南非开普敦举行。

本届大会以非洲航天为主题,议题包括太空监测非洲资源、南非乃至非洲太空活动等,大会还举行圆桌会议和各国宇航展览。这是该大会首次在非洲举行,也标志着国际宇航成员致力于在非洲发展航天项目。组织者说,本届大会会期正好与世界航天周相吻合。

中国两名专家当日在国际宇航大会上获得国际大奖。中国运载火箭和战略导弹专家刘纪原获得冯·卡门奖,这是国际宇航科学院最高奖项,也是中国专家首次获得这个大奖。作为国家宇航科学院院士,刘纪原为国际宇航科学做出了重要贡献,同时为中国早期运载火箭控制系统综合设计和实验工作做出了主要贡献。中国另一个宇航专家、导弹动力技术和航天工程管理专家王礼恒获得乌克兰的Mykhailo Yangel奖章,这个奖章是乌克兰授予那些为火箭发展和空间探索国际合作做出贡献的航天专家。

国际宇航大会是国际宇航联合会(IAF)、国际宇航科学院(IAA)和国际空间法学会联合主办的国际宇航界盛会,每年举办一届,每届大会收到上千篇相关科学论文。

国际空间法当前形势和未来发展学术研讨会在哈尔滨召开

由国防科技工业局军贸与外事司、外交部条约法律司和中国空间法学会共同主办的国际空间法当前形势和未来发展学术研讨会于2011年12月1日至2日在哈尔滨工业大学召开。来自主办单位和中国政法大学、北京航空航天大学、北京理工大学、香港大学及哈尔滨工业大学等院校的30余位专家、学者参加会议。

哈尔滨工业大学副校长丁雪梅出席开幕式并致辞。她指出，中国空间科学技术发展迅速，加强空间法的研究对保障我国国家利益有着重要的现实意义，相信本次会议的举行将对我国的空间法研究起到良好的促进作用。

国防科工局军贸与外事司副司长刘云峰、外交部条法司马新民参赞、中国空间法学会副理事长巴日斯分别致辞。

会议就"空间法发展的国际和国内形势"召开全体会议，并就"国际国内航天立法及重大航天活动涉及的法律问题""航天国际合作的法律问题""外空领域的国际法律秩序建设"等问题展开专题研讨。外交部条法司马新民参赞、中国空间法学会秘书长张振军在大会上做了主题报告。参会的空间法工作者、航天科技工作者在研讨会上作发言并展开讨论。

本次会议集中梳理并总结了当前国际空间法研究领域的一些热点问题，为有关学者、专家和航天管理部门的相关人员提供了一个交流的平台，对国际空间法律和政策研究起到了促进作用。

第一届亚太空间合作组织法律与政策论坛在北京举行

2012年6月,亚太空间合作组织(APSCO)和北京航空航天大学联合举办APSCO第一届空间法和政策论坛。来自APSCO成员国(或地区)(孟加拉国、中国、伊朗、蒙古、巴基斯坦、秘鲁、泰国和土耳其)代表,以及来自联合国外层空间事务办公室(UNOOSA)、欧洲空间法中心(ECSL)、国际空间法学会(IISL)、中国空间法学会、哈尔滨工业大学、北京理工大学、北京航空航天大学,深圳大学和香港大学的专家参加了此次论坛。

本次论坛主要讨论建立APSCO空间法研究中心的可选择性,相互交换了国家、地区和国家空间法发展的相关信息,并取得了丰硕的成果。同时,各国代表对中国首次将女宇航员送入太空表示祝贺。

联合国外空委及外空安全形势研讨会在北京举行

2012年7月13日,由国防科技工业局军贸与外事司主办,中国空间法学会协办的"联合国外空委安全形势"研讨会在京召开。国防科工局军贸外事司、系统工程一司、外交部条法司、军控司有关领导及专家,中国科学院有关单位专家,中国航天科技集团公司有关部门领导及专家,中国空间技术研究院、中国航天系统科学与工程研究院有关领导及专家,装备指挥学院、北京理工大学、北京航空航天大学、哈尔滨工业大学等有关高校专家学者参加了会议。会议议题包括:联合国外空委2012年度相关会议情况总结;外空活动长期可持续性问题研究;外空安全热点问题研究;我国空间碎片减缓措施及相关国际动态研究。

第55届国际空间法研讨会在意大利那不勒斯举行

2012年10月1—5日,第55届国际空间法研讨会在意大利那不勒斯举行。在此次会议中,哈尔滨工业大学赵海峰教授经全体会员选举,连任国际空间法学会理事。

本届大会的主题是"空间科学与技术造福民众"。一年一度的国际宇航联大会是宇航界最为重要的国际年会。在本届大会上,来自全球50多个国家的4 000名代表参加90场学术会议,讨论有关航天领域未来发展战略、星际探索和用于监测行星的新型卫星技术等。

开幕式后,召开了由各国航天机构首脑参加的会议,其中包括美国国家航空航天局局长查尔斯·博尔登,欧洲航天局局长多尔丹,中国国家航天局国际合作协调委员会副主任胡亚枫,加拿大航天局斯蒂夫·麦克莱恩,俄罗斯航天局副局长萨维利耶夫,印度空间研究机构代理主席 P. S. Veeraraghavan,意大利航天局局长埃里克·萨基斯,日本航空航天研究机构主席立川敬二。与会代表概述了各国的空间项目和未来规划,对当前形势下的航天发展和国际合作发表了自己的看法。

此外,会议期间还举行一系列展览以及旨在普及空间科技知识的公众开放日活动。

第 49 届国际航空与航天法会议在韩国首尔举行

2012 年 11 月 8—9 日,第 49 届国际航空和航天法会议在韩国首尔召开。韩国航空和航天法会员参加了本次会议。同时,本次会议还就韩国加入国际民用航空组织 60 周年开展了纪念活动。

哈尔滨工业大学法学院赵海峰教授参加了在韩国召开的 2012 年第 49 届国际航空和航天法年会,并就"中国空间工业和航天法的现状与展望"做了专题报告。

俄罗斯导航定位活动法

贾雪池[①] 译

2009年1月4日国家杜马通过
2009年2月4日联邦委员会批准

第1条 本法的适用范围

1. 本法确立实施导航定位活动的法律原则,旨在建立规则以满足对导航定位设备与导航定位服务的需求。

2. 本法调整因实施导航定位活动和提供定位服务而产生的关系,其中包括为保障俄罗斯联邦国防与国家安全而实施的导航定位活动。

第2条 本法使用的基本概念

为实现本法的立法目的,使用下列基本概念:

1. 导航定位活动——确立与使用客体的定位参数的相关活动。

2. 导航定位设备——用于形成导航信号、传输、接收、处理、保存导航信息与信息可视化的技术设备、装置与系统。

[①] 贾雪池,哈尔滨工业大学法学院副教授。

3. 导航定位活动的客体——是配置导航设备的客体和(或)为实施导航活动而利用导航设备的客体,以及保障导航设备功能实现的客体。

4. 导航定位活动的服务——是满足对导航设备与导航设备利用以及导航信息需求的活动。

5. 公开访问的导航定位信号——是用于完成定位与无限制导航保障的信号,该限制由核准进入访问的相关制度规定。

第3条 导航活动的法律关系主体

建造卫星导航设备与导航活动客体并使其发挥功能的国家权力机关、地方自治机关、自然人与法人,以及依据民事立法提供与获得导航活动服务的自然人、法人是导航活动的法律关系主体。

第4条 实施导航活动的特殊性(属性或性质)

1. 为保障俄罗斯联邦国防与国家安全,提高交通工具的管理效率,提高旅客、特种物品与危险品的安全运输水平,实施大地与地籍测量,交通工具、技术设备与系统(其中包括军事装备、军事与特种技术设备)应当配置导航设备,俄罗斯导航系统保障上述设备发挥功能。上述设备与系统的目录由俄罗斯联邦权力执行机关、俄罗斯联邦各主体的权力执行机关、地方自治机关依其权限制定。

2. 和平时期,备战时期与战争时期实施导航定位活动的特别规定,由俄罗斯联邦政府制定。

第5条 卫星导航设备与导航活动客体的所有权

1. 卫星导航设备与卫星导航活动的客体可以归俄罗斯联邦所有、俄罗斯联邦各主体所有、地方自治组织所有、自然人与法人所有。

2. 属于卫星导航系统并且由俄罗斯联邦预算承担费用建造的航天装置与宇航地面设施归俄罗斯联邦所有,禁止流通与转让。

第6条 导航活动的财政(资金)保障

1. 由于卫星导航活动的专用目标和资金需求数量众多,该活动的财政(资金)保障由俄罗斯联邦预算拨款、俄罗斯联邦各主体预算、地方自治组织预算,私人所有或吸收自法人与自然人的资金以及依据俄罗斯联邦立法的其他资金承担。

2. 法定授权解决导航活动问题的俄罗斯联邦权力执行机关、俄罗斯联邦各主体的权力执行机关、地方自治机关相应活动的财政保障是对应的俄罗斯联邦、俄罗斯联邦主体、地方自治组织的法定支付义务。

第7条 卫星导航活动的权限

1. 俄罗斯联邦总统确定卫星导航活动的国家政策的基本方向。

2. 俄罗斯联邦政府有权：

——为保障俄罗斯联邦国防与国家安全，为实现各经济部门的利益与保障在上述领域中俄罗斯联邦参与国际合作的利益，组织实施卫星导航活动的国家政策。

——为保障俄罗斯联邦国防与国家安全，建立、使用与发展卫星导航系统。

——为保障俄罗斯联邦国防与国家安全，提高交通工具管理效率、提高旅客、特种物品与危险品的安全运输水平，制定配置导航设备的规则。

——为保障对导航活动与导航服务管理的统一性，为联邦国家和其他需要，必要时建立网络操作人员队伍，并确定其任务与职能。

3. 俄罗斯联邦各主体的国家权力机关与地方自治机关依据其制定的规则有权获得导航方面服务。

第8条 自然人与法人参与导航活动的规定

自然人与法人为自身的需求可以实施导航活动，可以在全俄罗斯境内对没有精准度限制的导航活动客体提供导航服务。依俄罗斯联邦立法确定安全保障功能的特殊制度的区域与客体除外，上述区域与客体的目录由俄罗斯联邦政府确认。

第9条 提供开放式访问的导航信号的规则

无偿与无限制地向卫星导航活动法律关系的主体提供开放式访问的导航信号。

第10条 导航活动的信息保障

为实现对导航活动的信息保障,被授权的俄罗斯联邦权力执行机关在其互联网官方正式网站放置有关导航活动服务的信息。该服务提供依据国家标准和本法规定的标准。

第11条 有关导航设备与导航活动客体的信息保护

依据俄罗斯联邦立法,对有关导航设备与导航活动客体的信息实施保护,以使其免受非法入侵,使信息减少、变更、被封锁、复制、提供、扩展以及其他针对此类信息的非法行为。

第12条 本法的生效

1. 本法自正式公布之日起生效。本法第4条第1款除外。
2. 本法第4条第1款自2011年1月1日起生效。

Draft Code of Conduct for Outer Space Activities(2008)

Brussels, 17 December 2008
from : General Secretariat
to : Delegations
Subject : Council conclusions and draft Code of Conduct for outer space activities

Delegations will find attached annexes which have been approved by the Council on 8 ~9 December 2008:

—in Annex I, Council conclusions concerning the draft Code of Conduct for outer space activities,

—in Annex II, the text of the draft Code of Conduct for outer space activities, which will serve as a basis for consultations with third countries.

Council Conclusions on the draft Code of Conduct for outer space activities

As approved by the Council on 8 ~9 December 2008

The Council considers that strengthening the security of activities in outer space is an important goal in the context of the expanding space activities that contribute to the development and security of States. This objective is part of the European Union's space policy.

The Council supports the annexed European Union draft for a Code of Conduct for outer space activities, in which States would participate on a voluntary basis, and which includes transparency and confidence-building measures, as a basis for consultations with key third countries that have activities in outer space or have interests in outer space activities, with the aim of reaching a text that is acceptable to the greatest number of countries.

DRAFT
CODE OF CODUCT
FOR OUTER SPACE ACTIVITIES

As approved by the Council on 8 ~ 9 December 2008

Preamble

The Subscribing States,

Noting that all States should actively contribute to the promotion and strengthening of international cooperation relating to the activities in the exploration and use of outer space for peaceful purposes (hereinafter referred to as outer space activities).

Recognising the need for the widest possible adherence to relevant existing international instruments that promote the peaceful uses of outer space in order to meet emerging new challenges.

Convinced that the use of existing space technology, space telecommunications, and their applications, has important consequences in the economic, social and cultural development of nations;

Further recognising that space capabilities including associated ground and space segments and supporting links are vital to national security and to the maintenance of international peace and security;

Recalling the initiatives aiming at promoting a peaceful, safe and secure outer space environment, through international cooperation;

Recalling the importance of developing transparency and confidence building measures for activities in outer space.

Taking into account that space debris could constitute a threat to outer space activities and potentially limit the effective deployment and exploitation of associated space capabilities.

Reaffirming their commitment to resolve any conflict concerning actions in space by peaceful means.

Recognising that a comprehensive approach to safety and security in outer space should be guided by the following principles: (i) freedom of access to space for all for peaceful purposes, (ii) preservation of the security and integrity of space objects in orbit, (iii) due consideration for the legitimate defence interests of States.

Conscious that a comprehensive code, including transparency and confidence building measures could contribute to promoting common and precise understandings.

Adopt the following Code (hereinafter referred to as "the Code").

I. Core principles and objectives

1. Purpose and scope

1.1. The purpose of the present code is to enhance the safety, security and predictability of outer space activities for all.

1.2. The present Code is applicable to all outer space activities conducted by a Subscribing State or jointly with other State(s) or by non-governmental entities under the jurisdiction of a Subscribing State, including those activities within the framework of international intergovernmental organisations.

1.3. This Code, in codifying new best practices, contributes to transparency and confidence building measures and is complementary to the existing framework regulating outer space activities.

1.4. Adherence to this Code and to the measures contained in it is voluntary and open to all States.

2. General principles

The Subscribing States resolve to abide by the following principles:

—the freedom of access to, exploration and use of outer space and exploitation of space objects for peaceful purposes without interference, fully respecting the security, safety and integrity of space objects in orbit.

—the inherent right of individual or collective self defence in accordance with the United Nations Charter.

—the responsibility of States to take all the appropriate measures and cooperate in good faith to prevent harmful interference in outer space activities;

—the responsibility of States, in the conduct of scientific, commercial and military activities, to promote the peaceful exploration and use of outer space and take all the adequate measures to prevent outer space from becoming an area of conflict;

3. Compliance with and promotion of treaties, conventions and other commitments relating to outer space activities

3.1. The Subscribing States reaffirm their commitment to:

· the existing legal framework relating to outer space activities;

· making progress towards adherence to, and implementation of:

(a) **the existing framework regulating outer space activities**, **inter alia**:

—the Treaty on Principles Governing the Activities of States in the Exploration and Use of Outer Space, including the Moon and Other Celestial Bodies (1967).

—the Agreement on the Rescue of Astronauts, the Return of Astronauts and the Return of Objects Launched into Outer Space (1968).

—the Convention on International Liability for Damage Caused by Space Objects (1972).

—the Convention on Registration of Objects Launched into Outer Space (1975).

—the Constitution and Convention of the International Telecommunications Union and its Radio Regulations (2002).
—the Treaty banning Nuclear Weapon Tests in the Atmosphere, in Outer Space and under Water (1963) and the Comprehensive Nuclear Test Ban Treaty (1996).
—the International Code of Conduct against Ballistic Missile Proliferation (2002).

(b) **declarations and Principles, inter alia**:
—the Declaration of Legal Principles Governing the Activities of States in the Exploration and Use of Outer Space as stated in UNGA Resolution 1962 (XVIII).
—the Principles Relevant to the Use of Nuclear Power Sources in Outer Space as stated in UNGA Resolution 47/68.
—the Declaration on International Cooperation in the Exploration and Use of Outer Space for the Benefit and in the Interest of All States, Taking into Particular Account the Needs of Developing Countries as stated in UNGA Resolution 51/122.
—the Recommendations on the Practice of States and International Organisations in Registering Space Objects as stated in UNGA Resolution 62/101.
—the Space Debris Mitigation Guidelines of the United Nations Committee for the Peaceful Uses of Outer Space as stated in UNGA Resolution 62/217.

3.2. The Subscribing States also reiterate their support to encourage coordinated efforts in order to promote universal adherence to the above mentioned instruments.

II. General Measures

4. Measures on space operations
4.1. The Subscribing States will establish and implement national poli-

cies and procedures to minimise the possibility of accidents in space, collisions between space objects or any form of harmful interference with other States' right to the peaceful exploration and use of outer space.

4.2. The Subscribing States will, in conducting outer space activities:

· refrain from any intentional action which will or might bring about, directly or indirectly, the damage or destruction of outer space objects unless such action is conducted to reduce the creation of outer space debris and/or justified by imperative safety considerations.

· take appropriate steps to minimise the risk of collision.

· abide by and implement all International Telecommunications Union recommendations and regulations on allocation of radio spectra and orbital assignments.

4.3. When executing manoeuvres of space objects in outer space, for example to supply space stations, repair space objects, mitigate debris, or reposition space objects, the Subscribing States agree to take all reasonable measures to minimise the risks of collision.

4.4. The Subscribing States resolve to promote the development of guidelines for space operations within the appropriate fora for the purpose of protecting the safety of space operations and long term sustainability of outer space activities.

5. Measures on space debris control and mitigation

In order to limit the creation of space debris and reduce its impact in outer space, the Subscribing States will:

· refrain from intentional destruction of any on-orbit space object or other harmful activities which may generate long-lived space debris;

· adopt, in accordance with their national legislative processes, the appropriate policies and procedures in order to implement the Space Debris Mitigation Guidelines of the United Nations Committee for the Peaceful Uses of Outer Space as endorsed by UNGA Resolution 62/217.

III. Cooperation mechanisms

6. Notification of outer space activities

6.1. The Subscribing States commit to notify, in a timely manner, to the greatest extent feasible and practicable, all potentially affected Subscribing States on the outer space activities conducted which are relevant for the purposes of this Code, inter alia:

—the scheduled manoeuvres which may result in dangerous proximity to space objects;

—orbital changes and re-entries, as well as other relevant orbital parameters;

—collisions or accidents which have taken place;

—the malfunctioning of orbiting space objects with significant risk of re-entry into the atmosphere or of orbital collision.

6.2. The Subscribing States reaffirm their commitment to the Principles Relevant to the Use of Nuclear Power Sources in Outer Space as stated in UNGA Resolution 47/68.

7. Registration of space objects

The Subscribing States undertake to register space objects in accordance with the Convention on Registration of Objects launched in Outer Space and to provide the United Nations Secretary General with the relevant data as set forth in this Convention and in the Recommendations on the Practice of States and International Organisations in Registering Space Objects as stated in UNGA Resolution 62/101.

8. Information on outer space activities

8.1. The Subscribing States resolve to share, on an annual basis, and, where available, information on:

· national space policies and strategies, including basic objectives for security and defence related activities;

· national space policies and procedures to prevent and minimise the possibility of accidents, collisions or other forms of harmful interference;

· national space policies and procedures to minimise the creation of space debris;

· efforts taken in order to promote universal adherence to legal and political regulatory instruments concerning outer space activities.

8.2. The Subscribing States may also consider providing timely information on space environmental conditions and forecasts to other Subscribing States or private entities through their national space situational awareness capabilities.

9. Consultation mechanism

9.1. Without prejudice to existing consultation mechanisms provided for in Article IX of the Outer Space Treaty of 1967 and in Article 56 of the ITU Constitution, the Subscribing States have decided on the creation of the following consultation mechanism:

· A Subscribing State with reason to believe that certain outer space activities conducted by one or more Subscribing State(s) are, or may be, contrary to the purposes of the Code may request consultations with a view to achieving acceptable solutions regarding measures to be adopted in order to prevent or minimise the inherent risks.

· The Subscribing States involved in a consultation process will decide on a timeframe consistent with the timescale of the identified risk triggering the consultations.

· Any other Subscribing State which may be affected by the risk and requests to take part in the consultations will be entitled to take part.

· The Subscribing States participating in the consultations shall seek solutions based on an equitable balance of interests.

9.2. In addition, the Subscribing States may propose to create a mechanism to investigate proven incidents affecting space objects. The mechanism, to be agreed upon at a later stage, could be based on national information and/or national means of investigation provided on a voluntary basis by the Subscribing States and on a roster of internationally recognised experts to undertake an investigation.

IV. Organisational aspects

10. Biennial meeting of Subscribing States

10.1. The Subscribing States decide to hold meetings biennially or as otherwise agreed by Subscribing States, to define, review and further develop this Code and ensure its effective implementation. The agenda for such biennial meetings could include: (i) review of the implementation of the Code, (ii) evolution of the Code and (iii) additional measures which appear necessary.

10.2. The decisions will be taken by consensus of the Subscribing States present at the meeting.

11. Central point of contact

A central point of contact shall be nominated among Subscribing States to:

—receive and announce the subscription of additional States;

—maintain the electronic information – sharing system;

—serve as secretariat at the biennial meetings of Subscribing States;

—carry out other tasks as agreed by Subscribing States.

12. Outer Space Activities Database

The Subscribing States will create an electronic database to:

—collect and disseminate notifications and information submitted in accordance with the provisions of this Code;

—channel requests for consultations.

《2011年中国的航天》白皮书(中、英文)

2011年12月
中华人民共和国国务院新闻办公室

一、发展宗旨与原则

中国发展航天事业的宗旨是:探索外层空间,扩展对地球和宇宙的认识;和平利用外层空间,促进人类文明和社会进步,造福全人类;满足经济建设、科技发展、国家安全和社会进步等方面的需求,提高全民科学文化素质,维护国家权益,增强综合国力。

中国发展航天事业服从和服务于国家整体发展战略,坚持科学发展、自主发展、和平发展、创新发展、开放发展的原则。

——科学发展。尊重科学、尊重规律,从航天事业的发展实际出发,统筹兼顾和科学部署空间技术、空间应用和空间科学等各项航天活动,保持航天事业全面、协调、可持续发展。

——自主发展。始终坚持走独立自主、自力更生的发展道路,主要依靠自身力量,根据国情和国力,自主发展航天事业,满足国家现代化建设的基本需求。

——和平发展。始终坚持和平利用外层空间,反对外空武器化和外空军备竞赛,合理开发和利用空间资源,切实保护空间环境,使航天活动造福全人类。

——创新发展。把提高自主创新能力作为航天事业发展的战略基点,强化工业基础,完善创新体系,以实施航天重大科技工程为载体,集中力量,重点突破,实现航天科技跨越发展。

——开放发展。坚持独立自主与开放合作相结合,在平等互利、和平利用、共同发展基础上,积极开展空间领域的国际交流与合作,致力于推进人类航天事业的共同进步。

二、2006年以来的主要进展

2006年以来,中国航天事业实现快速发展,载人航天、月球探测等航天重大科技工程取得突破性进展,空间技术整体水平大幅跃升,空间应用的经济与社会效益显著提高,空间科学取得创新性成果。

(一)航天运输系统

2006年以来,"长征"系列运载火箭共完成67次发射任务,把79个航天器成功送入预定轨道,运载火箭的可靠性显著增强。"长征"系列运载火箭型谱进一步完善。新一代运载火箭工程研制取得重大进展。

(二)人造地球卫星

1. 对地观测卫星。基本建成"风云""海洋""资源""遥感""天绘"等卫星系列和"环境与灾害监测预报小卫星星座"。"风云"气象卫星具备全球、三维、多光谱的定量观测能力,"风云二号"静止轨道气象卫星实现双星观测、在轨备份,"风云三号"极轨气象卫星实现上午星和下午星的双星组网观测。"海洋"水色卫星成像幅宽增加一倍,重访周期大幅缩短,2011年8月发射的首颗"海洋"动力环境卫星,具备全天候、全天时的微波观测能力。"资源"卫星的空间分辨率和图像质量得到较大幅度提升。"环境与灾害监测预报小卫星星座"具备中分辨率、宽覆盖、高重访的灾害监测能力。2010年,正式启动实施高分辨率对地观测系统重大科技专项。

2. 通信广播卫星。突破大容量地球静止轨道卫星公用平台、天基数据中继与测控等关键技术,卫星技术性能明显提高,话音、数据和广播电视通信水平进一步提升。"中星十号"卫星的成功发射和稳定运行,大幅提高了中国通信广播卫星的功率和容量。"天绘一号"数据中继卫星的成功发射,使中国初步具备天基数据传输能力和对航天器的天基测控服务能力。

3. 导航定位卫星。2007年2月,成功发射第四颗"北斗"导航试验卫星,进一步提升了"北斗"卫星导航试验系统性能。全面实施"北斗"卫星导航区域系统建设。该系统由5颗地球静止轨道卫星、5颗倾斜地球同步轨道卫星和4颗中圆地球轨道卫星组成,2007年4月以来已成功发射10颗卫星,具备了向服务区(亚太地区)用户提供试运行服务的条件。

4. 科学卫星与技术试验卫星。研制发射多颗"实践"系列卫星和微小卫星,为空间环境探测、空间科学实验和新技术验证提供了支撑平台。

(三)载人航天

2008年9月25日至28日,成功发射"神舟七号"载人飞船,首次顺利实施航天员空间出舱活动,完成舱外空间材料试验、小卫星释放与伴飞试验,标志着中国成为世界上第三个独立掌握航天员空间出舱关键技术的国家。2011年9月和11月,先后发射"天宫一号"目标飞行器和"神舟八号"飞船,成功实施中国首次空间交会对接试验,为后续空间实验室和空间站的建设奠定了基础。

(四)深空探测

2007年10月24日,成功发射中国第一个月球探测器——"嫦娥一号",实现"精确变轨,成功绕月"的预定目标,获取大量科学数据和全月球影像图,并成功实施"受控撞月"任务。"嫦娥一号"任务的圆满完成,是继人造地球卫星、载人航天飞行取得成功之后中国航天事业发展的又一座里程碑,标志着中国已经跨入具有深空探测能力的国家行列。2010年10月1日,成功发射"嫦娥二号"月球探测器,获取了分辨率更高的全月球影像图和虹湾区域高清晰影像,并成功开展环绕拉格朗日L2点等多项拓展性试验,为深空探测后续任务的实施奠定了基础。

（五）航天发射场

中国已有的酒泉、西昌、太原3个航天发射场建设进一步完善，综合性试验能力和高密度发射能力明显提高，圆满完成载人飞船、月球探测器以及各类卫星的发射任务。目前，中国正在建设满足新一代运载火箭发射任务要求的海南航天发射场。

（六）航天测控

完善了地面测控站和远洋测量船，建立了由4个观测站和1个数据处理中心组成的甚长基线干涉测量网，初步具备了天基测控能力，基本建成天地一体、设备齐全、任务多样的航天测控网。目前，中国航天测控网正在逐步实现由陆基向天基、由地球空间测控向深空测控的拓展，不仅能满足卫星测控需求，还能为载人航天和深空探测等任务提供测控支持。

（七）空间应用

1.对地观测卫星应用。对地观测卫星应用的领域和规模不断扩大，业务服务能力不断提升，初步形成对地观测卫星应用体系。新建4个卫星地面接收站，提高了气象、海洋、陆地观测等卫星数据的地面接收能力；统筹建设对地观测卫星地面数据处理系统，提升了数据集中处理、存档、分发和服务能力；新建卫星环境应用中心、卫星减灾应用中心和卫星测绘应用中心等对地观测卫星应用机构，促进了对地观测卫星数据的推广应用；加强遥感卫星辐射校正场的定标服务，提高了对地观测卫星的定量应用水平。

目前，对地观测卫星数据已广泛应用于经济社会发展各领域。"风云"卫星系列实现对台风、雨涝、森林与草原火灾、干旱、沙尘暴等灾害的有效监测，气象预报和气候变化监测能力明显提升。"海洋"卫星系列实现对中国海域和全球重点海域的监测和应用，对海冰、海温、风场等的预报精度和灾害性海况的监测时效显著提高。"资源"卫星系列在土地、地质矿产、农业、林业、水利等资源及地质灾害调查、监测与管理和城市规划中发挥了重要作用。"遥感"和"天绘"卫星系列在科学试验、国土资源普查、地图测绘等领域发挥了重大作用。"环境与灾害监测预报小卫星星座"为地表水质与大气环境监测、重大环境污染事件处置以及重大自然灾害监测、评估与救援提供了重要的技术支撑。

2. 通信广播卫星应用。通信广播卫星应用稳步推进,形成一定的市场规模。卫星广播电视网进一步完善,2008年建立"村村通"直播卫星服务平台,实现中央人民广播电台、中央电视台节目和省级一套广播电视节目通过卫星播出,进一步提高了全国广播电视节目覆盖率。加强卫星远程教育宽带网和卫星远程医疗网的建设,在一定程度上缓解了边远地区教育与医疗资源短缺的问题。加强卫星应急通信保障能力建设,为抢险救灾、重大突发事件处置提供了重要支撑。

3. 导航定位卫星应用。导航定位卫星应用步入产业化发展轨道,正在进入高速发展时期。利用国内外导航定位卫星,在导航定位卫星应用技术的开发和推广等方面取得重要进展,应用范围和领域不断扩大,全国卫星导航应用市场规模快速增长。积极推进"北斗"卫星导航系统的应用工作,"北斗"卫星导航系统已在交通运输、海洋渔业、水文监测、通信授时、电力调度和减灾救灾等领域得到应用。

(八) 空间科学

1. 日地空间探测。中国的地球空间探测双星计划与欧洲空间局的星簇计划互相配合,获得大量新的科学数据,在空间物理学研究方面取得重要成果。

2. 月球科学研究。通过月球探测工程的实施,开展月球形貌、结构构造、月面物质成分、微波特性和近月空间环境等研究工作,对月球的科学认知进一步提高。

3. 微重力科学与空间生命科学实验。利用"实践"系列卫星和"神舟"飞船,开展微重力和强辐射条件下的空间生命科学、材料科学、流体力学等实验,进行航天育种实验研究。

4. 空间环境探测与预报。利用"神舟"飞船等航天器,进行空间环境主要参数及其效应的探测,开展空间环境监测与预报以及空间环境效应研究。

(九) 空间碎片

对空间碎片进行监测预警,为"嫦娥一号""嫦娥二号"月球探测器和"神舟七号"载人飞船等重要航天器的安全飞行提供了支撑;空间碎片减缓工作稳步推进,全面实施"长征"系列运载火箭的钝化,并对多颗废弃地球静止轨道卫星采取离轨处置措施;开展载人航天器的空间碎片防护工作。

三、未来五年的主要任务

未来五年,中国将加强航天工业基础能力建设,超前部署前沿技术研究,继续实施载人航天、月球探测、高分辨率对地观测系统、卫星导航定位系统、新一代运载火箭等航天重大科技工程以及一批重点领域的优先项目,统筹建设空间基础设施,促进卫星及应用产业发展,深入开展空间科学研究,推动航天事业的全面、协调、可持续发展。

(一) 航天运输系统

加强航天运输系统建设,不断完善运载火箭型谱,提升进入空间的能力。

增强现役运载火箭的可靠性和发射适应性,发展新一代运载火箭和运载火箭上面级,实现"长征五号""长征六号""长征七号"运载火箭首飞。"长征五号"运载火箭将完全采用无毒无污染推进剂,并具备近地轨道25吨、地球同步转移轨道14吨的运载能力。"长征六号"运载火箭是新型快速发射运载火箭,具备700千米高度太阳同步轨道不小于1吨的运载能力。"长征七号"运载火箭将具备近地轨道13.5吨、700千米太阳同步轨道5.5吨的运载能力。

开展重型运载火箭专项论证和关键技术预先研究。

(二) 人造地球卫星

重点构建由对地观测、通信广播、导航定位等卫星组成的空间基础设施框架,初步形成长期、连续、稳定的业务服务能力。发展新型科学卫星与技术试验卫星。

1. 对地观测卫星。完善已有"风云""海洋""资源"等卫星系列和"环境与灾害监测预报小卫星星座",研制发射新一代地球静止轨道气象卫星、立体测绘卫星、环境与灾害监测雷达卫星、电磁监测试验卫星等新型对地观测卫星,开展干涉合成孔径雷达、重力场测量等卫星的关键技术攻关。全面实施高分辨率对地观测系统重大科技专项。基本形成全天候、全天时、多谱段、不同分辨率、稳定运行的对地观测体系。

2. 通信广播卫星。完善固定通信业务卫星、电视广播业务卫星以及数据中继卫星,发展移动通信业务卫星,研制更大容量、更大功率的新一代地球静止轨道通信广播卫星平台。

3. 导航定位卫星。按照从试验系统,到区域系统,再到全球系统的"三步走"发展思路,继续构建中国"北斗"卫星导航系统。2012年前,建成"北斗"卫星导航区域系统,具备提供覆盖亚太地区的导航定位、授时和短报文通信服务的能力;2020年左右,建成由5颗地球静止轨道卫星和30颗非地球静止轨道卫星组成的覆盖全球的"北斗"卫星导航系统。

4. 科学卫星与技术试验卫星。研制发射硬X射线调制望远镜卫星、"实践九号"新技术试验卫星和返回式卫星。启动实施量子科学实验卫星和暗物质探测卫星等项目。

(三)载人航天

继续推进载人航天工程建设,加强关键技术攻关,为载人航天后续任务的圆满完成奠定基础。

发射"神舟九号""神舟十号"飞船,与已在轨飞行的"天宫一号"目标飞行器进行无人或载人交会对接。

发射空间实验室、载人飞船和货运飞船,突破和掌握航天员中期驻留、再生式生命保障及推进剂补加等空间站关键技术,开展一定规模的空间应用,为空间站建设进行技术准备。

开展载人登月前期方案论证。

(四)深空探测

选择有限目标,分步开展深空探测活动。

按照"绕、落、回"三步走的发展思路,继续推进月球探测工程建设,发射月球软着陆和月面巡视勘测器,实现在月球的软着陆和巡视探测,完成月球探测第二步任务。启动实施以月面采样返回为目标的月球探测第三步任务。

开展深空探测专项论证,推进开展对太阳系行星、小行星和太阳的探测活动。

(五)航天发射场

进一步提高航天发射场设施、设备的可靠性和自动化水平,增强航天发射场综合能力,满足发射任务需求。完成海南航天发射场建设并投入使用。

(六)航天测控

进一步完善航天测控网,建设深空测控站,发展先进的航天测控技术,全面提高航天测控能力,满足深空探测对远程测控的需求。

(七)空间应用

进一步完善卫星应用服务体系,扩大卫星应用规模,促进国家战略性新兴产业的发展,满足国民经济与社会发展需求。

1. 对地观测卫星应用。完善卫星数据接收、处理、分发、应用等地面设施,加强定标场等设施建设。加强对地观测卫星数据共享和综合应用,提高空间数据的自给率,引导社会资源积极发展面向市场的数据应用服务。实施应用示范工程,促进对地观测卫星的广泛应用和应用产业化发展。

2. 通信广播卫星应用。进一步加强通信广播卫星在公共服务领域和国民经济重点行业的应用。扩展卫星通信领域的增值服务业务。推动卫星通信的商业化进程,扩大通信广播卫星应用的产业规模。

3. 导航定位卫星应用。建设和完善地面测控段,推进覆盖全球的卫星导航系统的性能监测评估系统建设。加强导航定位卫星应用的技术研究、产品开发和标准体系建设,提高应用水平,促进位置服务市场发展,扩大产业规模,重点推动"北斗"卫星导航系统在国民经济建设各领域的应用。

(八)空间科学

加强空间科学研究体系建设,提升空间科学研究水平,加强对全民的空间科学科普教育。

通过月球探测工程的实施,开展月球着陆巡视区的月表特性原位分析、形貌探测、结构构造综合探测,以及月表环境探测和月基天文观测。

利用航天器,开展黑洞性质及极端条件下的物理规律研究,探索暗物质粒子的性质,开展量子力学基本理论的检验;开展微重力与空间生命科学实验;开展空间环境探测、预报与效应研究。

(九)空间碎片

继续加强空间碎片监测、减缓和航天器防护工作。

发展空间碎片监测与碰撞预警技术,开展空间碎片和近地小天体的监测与碰撞预警。建立空间碎片减缓设计评估系统,对任务后的航天器和运载火箭积极采取空间碎片减缓措施。开展空间碎片撞击数字仿真技术试验,推动航天器的空间碎片防护系统建设。

四、发展政策与措施

为确保完成既定的目标任务,中国政府制订了发展航天事业的政策与措施,主要包括:

——统筹规划、合理部署各种航天活动。优先安排应用卫星和卫星应用,适度发展载人航天和深空探测,积极支持空间科学探索。

——加强航天科技创新能力建设。集中力量实施重大航天科技工程,通过核心技术突破和资源集成,实现航天科技的重点跨越。积极构建以航天科技企业和科研机构为主体,产学研相结合的航天技术创新体系。加强航天领域的基础研究和若干前沿技术的超前研究,提高航天科技的持续创新能力。

——大力推动卫星应用产业发展。统筹规划与建设空间基础设施,推进卫星应用资源的共享,培育卫星应用企业集群、产业链和卫星应用市场,促进卫星应用产业快速健康发展。

——加强航天科技工业基础能力建设。加强航天器、运载火箭研制、生产、试验的基础设施建设。加强航天科技重点实验室和工程研究中心建设。加强信息化工作、知识产权工作和航天标准化工作。

——加强政策法规建设。积极开展国家航天法的研究,逐步制定和完善航天活动管理的法律法规和航天产业政策,指导和规范各项航天活动,营造更加有利于航天事业发展的政策法规环境。

——保障持续稳定的航天活动经费投入。逐步建立多元化、多渠道的航天投资体系,确保航天活动经费投入的持续稳定,重点加大对航天重大科技工程、应用卫星及卫星应用、前沿技术和基础研究的投入力度。

——鼓励社会各界参与航天活动。在国家航天政策指导下,鼓励科研机构、企业、高等院校和社会团体,发挥各自优势,积极参与航天活动。

——加强航天人才队伍建设。大力营造有利于人才发展的良好环境,以重大工程项目和重大基础研究为载体,培养造就航天领军人才,形成一支结构合理、素质优良的航天人才队伍。普及航天知识,宣传航天文化,吸引更多的优秀人才投身航天事业。

五、国际交流与合作

中国政府认为,自由探索、开发和利用外层空间及其天体是世界各国都享有的平等权利。世界各国开展外空活动,应有助于各国经济发展和社会进步,应有助于人类的安全、生存与发展。

国际空间合作应遵循联合国《关于开展探索和利用外层空间的国际合作,促进所有国家的福利和利益,并特别要考虑到发展中国家的需求的宣言》中提出的基本原则。中国主张在平等互利、和平利用、共同发展的基础上,加强国际空间交流与合作,促进包容性发展。

(一)基本政策

中国政府在开展国际空间交流与合作中,采取以下基本政策:

——支持联合国系统内开展和平利用外层空间的各项活动,支持政府之间、非政府之间空间组织为促进航天事业发展所开展的各项活动。

——重视亚太地区的区域性空间合作,支持世界其他区域性空间合作。

——加强与发展中国家的空间合作,重视与发达国家的空间合作。

——鼓励和支持国内科研机构、工业企业、高等院校和社会团体,在国家有关政策和法规的指导下,开展多层次、多形式的国际空间交流与合作。

——合理利用国内外两个市场和两种资源,开展积极、务实的国际空间合作。

(二)主要活动

2006年以来,中国积极开展多种形式的国际空间交流与合作,与多个国家、空间机构和国际组织签署多项和平利用外层空间的合作协定或谅解备忘录,参与联合国及相关国际组织开展的有关活动,支持国际空间商业合作,取得了积极成果。

双边合作

——中国与俄罗斯在总理定期会晤委员会航天合作分委会机制下,确定长期合作计划,双方已在空间科学、深空探测等领域签署多项合作协议。中国与俄罗斯互设国家航天局代表处。中俄双方在载人航天领域也开展了多项合作。

——中国与乌克兰在中乌合作委员会航天合作分委会机制下,开展广泛合作,共同签署《中乌航天合作大纲》。

——中国与欧洲空间局在中欧航天合作联合委员会机制下,共同签署《中欧航天合作现状和合作计划议定书》。在"嫦娥一号""嫦娥二号"月球探测任务实施期间,双方开展紧密合作。2011年9月,中国与欧洲空间局签署《关于测控网络及操作相互支持的协议》。

——中国与巴西在中巴高层协调委员会航天合作分委会机制下,统筹考虑中巴航天合作规划,积极推动中巴地球资源卫星的研制，继续保持中巴地球资源卫星数据的连续性，并扩大该卫星数据在区域和全球范围的应用。

——中国与法国在中法航天合作联合委员会机制下，签署中法空间及海洋科技合作框架协议，开展中法天文、中法海洋等卫星工程合作。

——中国与英国建立空间科学技术联合实验室，共同组织召开中英空间科学与技术研讨会，在月球探测、对地观测、空间科学研究与实验、人员培训等领域开展交流。

——中国与德国签署关于在载人航天领域开展合作的框架协议，在此协议机制下，中德双方在"神舟八号"飞船上开展了空间生命科学实验合作项目。

——美国国家航空航天局局长2010年对中国进行了友好访问，双方将继续开展在航天领域的对话。

——中国与委内瑞拉签署关于和平利用和开发外层空间技术合作的谅解备忘录，建立中委高级混合委员会科技、工业和航天分委会，在此框架下，推动了中委两国在通信卫星、遥感卫星以及卫星应用等方面的合作。

——中国与欧洲气象卫星开发组织为推进气象卫星资料共享和应用，共同签署《关于气象卫星资料应用、交换和分发合作协议》。

——中国与多个国家积极推动对地观测卫星数据的广泛应用。中国向多个国家赠送气象卫星广播系统接收站和气象信息综合分析处理系统，帮助南非建立了中巴地球资源卫星数据接收站，帮助泰国建立了中国环境减灾卫星数据接收站。中国并向以上国家提供相关对地观测卫星数据产品。

——中国与多个国家在卫星导航领域，开展频率协调、兼容与互操作、应用等国际交流与合作。

多边合作

——中国参加了联合国和平利用外层空间委员会及其科技小组委员会和法律小组委员会的各项活动。

——中国与联合国签署灾害管理与应急响应天基信息平台北京

办公室相关协议。目前,该办公室已正式挂牌成立。中国已通过该办公室为"非洲之角"提供旱灾风险监测产品,并且通过培训、能力建设、数据服务和灾害应急快速制图技术服务等多种方式为区域减灾做出贡献。

——中国在《空间和重大灾害国际宪章》机制下,与多个国家空间机构开展合作,通过该机制,为汶川地震、澳大利亚森林火灾等重大灾害救援工作提供了卫星数据支持。

——2008 年,在亚太地区国家的共同推动下,亚太空间合作组织正式成立。在该组织框架下,中国政府积极参与空间数据共享服务平台及其示范应用、地基光学空间目标观测网络、导航兼容终端等多个项目合作的研究,协助制定并发布亚太多边合作小卫星数据政策,促进了亚太地区国家空间领域的合作。

——中国参与全球卫星导航系统国际委员会、国际深空探测协调机构、机构间空间碎片协调委员会、国际地球观测组织、世界气象组织等政府间国际组织的各项活动,开展卫星导航、地球观测与地球科学研究、防灾减灾、深空探测、空间碎片等领域的多边交流与合作。"北斗"卫星导航系统成为全球卫星导航系统国际委员会认可的四大核心系统供应商之一,将逐步提供区域和全球导航定位服务,并加强与其他卫星导航系统间的兼容与互操作;中国将积极办好全球卫星导航系统国际委员会 2012 年第七届大会。中国自主开发的空间碎片防护设计系统被纳入机构间空间碎片协调委员会的防护手册。

——中国参与国际宇航联合会、国际空间研究委员会、国际宇航科学院等非政府间国际空间组织和学术机构的活动,组织召开世界月球会议等多个国际性学术会议,开展了深空探测、空间碎片等议题的研讨与交流。

商业活动

中国积极推进企业参与空间领域的国际商业活动。实现尼日利亚通信卫星、委内瑞拉通信卫星、巴基斯坦通信卫星的整星出口和在轨交付。为印度尼西亚的帕拉帕-D 卫星和欧洲通信卫星公司的 W3C 卫星提供商业发射服务。与玻利维亚、老挝、白俄罗斯等多个国家签订商业卫星及地面系统出口合同。

（三）重点合作领域

未来五年，中国将重点在以下领域开展国际空间交流与合作：

——空间天文、空间物理、微重力科学、空间生命科学、深空探测、空间碎片等领域的科学研究。

——对地观测卫星在环境与灾害监测、全球气候变化监测与预报、海洋监测等方面的应用。

——通信广播卫星在广播电视、远程教育、远程医疗等方面的应用。

——卫星导航系统的应用技术合作、终端设备研发、增强设施建设、特定行业服务等。

——载人航天工程空间实验室、空间站相关技术合作、空间科学研究与实验等。

——航天测控技术合作、航天测控支持等。

——卫星商业发射服务、卫星整星与零部件进出口、卫星地面试验设备进出口、卫星地面测控和应用设施建设及服务等。

——航天领域的人员交流与培训等。

China's Space Activities in 2011

The Information Office of the State Council on Thursday published a white paper on China's space activities in 2011.
Following is the full text:

I. Purposes and Principles of Development

The purposes of China's space industry are: to explore outer space and to enhance understanding of the Earth and the cosmos; to utilize outer space for peaceful purposes, promote human civilization and social progress, and to benefit the whole of mankind; to meet the demands of economic development, scientific and technological development, national security and social progress; and to improve the scientific and cultural knowledge of the Chinese people, protect China's national rights and interests, and build up its national comprehensive strength. China's space industry is subject to and serves the national overall development strategy, and adheres to the principles of scientific, independent, peaceful, innovative, and open development.

Scientific development. China respects science and the laws of nature. Keeping the actual situation of its space industry in mind, it works out comprehensive plans and arrangement of its activities regarding space technology, space applications and space science, in order to maintain comprehensive, coordinated and sustainable development of the industry.

Independent development. Keeping to the path of independence and self-reliance, China relies primarily on its own capabilities to develop its space industry to meet the needs of modernization, based upon its actual conditions and strength.

Peaceful development. China always adheres to the use of outer space for peaceful purposes, and opposes weaponization or any arms race in outer space. The country develops and utilizes space resources in a prudent manner and takes effective measures to protect the space environment, ensuring that its space activities benefit the whole of mankind.

Innovative development. China's strategy for the development of its space industry is to enhance its capabilities of independent innovation, consolidate its industrial foundation, and improve its innovation system. By implementing important space science and technology projects, the country concentrates its strength on making key breakthroughs for leap-frog development in this field.

Open development. China persists in combining independence and self-reliance with opening to the outside world and international cooperation. It makes active endeavors in international space exchanges and cooperation on the basis of equality and mutual benefit, peaceful utilization and common development, striving to promote progress in mankind's space industry.

II. Progress Made Since 2006

Since 2006, China has made rapid progress in its space industry. Breakthroughs have been made in major space projects, including human spaceflight and lunar exploration; space technology has been generally upgraded remarkably; the economic and social benefits of space applications have been noticeably enhanced; and innovative achievements have been made in space science.

1. **Space Transportation System**

Since 2006, Long March rockets have accomplished 67 successful launches, sending 79 spacecraft into planned orbits and demonstrating noteworthy improvement in the reliability of China's launch vehicles. The Long March rocket series have been improved, and major progress has been made in the development of new-generation launch vehicles.

2. **Man-made Earth Satellites**

1) Earth observation satellites

China has developed the Fengyun (Wind and Cloud), Haiyang (Ocean), Ziyuan (Resources), Yaogan (Remote-Sensing) and Tianhui (Space Mapping) satellite series, plus a constellation of small satellites for environmental and disaster monitoring and forecasting. Fengyun satellites are now capable of global, three-dimensional and multispectral quantitative observation. The Fengyun – 2 geostationary Earth orbit (GEO) meteorological satellite succeeded in double satellite observation and in-orbit backup; while the Fengyun – 3 polar orbit meteorological satellite succeeded in networking observation of morning and afternoon satellites. Ocean water color satellites have obtained their images of doubled width and their revisiting period reduced. The first Haiyang dynamics environmental satellite launched in August, 2011 is capable of all-weather and full-time microwave observation. The Ziyuan satellite series have seen their spatial resolution and image quality greatly enhanced. The small satellites for environmental and disaster monitoring and forecasting are now capable of disaster monitoring with medium-resolution, wide-coverage and high-revisit rate disaster monitoring. In 2010, China formally initiated the development of an important special project—a high-esolution Earth observation system.

2) Communications and broadcasting satellites

China has won successes in its high-capacity GEO satellite common platform, space-based data relays, tracking, telemetry and command (TT&C), and other key technologies, showing remarkable improvement in the technical performance of China's satellites and in voice, data, radio and television communications. The successful launch and stable operation of the Zhongxing – 10 satellite demonstrated a significant increase in the power and capacity of China's communications and broadcasting satellites. Similarly, the successful launch of the Tianlian (Space Chain)-1 data relay satellite demonstrated China's preliminary capability of both space-based data relays and space-based TT&C.

3) Navigation and positioning satellites

In February 2007, China successfully launched the fourth Beidou (Big Dipper) navigation experiment satellite, further enhancing the performance of the Beidou navigation experiment system. China has comprehensively launched the building of a Beidou regional navigation system, consisting of five GEO satellites, five inclined geosynchronous orbit (IGSO) satellites and four medium-Earth-orbit (MEO) satellites. Since April 2007, China has launched 10 such satellites and has been able to provide trial services for Asia-Pacific users.

4) Scientific satellites and technological test satellites

China has developed and launched several Shijian (Practice) satellites and small and micro satellites, providing supporting platforms for space environment exploration, space scientific test and new technology demonstration.

3. Human Spaceflight

From September 25 to 28, 2008, China successfully launched the Shenzhou-7 (Divine Ship – 7) manned spaceship. China also became the third country in the world to master the key technology of astronaut space extravehicular activity, completing a space material test outside the spaceship and an experiment on deploying and accompanying flight of a small satellite. In September and November 2011, China successively launched the Tiangong-1 (Space Palace-1) and Shenzhou – 8 spaceship, and accomplished their first space rendezvous and docking test, laying the foundation for the construction of future space laboratories and space stations.

4. Deep-space Exploration

On October 24, 2007, China successfully launched its first lunar probe, Chang'e-1, and achieved its objectives of "accurate orbital transfer and successful orbiting," also retrieving a great deal of scientific data and a complete map of the moon, and successfully implementing a controlled crash onto the lunar surface. The success of Chang'e-1 was another milestone for China's space industry, after man-made satellites and human spaceflight, signifying that China has become one of the countries capable of deep-space exploration.

On October 1, 2010, China successfully launched its second lunar probe, Chang'e-2, created a full higher-resolution map of the moon, and a high-definition image of Sinus Iridium, and completed several extended tests, including circling the Lagrangian Point L2, which laid the foundation for future deep-space exploration tasks.

5. Space Launch Sites

China has improved its three existing launch sites in Jiuquan, Xichang and Taiyuan, enhancing their comprehensive test capabilities and high-intensity launching capabilities. These sites have successfully launched manned spaceship, lunar probes and a variety of satellites. At present, China is building a new space launch site in Hainan to accommodate the launch of new-generation launch vehicles.

6. Space Telemetry, Tracking and Command (TT&C)

China has improved its TT&C ground stations and ships, and has established a very long baseline interferometry (VLBI) network comprising four observation stations and a data processing center, indicating that

China has acquired space-based TT&C capabilities; it has also established a multi-functioning TT&C network featuring space and ground integration, complete sets of equipment and ability to complete various tasks. At present, China's TT&C network is expanding from the ground to space, and from geospace TT&C to deep-space TT&C. The network is able to not only satisfy satellite TT&C demands, but also support human spaceflight and deep-space exploration.

7. Space Applications

1) Applications of Earth observation satellites

The fields and scope in which Earth observation satellites are used have been constantly expanding; these satellites' capabilities in providing business services have also been growing and an Earth observation satellite application system has initially taken shape. China has built four new satellite data-receiving stations, enhancing its ability to receive data from meteorological, ocean and land observation satellites. China has also established, based on comprehensive planning, the ground data processing system for Earth observation satellites, extending its ability in centralized data processing, data archiving, data distribution and services provision. China has established centers for environmental satellite application, satellite disaster-relief application, satellite mapping application and other application institutes for Earth observation satellites, promoting the spread and utility of Earth observation satellite data. China has improved calibration services of remote-sensing satellite radiation calibration fields, enhancing the quantitative application level of Earth observation satellites.

Today, Earth observation satellite data has been widely used in various fields for economic and social development. Fengyun satellites have effectively monitored typhoons, floods, forest and grassland fires, droughts, sandstorms and other natural disasters; their weather forecasting and climate change monitoring capabilities have also been enhanced remarkably. The ocean satellite series have monitored China's maritime territory and the world's key waters, and their forecasting accuracy for sea ice, ocean temperatures and wind fields have increased greatly, and their time efficiency in monitoring dangerous sea conditions has also been notably enhanced. The resource satellite series have played an important role in efforts to investigate, monitor and manage the resources of land, minerals, agriculture, forestry, and water conservancy, as well as geological disasters and city planning. Remote-sensing and Tianhui satellites have played an important role in scientific experiments, land censuses, mapping and other fields. The small satellites for environmental and disaster monitoring and forecasting have provided critical technical support for surface water quality and atmospheric environmental monitoring, major pollution events addressing, and major natural disaster monitoring, assessment and relief.

2) Applications of communications and broadcasting satellites

China has steadily promoted the applications of communications and broadcasting satellites, and has brought into being a market of certain scale. It has improved its satellite radio and TV network: in 2008 China established a satellite service platform to give every village access to direct broadcast and live telecasts. It also implemented satellite broadcasting and transmissions of China National Radio and China Central Television programs, and one channel program of provincial radio and TV stations, thus greatly increasing the radio and TV program coverage. China has strengthened development of its satellite tele-education broadband network and tele-medicine network, mitigating to some extent the problem of shortage of education and medical resources in remote and border areas. China has also strengthened its satellite capacity in emergency communications, providing important support for rescue and relief work and for major disaster management.

3) Applications of navigation and positioning satellites

China's applications of navigation and positioning satellites have embarked on the road of industrialized development, and are now developing at a high speed, and important progress has been made in developing navigation-and positioning-satellite applications. Through both domestic and foreign navigation and positioning satellites, China has been applying these technologies more broadly; as a result, the market for this industry has expanded rapidly. China strives to promote the application of its Beidou satellite navigation system, and the system has been used in transportation, sea fishing, hydrological monitoring, communications and timing service, power dispatching, and disaster reduction and relief.

8. Space Science

1) Sun-Earth space exploration

China has implemented the Double Star Program to explore the Earth's magnetosphere in concert with the Cluster Program of the European Space Agency (ESA), obtaining much new data and making important progress in space physics.

2) Lunar scientific research

Through lunar exploration projects, China has studied the morphology, structure, surface matter composition, microwave properties, and near-moon space environment, further enhancing its knowledge of the moon.

3) Experiments on microgravity science and space life science

Using the Shijian satellites and Shenzhou spaceship, China has carried out space experiments in life science, materials science, fluid mechanics and other fields under conditions of microgravity and strong radiation. It has also conducted experiments on crop breeding in space.

4) Space environment exploration and forecasting

Using Shenzhou and other spacecraft, China has explored the space environment's major parameters and effects, worked on space environmental monitoring and forecasting, and studied space environmental effects.

9. Space Debris

China has monitored space debris, and given early warnings against them, ensuring safe flight of Chang'e-1 and Chang'e-2 lunar probes, and Shenzhou-7 manned spaceship. China has steadily pushed forward its work on space debris mitigation, fully inactivating Long March rockets, and moving a few aging GEO satellites out of orbit. China has also worked on protecting manned spaceship from space debris.

III. Major Tasks for the Next Five Years

In the next five years, China will strengthen its basic capacities of the space industry, accelerate research on leading-edge technology, and continue to implement important space scientific and technological projects, including human spaceflight, lunar exploration, high-resolution Earth observation system, satellite navigation and positioning system, new-generation launch vehicles, and other priority projects in key fields. China will develop a comprehensive plan for construction of space infrastructure, promote its satellites and satellite applications industry, further conduct space science research, and push forward the comprehensive, coordinated and sustainable development of China's space industry.

1. Space Transportation System

China will build a stronger space transportation system, keep improving its launch vehicle series, and enhance their capabilities of entering space.

It will enhance the reliability and adaptability of launch vehicles in service, and develop new-generation launch vehicles and their upper stages, implement the first flight of the Long March—5, Long March—6 and Long March—7 launch vehicles. The Long March—5 will use non-toxic and pollution-free propellant, and will be capable of placing 25 tons of payload into the near-Earth orbit, or placing 14 tons of payload into the GEO orbit. The Long March-6 will be a new type of high-speed response launch vehicle, which will be capable of placing not less than 1 ton of payload into a sun-synchronous orbit at a height of 700 km. The Long March-7 will be capable of placing 5.5 tons of payload into a sun-synchronous orbit at a height of 700 km.

It will conduct special demonstrations and pre-research on key technologies for heavy-lift launch vehicles.

2. Man-made Earth Satellites

China will build a space infrastructure frame composed of Earth observation satellites, communications and broadcasting satellites, plus navigation and positioning satellites, and will develop a preliminary long-term, sustained and stable service capability. China will develop new types of scientific satellites and technological test satellites.

1) Earth observation satellites

China will improve its present meteorological, oceanic, and resource satellite series and its small satellites constellation for environmental and disaster monitoring and forecasting. It aims at developing and launching new-generation GEO meteorological satellites, stereo mapping satellites, radar satellites for environment and disaster monitoring, electromagnetic monitoring test satellites, and other new-type Earth observation satellites. It will work to make breakthroughs in key technologies for interferometric synthetic-aperture radar and gravitational field measurement satellites. It will initiate a high-resolution Earth observation system as an important scientific and technological project and establish on the whole a stable all-weather, 24-hour, multi-spectral, various-resolution Earth observation system.

2) Communications and broadcasting satellites

China will improve satellites for fixed communications services, television and radio service satellites and data relay satellites; develop satellites for mobile communication service; and develop a platform of higher capacity and higher power for new-generation GEO communications and broadcasting satellites.

3) Navigation and positioning satellites

Based on "three-step" development plan from experimental system to regional system and then to global system, China will continue building its Beidou satellite navigation system, implementing a regional Beidou satellite navigation system before 2012, whose navigation and positioning, timing and short-message services will cover the Asia-Pacific region. China aims at completing the global Beidou satellite navigation system by 2020, comprising five GEO satellites and 30 non-GEO satellites.

4) Scientific satellites and technological test satellites

China will develop and launch a Hard X-ray Modulation Telescope satellite, Shijian-9 new technology test satellite, and returnable satellites. It will begin to implement projects of quantum science test satellite and dark matter probing satellite.

3. Human Spaceflight

China will push forward human spaceflight projects and make new technological breakthroughs, creating a foundation for future human spaceflight.

It will launch the Shenzhou-9 and Shenzhou-10 spaceships and achieve unmanned or manned rendezvous and docking with the in-orbit Tiangong-1 vehicle.

China will launch space laboratories, manned spaceship and space freighters; make breakthroughs in and master space station key technologies, including astronauts' medium-term stay, regenerative life support and propellant refueling; conduct space applications to a certain extent and make technological preparations for the construction of space stations.

China will conduct studies on the preliminary plan for a human lunar landing.

4. Deep-space Exploration

China carries out deep-space exploration in stages, with limited goals. Based on the idea of "three steps" orbiting, landing and returning for continuing lunar probe projects, China will launch orbiters for lunar soft landing, roving and surveying to implement the second stage of lunar exploration. In the third stage, China will start to conduct sampling the moon's surface matters and get those samples back to Earth.

China will conduct special project demonstration in deep-space exploration, and push forward its exploration of planets, asteroids and the sun of the solar system.

5. Space Launch Sites

China will enhance the reliability and automation level of launch site facilities and equipment, strengthen the comprehensive capability of launch of spacecraft, and satisfy the launch demands. It will also complete the construction of the Hainan space launch site and put it into service.

6. Space TT&C

China will improve its space TT&C network, build deep-space TT&C stations, develop advanced TT&C technologies, and enhance its TT&C capabilities in all respects to satisfy the demands for remote TT&C.

7. Space Applications

China will further improve its satellite application and service system, expand satellites application scope, and promote the national new strategic industries, to meet demands of national economic and social development.

1) Applications of Earth observation satellites

China will improve its ground facilities for receiving, processing, distributing and applying satellite data, and will strengthen the development of calibration fields and other facilities. It will improve the sharing and comprehensive application of data retrieved from Earth observation satellites, make more self-obtained space data, and guide social resources to actively develop market – oriented data application services. It will implement application demonstration projects, and promote the wide utilization and industrialization of Earth observation satellites.

2) Applications of communications and broadcasting satellites

China will strengthen the applications of communications and broadcasting satellites in public service and major industries of the national economy. It plans to expand value-added business in the satellite communication field, further commercialize satellite communication, and expand the industrial scale of the application of communications and broadcasting satellites.

3) Applications of navigation and positioning satellites

China will build and improve ground TT&C segments and develop a system for monitoring and assessing performance of the global satellite navigation system, strengthen technological research, product development and standardization system of navigation and positioning satellites, enhance application level, promote position-based services, expand the industrial scope, and focus on promoting further use of the Beidou satellite navigation system in various fields of China's national economy.

8. Space Science

China will strengthen the development of its space science research system, upgrade the quality of space science research, and enhance popularization of space science knowledge in the whole nation.

By the implementation of lunar exploration projects, China will make in-situ analyses, morphological and structural surveys of the lunar surface in landing and roving areas, conduct environmental surveys of the lunar surface and make moon-based astronomical observations.

By using spacecraft, China will study the properties of black holes and physical laws under extreme conditions, explore properties of dark matter particles, and test basic theories of quantum mechanics. It will also conduct scientific experiments on microgravity and space life science, explore and forecast the space environment and study their effects.

9. Space Debris

China will continue to strengthen its work on space debris monitoring and mitigation and its work on spacecraft protection.

China will develop technologies for monitoring space debris and pre-warning of collision, and begin monitoring space debris and small near-Earth celestial bodies and collision pre-warning work. It will set up a design and assess system of space debris mitigation, and take measures to reduce space debris left by post-task spacecraft and launch vehicles. It will experiment with digital simulation of space debris collisions, and build a system to protect spacecraft from space debris.

IV. Development Policies and Measures

To ensure completion of the set goals and tasks, the Chinese government has formulated policies and measures to be taken for the development of China's space industry as follows:

Making comprehensive plans for and prudently arrange space activities. To give priority to applied satellites and satellite applications, develop human spaceflight and deep-space exploration properly, and give active support to space science exploration.

Strengthening innovation capability in space science and technology. To focus on implementing important space science and technological projects and to realize leapfrog development in space science and technology by way of making new breakthroughs in core technologies and resource integration. To actively build a space technology innovative system featuring integration of the space industry, academia and the research community, with space science and technology enterprises and research institutions as the main participants; to strengthen basic research in the space field and develop multiple advanced frontier technologies to increase sustainable innovative capacity in space science and technology.

Vigorously promoting development of the satellite application industry. To make comprehensive plans and construct space infrastructure; promote public sharing of satellite application resources; foster enterprise clusters, industrial chains and market for satellite applications.

Strengthening basic capability in space science, technology and industry. To strengthen construction of infrastructure for development, production and test for spacecraft and launch vehicles. To strengthen construction of key laboratories and engineering research centers for space science and technology. And to strengthen work on informatization, intellectual property rights and standardization of space activities.

Strengthening legislative work. To actively carry out research on a national space law, gradually formulate and improve related laws, regulations and space industrial policies guiding and regulating space activities, and create a legislative environment favorable to the development of space activities.

Guaranteeing the sustainable and steady financial investment for space activities. To gradually establish a diverse, multi-channel space funding system to ensure the investment sustainable and steady, especially to provide larger amounts for important space scientific and technological projects, applied satellite and satellite applications, frontier technologies and basic researches.

Encouraging organizations and people in all walks of life to participate in space-related activities. To encourage scientific research institutes, enterprises, institutions of higher learning and social organizations, under the guidance of national space policies, giving full play to their advantages and taking an active part in space activities.

Strengthening training of professionals for the space industry. To vigorously develop a favorable environment for the development of professional personnel, fostering leading figures in the space industry and forming a well-structured contingent of highly qualified personnel in the course of conducting the important projects and basic researches. To publicize space knowledge and culture, and attract more outstanding personnel into the space industry.

V. International Exchanges and Cooperation

The Chinese government holds that each and every country in the world enjoys equal rights to freely explore, develop and utilize outer space and its celestial bodies, and that all countries' outer space activities should be beneficial to economic development, the social progress of nations, and to the security, survival and development of mankind.

International space cooperation should adhere to the fundamental principles stated in the "Declaration on International Cooperation in the Exploration and Use of Outer Space for the Benefit and in the Interest of All States, Taking into Particular Account the Needs of Developing Countries." China maintains that international exchanges and cooperation should be strengthened to promote inclusive space development on the basis of equality and mutual benefit, peaceful utilization and common development.

1. Fundamental Policies

The Chinese government has adopted the following fundamental policies with regard to developing international space exchanges and cooperation:

Supporting activities regarding the peaceful use of outer space within the framework of the United Nations. Supporting all inter-governmental and non-governmental space organizations' activities that promote development of the space industry.

Emphasizing regional space cooperation in the Asia-Pacific area, and supporting other regional space cooperation around the world.

Reinforcing space cooperation with developing countries, and valuing space cooperation with developed countries.

Encouraging and endorsing the efforts of domestic scientific research institutes, industrial enterprises, institutions of higher learning, and social organizations to develop international space exchanges and cooperation in diverse forms and at various levels under the guidance of relevant state policies, laws and regulations.

Appropriately using both domestic and foreign markets and both types of resources, and actively participating in practical international space cooperation.

2. Major Events

Since 2006, China has implemented international space exchanges and cooperation in various forms. It has signed a number of cooperation agreements and memoranda on the peaceful utilization of outer space with a host of countries, space agencies and international organizations. China has taken part in relevant activities sponsored by the United Nations and other relevant international organizations and supported international space commercial cooperation. These measures have yielded positive results.

1) Bilateral cooperation

China has established a long-term cooperation plan with Russia through the mechanism of the Space Cooperation Sub-committee under the Prime Ministers' Meeting between Russia and China. The two nations have signed a number of cooperation agreements on space science, deep-space exploration and other areas, and their national space administrations have opened representative offices mutually. In the field of human spaceflight, the two nations have also carried out many cooperation projects.

China has undertaken extensive cooperation with Ukraine under the Space Cooperation Sub-committee mechanism of the Sino-Ukrainian Cooperation Commission, and the two sides have signed the "Sino-Ukrainian Space Cooperation Program."

China and the European Space Agency (ESA) have signed the "Status Quo of China-Europe Space Cooperation and the Cooperation Plan Protocol" under the mechanism of the China-Europe Joint Commission on Space Cooperation. The two sides cooperated closely during the lunar exploration missions of Chang'e-1 and Chang'e-2, and signed the "Agreement on Mutual Support for the TT&C Network and Operation" in September 2011.

China and Brazil, through the mechanism of the Space Cooperation Sub-committee of the Sino-Brazilian High-level Coordination Commission, have worked out a comprehensive bilateral space cooperation plan, actively promoted the research and development of the China-Brazil Earth resources satellites, continued to maintain data consistency of their Earth resources satellites and expanded the application of their data into regional and global application.

China has signed a cooperation framework agreement on space and marine science and technology with France under the mechanism of the Sino-French Joint Commission on Space Cooperation, aiming at developing bilateral cooperation on astronomic satellite, ocean satellite and other satellite programs.

China and Britain have established a joint laboratory on space science and technology, jointly organized a seminar on space science and technology, and conducted exchanges on lunar exploration, Earth observation, space science research and experiment, personnel training and other areas.

China has signed a framework agreement with Germany on bilateral cooperation in the field of human spaceflight. Under the framework, the two countries have carried out a cooperative experiment project on the Shenzhou-8 concerning space life science.

The director of the U. S. National Aeronautical and Space Administration (NASA) visited China and the two sides will continue to make dialogue regarding the space field.

China has signed a memorandum of understanding on technological cooperation in the peaceful utilization and development of outer space with Venezuela, and the two nations have established a technology, industry and space sub-committee under the China-Venezuela Senior Mixed Committee. Under this framework, the two nations have promoted bilateral cooperation in communications satellites, remote – sensing satellites, satellite applications and other areas.

China has signed the "Cooperation Agreement on the Application, Exchange and Distribution of Meteorological Satellite Data" with the European Organization for the Exploitation of Meteorological Satellites (EUMETSAT), to promote the sharing in and application of meteorological satellite data.

China has actively promoted the extensive applications of Earth observation satellite data with various countries. China has given to many countries free receiving stations for meteorological satellite broadcasting systems and comprehensive systems for meteorological information analysis and processing. With China's help, a data receiving station of the Sino-Brazilian Earth Resources Satellite Program was established in South Africa, and another station for receiving environmental and disaster data from Chinese satellites was set up in Thailand. China has provided related earth observation satellite data products to the above-mentioned countries.

China has implemented international exchanges and cooperation with a number of countries in frequency coordination, compatibility and inter-operability, applications and other international exchanges and cooperation in the area of satellite navigation systems.

2) Multilateral cooperation

China has taken part in activities organized by the United Nations Committee on the Peaceful Uses of Outer Space (UN COPUOS) and its Scientific and Technical Sub-committee and Legal Sub-committee.

China has signed relevant agreements with the United Nations on disaster management and emergency response based on the space-based information platform. A Beijing office of the program has been established. Through this office, China has provided drought risk-monitoring products to the "Horn of Africa", and contributes to the regional disaster mitigation effort by offering training, capacity building, data service, disaster emergency response, QDGS (Quick Draw Graphics System) and other services.

China has cooperated with the space institutes of various countries through the mechanism of the "International Charter on Space and Major Disasters." Through this mechanism, satellite data support was provided to the Wenchuan earthquake, the forest fire in Australia and other major disaster relief work.

In 2008, the Asia-Pacific Space Cooperation Organization (APSCO) was established with the joint effort of Asia-Pacific nations. Under the APSCO frame, the Chinese government actively participates in the cooperation and study of various projects, including the development of a space data-sharing platform, its demonstration and application; an Earth-based optic space target observation network; compatible navigation terminals. China assisted APSCO in the formulation and release of its policy on small satellite data in Asia-Pacific multilateral cooperation, and has promoted space cooperation in the Asia-Pacific region.

China participates in activities organized by the International Committee on Global Navigation Satellite Systems, International Space Exploration Coordination Group, Inter-Agency Space Debris Coordination Committee, Group on Earth Observations, World Meteorological Organization and other inter-governmental international organizations. China has also developed multilateral exchanges and cooperation in satellite navigation, Earth observation and Earth science and research, disaster prevention and mitigation, deep-space exploration, space debris and other areas. China's Beidou satellite navigation system has become one of the world's four core system suppliers accredited by the International Committee on Global Navigation Satellite Systems, and will gradually provide regional and global navigation and positioning service as well as strengthened compatibility and interoperability with other satellite navigation systems.

China will do its best to host the Seventh Meeting of the International Committee on Global Navigation Satellite Systems in 2012. The nation's independently developed space debris protective design system has also been incorporated into the protection manual of the Inter-Agency Space Debris Coordination Committee.

China takes part in activities organized by the International Astronautical Federation, International Committee on Space Research, International Academy of Astronautics, and other non-governmental international space organizations and academic institutes. It has also organized a series of international academic conferences, including the Global Lunar Conference, and has fostered discussion and exchanges in deep-space exploration, space debris and other issues.

3) Commercial activities

China actively promotes the participation of Chinese enterprises in international commercial activities in the space field. China has exported whole satellites and made in-orbit delivery of communications satellites to Nigeria, Venezuela and Pakistan; provided commercial launch services for the Palapa—D satellite of Indonesia and the W3C satellite of Eutelsat, and signed commercial satellite and ground system export contracts with Bolivia, Laos, Belarus and other countries.

3. Key Cooperation Areas

In the next five years, China's international space exchanges and cooperation will be mainly in the following areas:

Scientific research on space astronomy, space physics, micro-gravity science, space life science, deep-space exploration, space debris and other areas.

Applications of Earth observation satellites in environment and disaster monitoring, global climate change monitoring and forecasting, marine monitoring and other areas.

Applications of communications satellites in broadcasting and television, long-distance education, telemedicine and other areas.

Applied technological cooperation, research and development of terminal equipment, reinforced facility building, specific industrial services and other areas of satellite navigation systems.

Technological cooperation on a space lab and a space station in China's human spaceflight program; space science research and experiments and other areas.

Space TT&C cooperation, support and others.

Commercial satellite launch service, import and export of whole satellites, satellite parts and components, import and export of ground test equipment, and building and service of satellite ground TT&C and satellite application facilities as well as related services, etc.

Personnel exchanges and training in the field of space.